KU-508-936

Kris Jenner is executive producer and star of the wildly popular *Keeping Up with the Kardashians*, a reality show about her famous family that appears in 150 countries and is one of the most successful shows in the E! network's history. The mother of Kim, Kourtney, Khloé and Robert Kardashian, Jr., she was formerly married to lawyer Robert Kardashian, who was widely known as a member of O.J. Simpson's defense Dream Team. She and her husband, Olympic decathlon champion Bruce Jenner, have two children, Kendall and Kylie Jenner.

Praise for Kris Jenner — from the people who know her best!

"My mom is my best friend; I thought I knew everything about her until I read this book! She shares so many special stories I think everyone can relate to! I love you, Mom!"

—Kim Kardashian

"My mom has raised us to be very family oriented. Everything we do is as a family. Don't worry about all the superficial things going on around this world because at the end of the day you have your family."

—Rob Kardashian

"My mom amazes me every single day. She has truly taught me so much about life, love, celebrating, grieving, and having a lot of fun and in her book, you will see how she manages to do it all!"

—Kourtney Kardashian

"My mother has always been such an inspiration to me and in my life. She is the one who gets us through every obstacle in life, and she is the glue that keeps our family together. I'm so excited for the world to finally get a small glimpse into my mom's past and how incredibly hands-on she is with her children."

—Khloé Kardashian Odom

"Since the moment I met Kris, she has welcomed me into her family with open arms. This book details all the important relationships in her life and the strong family values that she instills in all of her children, which is one of the qualities I admire most about her. I am truly blessed to have her in my life."

—Lamar Odom

Kris Jenner

. . . and All Things

Kardashian

Kris Jenner

**SIMON &
SCHUSTER**

London · New York · Sydney · Toronto · New Delhi

A CBS COMPANY

First published in Great Britain by Simon & Schuster UK Ltd, 2011
This paperback edition published by Simon & Schuster UK Ltd, 2012
A CBS COMPANY

10

Simon & Schuster UK Ltd
1st Floor
222 Gray's Inn Road
London WC1X 8HB

www.simonandschuster.co.uk

Simon & Schuster Australia, Sydney
Simon & Schuster India, New Delhi

A CIP catalogue record for this book is available from the British Library

ISBN: 978-1-84983-750-7

Designed by Joy O'Meara

Printed and bound by CPI Group (UK) Ltd, Croydon, CR0 4YY

To the loves of my life:
My children, Kourtney, Kimberly, Khloé, Robert, Kendall,
and Kylie . . . and my husband, Bruce.
You are my heart.
Thank you for loving me unconditionally.

Introduction

I know this sounds crazy, but this is exactly where I'm supposed to be: screaming through the streets of Paris in a chauffeur-driven Mercedes with my daughter Kimberly, on our way to see the *Mona Lisa* in the Louvre. How I got here has been a long, wild, and winding road, which we will get to in a moment. For now, I'm going to ask you to sit back and experience the ride.

It was September 2010, and Kim and I were in Paris to meet the international media to celebrate the fifth season of *Keeping Up with the Kardashians*, the hit reality show about our family, shown in many languages in 150 countries around the world.

The show's producers, E! and Comcast Entertainment Group, flew us to Paris first-class on British Airways. From Paris we were flown in a shiny, sexy private jet (which looked just like a beautiful black Chanel handbag), along with our glam squad, to eight European cities for the media tour. The jet was stocked with my favorite champagne, Kim's favorite snacks, and all our favorite blankets and movies. *Fabulous*.

Our show is the most-watched series in E! history, and by the end of 2010, Kim would be among the world's most-searched people on the Internet. Her Twitter account, with almost ten million followers, as of this writing, would be among the five most followed in the world, along with those of President Barack Obama and Lady Gaga. And Kim would be named one of *People* magazine's Most Beautiful People.

As for me, I'm a unique combination of mother and manager. I've actually trademarked the term "Momager," which is what I am. I spend endless eighteen-hour days creating, nurturing, and juggling the insanely busy careers, endless personal appearances, and business enterprises of my six children—Kourtney, Kim, Khloé, Rob, Kendall, and Kylie—my husband, Bruce Jenner, my son-in-law Lamar Odom, and myself. Some of the many hats I wear include those of producer, creator, and star of our reality television series for E!, from which we have launched three spin-off hit television series. There are brand endorsements to run along with our own clothing lines, including the Kardashian Kollection for Sears. I also oversee several businesses, such as our skin care line, PerfectSkin; our diet and nutrition supplement business, Quick Trim; the fragrances Kim Kardashian, Kim Kardashian Gold, and Reflection, along with Khloé and Lamar's fragrance, Unbreakable. Oh, and did I mention I have my own clothing line launching on QVC this fall, the Kris Jenner Kollection? And I finally launched my very own blog, www.OfficialKrisJenner.com. *Whew!*

My favorite hat, though, will always be "Mom." In the midst of our media blitz through Europe, Kim and I were still a mother and daughter in Paris, and I kept insisting that we see the city. "We're in Europe. We must do things that are really special," I told her. "We can't come all this way and not do a little sightseeing. We have to remember to always experience life and live it to the fullest."

So I arranged a special trip to see the *Mona Lisa* at the Louvre. We awoke that morning with a special surprise planned by the general manager of the famous Ritz Hotel, Omer Acar.

"Before you visit our beautiful Louvre, I've planned something truly spectacular that I know you will both love," he told us.

As Kim and I left our luxurious suite, we were escorted to another floor at the Ritz. The next thing I knew, we were inside the suite where Coco Chanel lived until her death in 1971. The day before, we had been taken to Azzedine Alaïa's atelier with him in the trendy Marais district. Now to be in Madame Chanel's suite! Kim and I were pinching ourselves.

As we exited the Ritz, I sadly remembered the last picture the world saw of Princess Diana before her fatal car accident—in the exact place where we were walking. Kim and I were taken aback by the blinding flash of dozens of photographers outside the hotel, as uniformed security guards hurried us to a waiting Mercedes. The cameramen climbed onto their motor scooters as we drove off in the Mercedes, and with police escorts in front and behind, their sirens blaring, we raced the paparazzi to the Louvre. Arriving at the famous museum's pyramid, we were greeted by a team of escorts and security. They led us through private tunnels, up some stairs, then down some others. A door suddenly opened and we were standing behind a velvet rope, beyond which stood the world's most famous woman: Leonardo da Vinci's masterpiece of beauty and mystery, the *Mona Lisa*. Oh my God, pinch us again!

The curator of the Louvre whispered in my ear, "We do not allow pictures with the *Mona Lisa* except on special occasions." Then she gave us the okay to take a picture or two. So Kim and I stood to the side of the velvet rope as a large crowd gathered, whispering our names and waving to us wildly. We took pictures alongside the famous painting, as everyone else began taking pictures of us. *Incredible!*

When we left through the same side door we had entered, a crazy, chaotic crowd had gathered. It wasn't until we were ushered away from the *Mona Lisa* that I realized I was numb, floating.

As I walked toward the car, my mind wandered back to 1978 when I stood in the exact same place in the exact same city on the *other* side of the same velvet rope, holding hands with my husband, Robert Kardashian. We were on our honeymoon and I was a twenty-two-year-old American Airlines flight attendant. I thought, *Who could have imagined that I would be back thirty-something years later, and this would be my life?* I had come full circle. Now, the road I had traveled was nothing I had ever expected or planned.

I know: the *Mona Lisa* will be here long after the Kardashians are gone. As I always tell my kids, "You're going to meet the same people on the way down as you did on the way up. So be grateful and humble for the blessings that have been given to you." Still, I had to admit that trip to the Louvre was one of the headiest experiences of my life.

I kept thinking: *This is where I'm supposed to be.*

I am a wife and a mother (believe it or not, I always dreamed of having six kids). I'm not only living that dream, I'm lucky enough to be living it on a huge stage. I've been blessed.

I made it through adversity, through personal storms, tremendous personal loss, a devastating divorce, and seemingly insurmountable tragedy, and managed to pick myself up and find love and happiness without ever losing my true self or my motivation to do something with my life and become the best person that I could be.

My mother told me I could do anything I set my mind to, and she taught me to set the bar high. She taught me to dream big and showed me through her strength and perseverance. My grandmother always said: "Do your best!" no matter how big or how small the job. And, of course, my lifelong motto is: "If someone says no, you're talking to the wrong person." Yet I would live two distinctly different lives—the first derailed by turmoil, tragedy, and wasted opportunities, the second as a wife and mother who not only reclaimed her power and lifelong love of family but went on to build the unlikely empire called the Kardashians.

Coming from humble yet wonderful beginnings in Southern California, I was lucky to meet a man who should have been the love of my life, a young and successful lawyer named Robert Kardashian. He transported me into a Beverly Hills dream life and helped me foster a close relationship with God. Then I threw it all away for a crazy love (or lust) affair that left me flattened. I lost my husband, my friends, my home, and nearly my mind, only to reassemble my life and my family with my second husband, the Olympic champion Bruce Jenner.

Shortly after Bruce and I were married, tragedy struck again: My dear friend Nicole Brown Simpson was found stabbed to death on the front steps of her home, and O.J. Simpson—another close friend whom I had known since Robert Kardashian and I were married and with whom I would be reunited during my marriage to Bruce Jenner—went on trial for her murder.

Through the grace of God, I landed on my feet with a second life, a second chance. Standing before the *Mona Lisa* in the Louvre, I could reflect on it all and what we had accomplished: turning the life and times of a Southern California family into a business, an international brand, that connects with millions of people around the world through our laughter, craziness, and, most important, our love for one another.

Yet, like the famous lady in the frame, to many we remain a mystery.

How did we get here? What is the mystique, the magic, the story behind the smiles? Who am I to manage my family as a business and produce a hit television series, which has spawned, as of this writing, three hit spin-off series, all supported by a seemingly endless stream of endorsements, modeling contracts, clothing and fragrance lines, magazine covers, and TV appearances?

It has taken me half a lifetime to live the story in these pages, one that I hope will show people you can follow your dreams—no matter how big—and still become whatever it is you set your mind to through hard work and perseverance, no matter your age or circumstances. And, as with any story worth telling, I have to start at the beginning . . .

Kris Jenner

... and All Things

Kardashian

CHAPTER ONE

The Candelabra

I remember the candles. Thousands of them. Green and blue and silver and gold. Candles in all sizes and shapes—angels, pillars, balls, and flowers—made of beeswax and paraffin, all so beautiful and smelling divine.

Most of all, I remember the Gloomchasers: crushed colored glass glued onto a jar, grouted in gold, then polished and placed on teak stands with glass votive candles inside. When the votives were lit, the candles would glow and the colors would glisten, and supposedly any gloom in the room would be immediately chased away. The Gloomchasers were gorgeous, and we could not make them fast enough or keep them in stock.

We were the candle family of La Jolla, California. In 1963, my grandparents Lou and Jim Fairbanks along with my mom, Mary Jo, opened one of the first candle stores in California. My grandfather Jim would come home after working all day at San Diego Glass and Paint and help my grandmother Lou Ethel make the Gloomchasers in their garage. At their candle store, the Candelabra, my grandmother had a room as big as a walk-in closet exclusively for Gloomchasers, all of them lit, all of them magical.

The candles are my most vivid memory of my perfect childhood in the perfect world we had in Southern California, before it all began to fall apart . . .

My father, Robert Houghton, was an engineer for Convair, an aircraft design and manufacturing company. He and my mom had me on November 5, 1955, and my sister, Karen, three years later. We lived in Point Loma, a really tony area of San Diego, in a big, beautiful white house like you see in the movies.

Karen and I were extremely close in the fabulous *Gidget* dream of an early childhood that we shared. We looked very different. She had light brown hair, and I had jet-black hair—and she was smaller than I was. There's a definite family resemblance, though. It's obvious that we come from the same parents. We also had different personalities. Even though we grew up under the same circumstances and in the same environment, we just approached goals and situations differently, even in childhood. With my big, chatty personality, I'm sure I entertained my quieter sister. We loved each other, and we were there for each other through thick and thin, and to this day we are part of each other's lives.

When I was seven, our parents had an argument, and soon they were arguing all of the time. Finally, in 1962, my father packed his bags. He was "going away," our parents told us, but he would be back. That's how you did it in those days. There wasn't a therapeutic plan for how to tell a seven-year-old and her four-year-old sister that life as they knew it was over. Soon we realized that our parents were getting divorced and our father was never coming back. We had a great relationship with him until Convair moved to Long

Beach in the mid-seventies, and took my father with it. We saw him rarely after that.

The divorce was tough for me and had lasting effects. It was very, very hard for me to wrap my head around my parents not living together anymore. My dad would come visit us at our house in Point Loma, the one that we used to all live in together. That was really hard, because we were young. He would come to visit us and then leave again. That was really weird for me. I wondered, *Why is he leaving? Is he going to stay? Is this going to work out?* When you are a child and your parents separate, you're always hoping that they are going to get back together.

My mother was such a pillar of strength through that time. I didn't realize it then, but watching her remain that strong and upbeat through such a personal storm was very influential on me. She wasn't going to let that divorce get her down. We moved from Point Loma to Clairemont, where my grandparents lived. My mom bought this amazing 1956 T-Bird convertible. She used to throw us in the back of the car and drive us to the beach in La Jolla. In those days you didn't have to wear seat belts, and we'd sit in the tiny area in the back of the car with the picnic lunch she had packed. Her girlfriends would meet us at the beach, and we'd eat our picnic lunch. She did so many fun things on the weekends with us, and it was clear we were going to persevere. The three of us were going to be just fine.

My mother raised us with rules. She wasn't going to let us run amok. There were rules and regulations: we had to make our beds, and we had to wash our sink out when we brushed our teeth like my grandmother taught us, and we had to help her vacuum, and we had to clean the house a couple of days a week. We had to take care of our own rooms and belongings. She taught us to be responsible for ourselves, and that that was the way to overcome adversity. She taught us to just pick ourselves up by the bootstraps and soldier on with a smile. We were going to have fun, and things were going to be great. They might not be perfect, and we might not have a dad, but life was still fabulous.

Just after my parents' divorce in 1963, I was walking home from school in second grade, passing the huge mansion with the circular driveway near our house in Point Loma, as I did every day. For some reason I hit the inside of my left shin on a retaining wall. It hurt all night long. When I woke up the next morning, I had a bump on my leg the size of a large lemon. The doctor said we needed to do some X-rays, and when the results came back, it showed I had a bone tumor. My parents had to sign a piece of paper before I went into surgery, stating that if the doctors found cancer in my bones, they had approval to amputate my leg at the hip, or wherever the doctor determined the cancer began.

Mom and Dad didn't think I could hear them talking about this, but I could. So all I could think about when I went into this surgery was the doctors amputating my leg at the hip. I was scared to death. But I came out of the surgery, with my mom and my grandmother in the waiting room, and I still had my leg.

That was when I realized how loving my family was and how appreciative I was to have them help me get through something so traumatic. It was also the first time my dad had come back since the divorce. He came to the hospital and brought me a transistor radio in a black case. I have it to this day. The end of the divorce had been rough, so he had stayed away for a while, and his visit meant a lot to me. My mom gave me a stuffed monkey named Anabelle, and that monkey has lived in every closet in every home I've had since.

From the moment my parents divorced, my mom worked full-time. She loved to work, and we learned from her that work was a positive thing. She had to sell our beautiful house in Point Loma, but my grandmother helped her get a house on Deer Park Drive in

Clairemont, just three blocks away from Longfellow Elementary. I walked to school and was a Brownie. My grandfather Jim came over and built my sister and me a real playhouse. I'll never forget how amazing that playhouse was, right in front of our house. We were really happy. Every day after school, my mother would give us a dollar each, and Karen and I would walk up to the little strip mall at the other end of the street and buy candy as an after-school treat.

My mom worked in many places after my parents' divorce, but the job I most remember was in a pro shop at a golf course. My mom is and always has been so beautiful: she's tall, and she has such a beautiful figure. And she's always dressed to the nines. When I was a little girl, my mom dressed like all women did in the '50s with the fashion and the drama—the hats and the gloves, everything. My mom didn't have a lot of money in those days, but somehow she always figured out a way to look really fashionable. She went to work every day dressed like Jacqueline Kennedy. She was the mom doing the housework and making dinner, but at the same time, she was wearing these gorgeous dresses cinched at the waist. She always looked like she had on some fabulous Chanel ensemble. And her hair was perfect. She was so beautiful, and I adored and admired her.

But it was my grandmother who was most instrumental in my upbringing. My grandmother was my hero. She was born in Hope, Arkansas, and her first husband, my biological grandfather, cheated on her. So she packed up my mother and had the gumption to leave. She was very strong-willed and stubborn. She decided she didn't need a man, and she moved with her daughter to San Diego. She was so confident, so smart, and she had a strong sense of self. She met my grandfather Jim while working as an accountant on a naval base in San Diego. She wasn't afraid to roll up her sleeves and get to work.

She and my grandfather lived in an upper-middle-class neighborhood with an avocado tree and a birdbath in the backyard. Since my mom was busy with work, Grandma and I really bonded. After my father moved, my grandfather became the male figure in my life. He was pure working-class Middle America. Every day he put on a uniform—khaki pants, khaki shirt—and went to work for San Diego Glass, driving one of those trucks that carried big panes of glass on their sides.

My grandma bought our school clothes, cooked the greatest dinners, and bathed and groomed her two toy poodles, Bridgette and Toulouse, who were supposed to be my dogs. My mother wouldn't let me keep them because they were too much work, so my grandmother kept them for me.

My grandmother was gorgeous like my mom, but she had blond hair and green eyes. Until the day she died, my grandmother wore a matching outfit every single day. She always wore beautiful slacks with a matching blazer and the perfect blouse and shoes. My family members, every last one of them, were always fashion-forward, and my grandmother was the matriarch. Fashion and grooming were both very important to her. Even if we were going to Disneyland, she made sure to take us shopping a few days beforehand to buy us new outfits for the outing. My grandmother took us shopping while my mom was at work, and if we had a friend with us, she got a new outfit too. It was always important to my grandmother and my mother that we looked our best.

I remember how special my grandmother used to make our holidays—big, perfect, and glorious, a tradition that I would eventually assume and take to an even bigger level. We celebrated everything endlessly. At Easter, for instance, there were Easter cupcakes and Easter cookies and Easter eggs. She always entertained as if she were expecting a party of fifty guests, even when she was having only my little sister and me. I grew to love that quality, and I think she passed it on to me. When I grew up and got married and had kids of my own, I wanted to do all the same kinds of things for my own kids. Of course, I ended up carrying on the traditions my grandmother taught me, except on steroids. Doing everything for my kids is something I learned from my grandmother. She sparked a dream in me early on: to someday have a ton of kids and become a wonderful mother.

Grandma also taught me the value of hard work.

The Candelabra was right in the middle of La Jolla, just across from the ocean. She just *loved* candles. A great deal of my childhood was spent in that store. My mom often worked there with my grandmother. The older I got, of course, the more often they would drag me along with them to work. I would be in the back room, doing my little chores: wrapping gifts for customers, making candles, and doing whatever else needed to be done.

The Candelabra did so well that my mother opened up her own shop in 1976, called the Candles of La Jolla. So there was the Candelabra on Prospect Street and the Candles of La Jolla on Gerard, next to John's Waffle Shop.

Candles became our family business. I grew up working in both shops. When I was old enough to drive, I drove myself to work there. My whole childhood, beginning at age ten, was spent working in those two stores. By the time I was thirteen, I was getting a little paycheck and really contributing to the business by being there at Christmastime. During Christmas vacation, I spent my days at the candle store, wrapping gifts as fast as I could.

My grandmother actually did so well at her candle store that she was able to keep her home decorated in a just-2die4-style, as did my mother. They liked beautiful things, and everything had to be just so. They were both perfectionists. "As soon as you finish using the sink, wash it out with Comet," my grandmother would tell me.

"Clean the sink and polish it." It was the era of "Cleanliness is next to Godliness," and that was how I was raised: with a "Whistle while you work" mentality, like in *Snow White and the Seven Dwarfs*.

Because of all of that, I never complained about hard work; I thrived on it. From a young age I learned that if I wanted to get ahead in life, I needed to work. It was a pretty perfect world: hard work, beautiful candles, and lots of love.

A few years after my parents had divorced, my mother met Harry Shannon. Harry was a great guy, and he quickly became *her* guy. They fell completely in love. It started off great, but for a while the candles in our lives began to flicker and came close to blowing out.

Harry was a drinker and he loved to party. It was the era of the Rat Pack, of course, and everybody went to cocktail parties on the weekends. Even my grandmother would have her friends over regularly. But Harry Shannon took it to an extreme. He was an alcoholic. Still, my mom loved him, dating him on and off, but always breaking up with him because she had two little girls to take care of and would lose patience with his problems with alcohol.

Harry had money. He was a yacht broker and taught his clients how to sail. He was an excellent sailor, and he was definitely a businessman. He walked around in fabulous white linen slacks, jackets, and fabulous loafers. He was the coolest, most beautiful dresser. He always looked like a Ralph Lauren ad.

He was in love with my mother. But when Harry drank, he misbehaved. Once when they were dating, my sister and I were sleeping in my mom's bed because she had gone out that night and left us with a babysitter. When she came home, she crawled into bed with us and we all fell asleep. An hour or so later, we heard banging at the bedroom window. Harry Shannon was trying to get into the house. He was drunk as a skunk. We went to the front door and peeked through the curtain to see him pounding on the door and screaming, "Let me in, Mary Jo! Let me in!"

"Go home, Harry, and come back when you sober up!" she screamed through the door. "You're in no shape to be here."

"Let me in!" he continued.

My sister and I were, of course, scared. We crawled into my mother's bed and sat there shivering under the covers, wondering what was going to happen next. Every once in a while, we would get out of the bed and peek out the window. He kept banging and he was banging so hard, we thought he might knock down the house. It was that bad. Finally, he went home.

That night, my mother promised us that she would never subject us to anything like that again. Harry Shannon was out of her life until he sobered up. A day or two later, Harry came crawling back on hands and knees, apologizing profusely. A short time after that, he proposed. My mother finally gave him an ultimatum: quit drinking and we'll get married.

That very day, he quit. He wouldn't have another drink until the day he died. Just like Elizabeth Taylor and Richard Burton, Harry and Mom flew to Puerto Vallarta and got married, taking a few friends along for the ride. It was June of 1968, and I was thirteen. My sister and I stayed with my grandparents. We were standing there with my grandparents when Mom and Harry returned, thinking, *Wow, we have a stepdad!* From that day forward, I called Harry "Dad." He embraced my sister and me as if we were his own. Harry taught me a big lesson in life: if you want something bad enough, and are willing to change your life for it, you can do anything. Harry taught me how to find inner strength.

Soon after their marriage, Harry announced that he was going to invest in a new company. "We're going to move to Oxnard, California," he said. "And we're going to harvest abalone."

"Abalone?" I asked. "What's abalone?"

He explained: abalone is a big, red, edible sea snail.

Ugh!

I had lived in the San Diego area my whole life. I was in junior high, and we were all very happy. But here was Harry Shannon talking about giving it all up for sea snails, abalone, something we had never heard about before, and my mother telling us it was a done deal. Harry, my mom, Karen, and I were all moving to Oxnard—the strawberry and lima bean capital of California, 155 miles north of San Diego—where Harry could invest in something called the Abalone Processing Plant. Mom put her candle shop on hold—she had someone work there for the summer—and we moved up to Oxnard. We moved into this small apartment. We had no friends. We didn't know anybody.

I *hated* abalone.

I hated the idea of abalone harvesting: of fishermen catching abalone and bringing abalone back to Harry and his partners' plant. He had people there pounding and preparing the abalone for sale. We would go to these restaurants and eat abalone burgers. Again, *ugh!* Why couldn't he have bought a McDonald's franchise? *That* would have been a great idea to a girl of thirteen. Burgers, yes. But abalone? *What?* The whole move was just a big hot mess.

That same year, I started my period. I was away from my friends, away from any family, stuck up in Oxnard, surrounded by abalone. I was yearning for my grandmother, missing my old life and that part of my family. I wrote her probably three hundred letters during that miserable Oxnard summer. I cried my eyes out every single night, missing her. I could have said, "Oh, I'm getting the next train to La Jolla." I guess I could have lived with my grandmother. But that was my mother's first year of marriage, and I was part of a family unit. Still, all I could think about was getting out.

The only highlight of this time was when a girlfriend from San Diego called and said she and her dad were going into Los Angeles to a big sale at Judy's. Now, Judy's I loved. Judy's was famous. Shopping there was fantastic. So I met my girlfriend at Judy's in L.A. with some cash that my grandmother had sent me, and I had the best time. I felt like such a big girl, such an independent woman, who could go into a big city all by herself with a girlfriend and go shopping. *I could get used to this,* I thought. I liked the independence of making my own decisions.

But when I got back home it was still Oxnard. And abalone. In some ways, the move to Oxnard was my first step toward me being independent. I thought, *Okay, life isn't going the way I expected it to. I'm stuck up here.* It made me think that I never wanted to be "stuck" again. I couldn't wait to be able to make decisions for myself after that. I never forgot the things I learned in Oxnard, most important that I never again wanted to be in the position of being completely powerless to do something about a situation I didn't want to be in.

Then the unthinkable happened: three months after our move to Oxnard, Harry's partner took all of the money in the company—$15,000—and skipped town, never to be heard from again. My parents kept it quiet at first. We were young and they didn't want to worry us.

I was happy when I found out. Not for the loss, but I was *so* excited to be going home. We were packing up and moving back to San Diego almost immediately. I couldn't pack fast enough.

It was a major failure for Mom and Harry. He'd lost everything he had invested. We weren't broke—we still had the candle store—but Mom and Harry were essentially starting over. That was scary. But still, I was thrilled to be going back home and my parents were ready to make something wonderful happen for them again.

We rented a house across the street from my grandparents' in Clairemont. I was not only back in San Diego, I was also living across the street from my beloved grandmother. I spent time with her every single day. It took Harry a while to financially recover from his Oxnard/abalone fall. First he went to work for his brother, who had a very successful car dealership in San Diego. Harry was very entrepreneurial. He bought a car rental franchise called Ugly Duckling Rent-A-Car and started renting out cars across the street from Sea World. It was in a little run-down building, but he and my mom fixed it up. Eventually they opened an antenna installation company as well, and Harry would crawl up onto people's roofs like Spider-Man and install television antennas.

After that, Harry heard about a new business: car striping. People were taking tape and striping their cars with pinstripes. Remember that? That became Harry's newest venture. He became the best car striper in San Diego. He went from car dealership to car dealership, becoming "the Car Striper Guy" and striping five cars a day at dealerships all over the area.

Harry taught me that if someone says no, you are talking to the wrong person. It's a mantra I have made my own. Just like my grandmother, Harry showed me how to do whatever it takes to get the job done and make a living. Nobody handed him anything on a silver platter. Harry thrived on hard work.

The whole experience—Harry's alcoholism and recovery/Oxnard/abalone/car rental/car striping—was a kind of wake-up call for me. It taught me how fast your life can turn around on a dime. I learned a lot of lessons I was able to use later. One minute I was with my grandmother, my mom was off getting married in Puerto

Vallarta, and life was dandy. I went to school, I got good grades, I had lots of friends. I was a very stable kid, really responsible. The candles were burning bright. So when my life became so unorganized and messy, it made me uncomfortable. The years after the debacle in Oxnard were wonderful for all of us, and highlighted what a wonderful man Harry Shannon really was. My biological dad, at that point, was gone. He was a really good guy, but we had lost touch with him. He moved back east and then to the Midwest, moving all over, trying to find work. I didn't even know where he was or what he did at that point. He called or sent letters periodically, but he was really just doing his own thing.

Harry, meanwhile, treated us as if we were his own kids. He showed us unconditional love. He redefined for me what family means. He showed me what it meant to be a good husband and contributor. When my mom wanted a new patio for the backyard, for example, he went out and brought home a truckload of bricks and laid my mom a gorgeous new patio for her new backyard. He was just a *doer.* If my mom needed something ironed, he did it. He was the family ironer. He was the best at ironing in the world. He would make it look like a professional job! He taught us by example what it meant to be an active part of a happy family.

Mom and Harry's businesses were doing well, and soon we were moving into a beautiful house in University City, a brand-new neighborhood where an entire area had been leveled—acres and acres and acres—to create a new development. Everything was new. It was a neighborhood full of kids with brand-new schools, brand-new houses, brand-new everything. Our new house had red shag carpeting, gorgeous in those days. On Fridays, my mom would make me rake the rug to fluff it up before I could go out with my friends.

By that time I had a second job, other than the candle business. I worked in a doughnut shop. I would report to work at five a.m., where I would literally scrape the glaze off the floor and sell coffee to customers. Then I would walk across the street and catch the bus to school. After school, I would work in the candle shop. When I came home, I would rake the carpet before I was allowed to go out with my friends. I never complained about the work. By the time I was a teenager, I knew that I had a beautiful life in La Jolla and I wanted to keep it going. I was determined to make something of myself one day. But in those days my idea of success was getting married and having babies. Six babies.

Boyfriends? Sure, a few. Just like any normal teenage girl, I loved hanging out with my friends. But mostly in groups. Weekends at the beach. Surfing at La Jolla Shores. Every day during the summer. But no real serious relationship yet. I always saw myself as being with an adult. I was biding my time.

When I turned sixteen, Harry surprised me with a brand-new car, a red Mazda RX-2. I would often drive that red Mazda east on the freeway that connects La Jolla with Clairemont, thinking about my plan. I always had to have a plan. I believed in dreaming big, working hard, and setting goals.

At that age, most girls were thinking about the prom. I was thinking, *Fuck the prom. I want to get married and have six kids.* I felt like life would start when I got that done. I graduated from Clairemont High, but I didn't go to college. No interest. School wasn't my thing. I had already set goals for my life, and college wasn't part of it.

I wanted to get out into the world.

CHAPTER TWO

R.G.K.

My best friend in high school was Debbie Mungle. We hung out together every single day. Debbie had great style and was always so much fun. Her mother was the business manager for a professional golfer named Phil Rodgers. Phil was like a part of Debbie's family, and he was very well-known. Debbie and I had been to many golf tournaments with Phil. And for our high school graduation, Debbie's mom bought us tickets to Hawaii so that we could go with Phil to the Hawaiian Open.

"You'll stay at the hotel, and it will be lots of fun," Phil told us.

I was seventeen, and I am still shocked my mother let me go.

In Hawaii, I met a professional golfer I'll call Anthony.

He was twelve years older than me.

He was tall, dark-haired, funny, and successful, and he represented this glamorous world of golf. Maybe I was just a golf groupie, but I liked him immediately. He made all the boys I'd hung out with in high school seem like, well, boys.

He was on the PGA tour with Phil. He was my first grown-up, non–high school boyfriend. I was very young, and I think my mother probably thought it was a phase and I would grow out of it, which I eventually did. I don't think she ever really thought that Anthony would be the person I would end up with for the rest of my life, because I was very, very young. She was smart enough to let me go through the motions and figure it out for myself. Even more, my mom and dad actually came to love Anthony, as did my grandmother. In my family, if the matriarch says something is okay, then it is okay. And everyone falls in line. They thought he was great because they had gone to so many of his golf tournaments. They loved going to the golf tournaments—especially Harry and his brother, Jim, who actually ran a golf tournament that Anthony always played in Torrey Pines. Harry and my mom used to take care of the scoreboard. They would go down to the eighteenth hole, and there was this huge board, and Harry would get up there and change the board. He had so much fun.

My parents loved golf. They loved that whole lifestyle, so when I ran off to golf tournaments with my girlfriend Debbie, my mom just said, "Have fun!" My parents weren't strict when it came to things like that. They knew that I was going to be that independent person, so they just followed that old philosophy that if your kids want to do something, they're going to do it with or without your blessing. So that is what I did, and Anthony went along with the whole golfing experience. We had many adventures together.

Anthony courted me; he showed me things I had never seen, taking me to PGA events in these beautiful places and resorts. I had grown up going to the La Costa Country Club with my dad and uncle, and I thought those big golf events were so glamorous and exciting. But that was nothing compared to Anthony's world. Soon I was traveling with Anthony to Japan, Scotland, London,

Mexico City. I spent a year traveling with him. Dating someone who was a professional golfer was thrilling. Anthony was hanging out with the likes of Lee Trevino, Ben Crenshaw, and Tom Watson.

After we had dated for a year and a half, Debbie and I convinced Anthony to let us live in his town house in Mission Beach—free of charge, of course. I have to admit, we were little con artists. We told Anthony that since he was on his way to being a *truly* bigtime golfer, he needed us to live in his house and watch his plants and take care of things for him. So while Anthony was out on the road, Debbie and I lived in his house. I was able to save money by continuing to work at my mom and grandmother's candle stores, as well as a little dress shop in La Jolla. I was already multitasking.

One day, in the midsummer of my eighteenth year, while Anthony was out of town at a golf tournament, Debbie and I decided to go to the horse races. That was the fateful day I met a young L.A. lawyer named Robert George Kardashian.

Every year, my mother would go to the Del Mar Thoroughbred Club, very close to San Diego, on opening day. Going to Del Mar was exciting because it was such an example of wealth and high society. The clothes were amazing and the fashion was over-the-top. We lived in a beautiful neighborhood in San Diego, but I wasn't used to going to big events. Naturally, I jumped at the chance to go to Del Mar with my mom.

Mom took us a couple of times over the years, but that summer we were living in Anthony's place, Debbie and some other friends of ours went to the track on our own. It was a beautiful day in Del Mar. I was beside myself with excitement. The women were all in gorgeous white with big hats and giant sunglasses. I was wearing a white pantsuit with a huge hat and sunglasses, like some 1920s movie star. Around my neck was a gold necklace with a pendant that spelled out the words "OH, SHIT." (I still have that necklace.)

We were having lunch at the Turf Club, the private club at Del Mar. I walked out to make a $2 bet. After I placed my bet, I stood next to a nearby pillar to wait for Debbie to place her bet. That's when I noticed a guy standing in front of me.

"Hi, is your name Janet?" he asked.

"That is the worst pickup line I have ever heard!" I replied.

"No, I'm serious. Is your name Janet?" he continued. He was dressed in a blazer and slacks, platform shoes, with slicked-back hair and had this big mustache. He looked very successful, and a lot like the singer Tony Orlando.

"No, my name is not Janet," I told him.

"Well, then what is it?" he asked.

"What's *your* name?" I shot back.

"I'm Robert Kardashian."

"Okay, my name is Kris."

"What's your last name?"

"Why do you want to know?"

"Because you look exactly like a girl I used to go out with."

"If you used to go out with her, you should know her last name."

"Come on, tell me your name."

"It's Kris Houghton."

"How do you spell that?"

"K-R-I-S-H-O-U-G-H-T-O-N."

"Where do you live?"

By then I'd had enough. He was so bold. He was hitting on me! I thought he was cute. I also thought he was way too old for me.

"San Diego," I said.

"Oh," he said, and paused. "Well, would you ever consider going out with me?"

"No!"

He stared down at my necklace, which, of course, spelled out "OH, SHIT."

"Nice necklace," he said.

"Thanks," I said. I have to admit, I was snobby. I knew I looked pretty cute. I was on my game that day, and I knew it. I turned to go back to the Turf Club.

"Maybe I'll call you sometime. What's your phone number?" he called out after me.

"I'm not giving you my phone number," I replied firmly, and that was that.

I felt his eyes on me for the rest of the day. I would look around and find him practically stalking me, standing in the corner, staring at me. When a race was about to begin, I would go to the window to place another bet. Sure enough, there's Robert Kardashian, waiting for me to show up. This time he had brought his brother.

"I'd like to introduce you to my brother, Tommy," he said. He and Tommy and their father, Arthur, came to the races every year, just like we did.

"Nice to meet you," I said to Robert's brother. Then to Robert: "See you later."

"Are you still not going to give me your number?"

"Nope, not going to give you my number."

Back in the early '70s, you could look up just about anybody in the phone book. I wasn't listed, though, because Debbie and I had just moved into Anthony's house about six months before. We had a new phone line of our own. It was just an old-fashioned one-line dial-up phone.

One day, Debbie was at work when the telephone rang.

"Hi there, Kris! It's Bob Kardashian," he said. "Remember? The races?"

I remembered all too well. "How did you get my number?" I asked.

"My friend Joni Migdal works for the telephone company," he said. "She just looked up your records and saw that you have a brand-new number and she gave it to me."

Oh my God! I thought. But I just said, "Well, hi."

I put him off for weeks and weeks as he kept trying to convince me to go out with him. He called me twice a week. Then weeks turned into months. He had this low voice, and it was so adult and grown-up. He actually scared me a little bit. He was a little intimidating.

I got to know him a little over the phone, even though I really didn't want to for some reason. Robert said that he lived in Beverly Hills, and he had a really nice house. He told me about his close Armenian family. But every time he would get around to asking me out, I would say, "I really can't." I never told him the full story about Anthony, but I did eventually tell him that I was dating someone else, and that his name was Anthony and that he was a PGA golfer.

Months passed. I hadn't seen Robert again, but I had continued to speak to him by phone. One day, Debbie and I went up to Los Angeles to watch Anthony and Phil play in the Los Angeles Open at the Riviera Country Club. We checked into the round Holiday Inn on the corner off the 405 and got all dolled up. I remember I wore a pair of new sunglasses I had just bought at Judy's—really great movie-star sunglasses—and I had this little purse with a wooden handle so that you could change out the purse itself and just attach different bags to the wooden handle, gray flannel or black-and-white check or black leather. Every golfer's wife had that purse. I thought I looked pretty cute with my golf shoes and my fabulous outfit and my little sweater. We had VIP passes and *the* purse, just like the other professional-golfer wives.

We headed to the golf course. Anthony was playing a round with Arnold Palmer. Arnold Palmer had fifty bazillion followers—

"Arnie's Army," they called them—and they were his fan club. I followed Anthony around with my little stick seat, which unfolded out into a chair. With my little seat and my cute outfit, I looked like I had been out on tour for ages. Debbie and I floated around between Anthony and Phil. The round Anthony played with Arnold Palmer was crazy—there were so many people around. It was like having your boyfriend play against Tiger Woods.

I was walking down the fairway when I felt a tap on my shoulder. I turned around and there he was. "Remember me? Bob Kardashian," he said.

I was shocked, but he kept talking. "This is my friend Joni Migdal," he continued, introducing me to the woman who had found my phone number for him.

"What are you guys doing here?" I said, my mind racing. I was trying to put it all together. Did he just run into me accidentally? Was Joni Migdal actually his girlfriend? Robert and Joni started to follow me around the fairway. I found Debbie, but it was clear Robert and Joni were not planning to leave.

Around this time, Anthony walked by and saw the little parade on my tail. "Oh, who are your friends?" he asked.

"This is Robert Kardashian and Joni Migdal," I said.

Robert turned to me and said, "Cute glasses."

I smiled at that; I *loved* those sunglasses.

"They're filthy. You better clean them," he added.

I took them off and, sure enough, they *were* filthy, smudged, and I was so embarrassed. I thought I was so cool and so meticulous, and here I was, wearing a dirty pair of sunglasses. Robert thought it was so funny. I cleaned them immediately and we all walked around together for the rest of the day. Finally, Robert said, "I'll call you."

"Isn't Joni your girlfriend?" I asked when she was out of earshot.

"No, she's my friend," he answered. "We came out here to find *you*!"

I had been blowing Robert off every single phone call, but apparently when I told him I was going to the Los Angeles Open, he decided he would come there to find me. After they left, I had to admire Robert's persistence. Here I had blown him off for a year, and he still kept calling me. The Anthony thing seemed serious, but I think I loved the lifestyle more than the man. So the next time Robert called and asked, "Will you *finally* go out with me?" I relented.

"If you come to San Diego and take me out on a real date, I will go out with you," I told him. I didn't tell Robert that I had agreed to marry Anthony.

Anthony proposed, and I had been having so much fun dating him that I thought that saying yes was the right thing to do. But as time passed, I started to realize that I didn't really want to marry Anthony. At nineteen, I was too young to be engaged to anyone. I had also reconnected with my biological father. My dad had moved back to San Diego, and I reached out to him a lot. My dad became not just the dad who didn't get along with my mom when I was a child; he became more like a friend. He was a really cool guy, and I really enjoyed the time I would spend with him. We formed this really amazing bond during that time.

Also around this same time, I fell in love with cooking. Debbie and I entertained at Anthony's house on his tiny patio, taking turns hosting parties. Debbie would make the best tacos and peach margaritas and amazing dips and guacamole, and I would make steaks, Caesar salads, and baked potatoes. We invited our friends over, and I started inviting my dad. Dad got to know Anthony a bit, and he already knew Debbie. When I told him about Robert, he wanted to get to know him too.

But it wasn't meant to be.

The night of our big, long-awaited first date, Robert picked me up and said, "Let's go to the movies." He had actually flown from Los Angeles to San Diego just for our date that night. After the movie, we ended up back at my house, which was also, of course, still Anthony's house. Debbie was working that night, so Robert and I were alone, and somehow we made our way upstairs. We were messing around and heading in the direction of some major hanky-panky when we heard the front door open. *Anthony was home!*

"Kris!" I heard him calling from downstairs. I looked at Robert, and Robert looked at me. *Oh, shit.* We were so busted. We flew to our feet, but we were stuck upstairs in Anthony's town house. And we are not talking about the Taj Mahal here—it wasn't a big place. *How are we getting out of here?* I thought. We couldn't jump out of a second-story window. I couldn't hide Robert in the closet. Thank God we had our clothes on.

"Let's make a run for it!" I said, and we went running down the stairs, right past Anthony, and headed for the front door. It was stupid and immature of me to think we could get away with that.

"What are *you* doing here?" Anthony yelled at Robert.

I stopped, turned around, and I answered, "Oh, this is my friend Bob."

"What are you doing here, man?" Anthony repeated, and he and Robert got into it. Anthony started to grab Robert, and I immediately realized Robert was not a fighter. He was standing there in his designer jeans, Gucci loafers, and a gorgeous Gucci sweater with an anchor knitted into it. Anthony grabbed the sweater first.

"Don't touch the sweater!" Robert screamed. "It's my brother's!" He had stolen his brother's brand-new Gucci sweater out of his closet to wear for our big first date, not thinking he might get attacked by a really pissed-off professional golfer while wearing it. Anthony didn't give a damn. He grabbed the sweater and ripped it, stretching it out terribly and ruining it. Robert just broke away and went hauling down the street, running for his life.

I ran past Anthony, grabbed my car keys from the front table, jumped in my little red Mazda, locked the doors, and took off after Robert. When I reached him, we were both shaking. "Get in the car! Get in the car!" I yelled. He hopped in, and we could see Anthony in the rearview mirror, chasing us down the street.

"I am never coming back here again," Robert said.

"I'm sorry, I'm so sorry," I said. I was so upset. I thought he would never speak to me again. I had told him that Anthony and I weren't getting along, but I never meant to put him in such a situation.

"Where do you want to go?" I asked him.

"Just take me to the airport," Robert said. "When you get things straightened out with this guy, or decide what you want to do, we'll talk. But that was scary."

I dropped him off and he flew back to L.A. I didn't hear from him again for a really long time. He had probably never been in a fight in his life before that night.

That same year, on Easter Sunday evening of 1975, I was standing in the kitchen at Anthony's house when the phone rang. It was my paternal grandfather.

"I have some really bad news," he said. "Your dad's been in a terrible accident, and he didn't make it."

He told me the awful details: He was with his girlfriend in his vintage yellow Porsche—his pride and joy—and was run off the road by a jackknifed semitruck in a remote, deserted area of Mexico. A group of nuns found the wreckage by the side of the road and took him to the closest medical facility. My father's girlfriend survived, but he suffered severe internal injuries. He was only forty-two years old.

I screamed, dropped the phone, and was just crying, crying, crying, hysterically crying. A few nights before, my father had called me. "I'm going to Mexico for Easter break and I'm taking my girlfriend. I would love to see you tonight, honey. Are you busy?" he asked. I hadn't been busy, but I was tired. When I told him that, he said, "It's okay, I'll just see you when I get back. It's fine." And now he was dead. He was the first significant person in my life who had died, and when he had wanted to spend time with me, I had blown him off.

It was an important lesson about love. Love your family; try to do as much as you can. I think that's why I'm always trying to burn the candle at both ends now. I want to be there for my family and for my loved ones, and if somebody needs me or wants to be with me, I feel really bad or guilty if I can't be there for them. You never know when it might be the last time you see somebody.

My dad was a lot of fun. He liked to have a good time. He was very social. I remember that one time when I was a teenager he invited me up to spend the weekend with him in Long Beach. He took me to Venice Beach, and he thought that was so cool. He would always try to think of the cool thing to do that would help him relate to me at whatever particular age I was at the time. I was probably sixteen and I had just started driving when he invited me to come up and see his place that weekend. I didn't appreciate it at the time, but when I look back at that moment, I realize how much thought he put into where he could take me instead of just maybe another movie or a dinner. He wanted to make sure I had a good time.

My father was cremated.

At the funeral, I remember someone told me that my paternal grandmother had seen his body the day before. I thought, *Nobody asked me if I wanted to see him one last time*. That hurt. Not just that I wasn't asked, but that they seemed to view me as a child. My mom took us to the funeral and I remember how strong she was in supporting my sister and me.

I found myself thinking about how much I wished my dad had met Robert Kardashian. He had begun calling again. I didn't know what to do. I was still engaged to Anthony and I didn't know how to juggle the two.

"Maybe we should get together," Robert would say, and I would hem and haw and answer, "Maybe we should. I'd love to see you. But let's see what happens."

We would make a plan. But every time I would cancel at the last minute. "I just can't come," I would say in a phone call the night before or the morning of the planned rendezvous. I came up with the stupidest excuses. I had a toothache or whatever, but how many toothaches can one person have? When I ran out of teeth, I told him I had sprained my ankle or I had the flu. It became ridiculous.

The whole situation came to a head when Anthony was invited to play in the British Open. Tom Watson was playing there, too, and he and his wife, Linda, had rented a house on the golf course in England. "Why don't you and Anthony get married in our backyard here?" Tom and Linda told us. "How much fun would that be!" they said. "That's a great idea!" Anthony replied. I was thinking, *Not so much*.

I didn't want to marry Anthony. We eventually decided that perhaps a European wedding without my family wasn't such a great idea. Still, I was up for the trip.

Right before I left for Europe, Robert called me and said,

"I bought a new house in Beverly Hills, and my brother and I are having a housewarming party. I would really like you to be my date, and it's really important to me that you give me a yes or a no."

At that point I had decided that I was going to break things off with Anthony in Europe and see if I wanted to date Robert after doing that. I told Robert about my plan to break up with Anthony in Europe and come home by myself, and told him, yes, I would be his date to his big, important party.

He immediately told everyone he knew that he had met a fabulous girl and she would be his date to his housewarming party. But once I was in Europe with Anthony, I couldn't figure out how to get out of there. I had no backbone. I couldn't figure out how to tell Anthony it was over and that I was going home on my own. Finally, the day of Robert's party came, and instead of meeting him on the 5:00 p.m. plane from San Diego to Los Angeles as I had promised, I was still in Europe with Anthony. I didn't even have the guts to call Robert and tell him I wasn't coming.

Robert was at the airport waiting for me, standing at the gate with two dozen red roses. He waited until every single person came off that plane before giving up on me. He turned around, walked to the trash can, and threw the roses away. He walked to his car alone and cried all the way home.

At his party, he had to face all his friends who were expecting to meet this great new girl he had told them all about. I had made him look like a fool. He didn't have a girlfriend, he didn't have a date. This was his big, huge party, and I had blown him off.

I was so young, and I had a lot to learn. When I called him the next day to say "I'm so, so sorry," I could hear him crying on the other end of the line. "I just don't know what to do."

Suddenly he turned angry. "You embarrassed me," he said. "You made me look bad. When you finally figure this all out, give me a call."

Then he hung up.

I returned from Europe with Anthony, still unable to figure out how to call things off. Fortunately, Anthony made it easy for me. His next tournament was in Pebble Beach. I went with him and took my parents, and after the tournament I left with my parents for a trip down the coast to the Hearst Castle. Anthony couldn't come along, he said, because he had to get to the next city on the tour.

When I got back to his house, though, I received a letter in the mail. Inside was a hotel receipt from Carmel showing that Anthony had stayed in Carmel four days longer than he had told me. Then a young woman started calling the house, looking for Anthony. She wanted to know who I was and why I was answering his phone. "Who the hell are *you*?" I asked. She told me she had spent four days with Anthony in Carmel, after which he left for his next golf tournament. Now she couldn't find him. He wasn't returning her phone calls. She was pissed, which was why she called me.

I was *so* mad, but also glad. Now I had a backup plan. I had been too weak to break up with him. Now Anthony had made things easy for me. I packed my bags and put everything in my car, thinking, *I wasn't raised to be a victim. I was raised to be a strong, confident girl who knows when it is time to fold 'em.* I waited until he came home, and when he walked through the door, I told him that we were done, and I told him why. He denied, denied, denied.

"I really don't care," I said. "I'm out of here."

I went to my mother's house and called Robert. "It's over, I'm done," I said.

"Okay, if you're done, then why don't you come see me this weekend?"

"Great. I'll be there," I said.

I got dressed, got on a plane, and flew to L.A., where I rushed out of the airport to meet Robert Kardashian for our first legitimate date. Sitting in a green Mercedes, waiting for me at the curb at the airport, were Robert and O.J. Simpson.

"This is O.J., my best friend," Robert told me, introducing me to the famous football player, while I'm thinking, *Oh my God. Oh my GOD!* We drove back to Robert's house in Beverly Hills: Robert Kardashian, O.J. Simpson, and me.

CHAPTER THREE

Flying High

R obert and his brother, Tommy, had bought a beautiful house on Deep Canyon Drive in Beverly Hills. It had a tennis court and a swimming pool, and they were living *the life*. Judy Wilder, a really well-known interior designer, decorated the house. If you had your house decorated by Judy Wilder, you were stylin'. Tommy ran the family meatpacking business, and Robert was an attorney with a group of Armenian lawyers, Eamer, Bedrosian & Kardashian. He worked with all kinds of people, including O.J. Simpson.

Robert took me back to his house and showed me around, and then he took me to his mother's house, where I met his mother and practically his entire family. I could not believe what a nice family he had and what wonderful family values they embodied. They loved one another so much. His mother had made this thing called *beeshee*, an Armenian breakfast pastry. It's a big, flat, fried pancake with sugar or syrup on top. My daughter Kourtney got the recipe from Robert's mother before she died, and now we make it for family occasions. It's one of my most favorite things in the world now because of the strong family values it represents. Plus, it's absolutely delicious.

So Robert's mom had made *beeshee*, and they had people and friends stopping in to meet me. Afterward, we went back to Robert's house and I met a few more of his friends as well as his brother Tommy's friends. It was a turning point. I thought, *This could very well be the guy for me.*

Every weekend for three weeks after that, I flew up to visit Robert. That first weekend, I met his friends and his parents, and had the time of my life. The second weekend, I met more of his friends and stayed at his house. The third weekend, he sat me on his lap on the chair behind his bedroom desk and said, "Will you marry me?"

"What?!" I said.

"Will you marry me?" he repeated.

I stammered something to the effect of "I don't think I can marry you right now. I mean, it's kind of soon."

He was beyond upset; he was devastated. When I said no, Robert's face just fell. He had me sitting on his lap and he was so excited. He had experienced this revelation that he had finally found the love of his life, and I just didn't understand. I later learned that he had told all his friends and colleagues about me, telling them that I looked like Natalie Wood. (I found that funny!) Now I was making him look bad, because I was refusing his proposal. But I had just been through this crazy thing with Anthony, and I wasn't ready to jump back into another engagement so soon. After all, I wasn't even twenty.

Robert and I continued dating, but he was angry and took serious issue with me for declining his marriage proposal. I returned to San Diego and decided that I was going to take control of my life. I started by deciding to apply to become an American Airlines flight attendant instead of going to college. The only part of high school I enjoyed was the social aspect. I was just not into school. I wanted to get on with my life.

Within a week, I applied for, interviewed for, was offered, and accepted a job. American immediately flew me to Fort Worth, Texas, to begin six weeks of flight attendant school.

Robert wasn't happy. He took it personally and believed that by turning him down and preparing to fly off into the sunset with American, I was slamming his character and who he was as a human being. I still felt like I had made the right decision, and I certainly didn't think he would jump back into the dating scene immediately. When I flew away, he began dating someone else right away: *Priscilla Presley.*

Robert and Tommy Kardashian were two of the most eligible bachelors in Beverly Hills at that time. They were at the top of their game: cool, successful, good-looking, and from a great family. Everyone wanted to date them. Tommy was dating Joan Esposito, the ex-wife of Elvis Presley's close friend Joe Esposito. Tommy and Joan decided that it would be a great idea to set up Robert with Priscilla. Robert was instantly smitten with Priscilla, and she apparently was smitten with him. They quickly moved in together.

Payback is a bitch.

I was living in a flight attendants' dormitory in Fort Worth, bummed that Robert was going to end up with Priscilla Presley. She was *gorgeous*, of course, petite and perfect and beautiful and famous. I would see pictures of her and just die. Any woman would be thrilled to look like Priscilla Presley.

I was at flight school, doing my thing, but again, I was bummed. Not devastated—*I* had been the one to turn *him* down, after all— but disappointed, because deep in my heart I was still hoping that Robert would end up being the guy for me.

We became telephone buddies again. We would talk every

night, me on the public telephone in the hallway of my dorm, Robert in Beverly Hills. I had to keep putting quarters into the pay phone to finish our conversations and kept rolls of quarters and dimes on hand for my nightly phone calls with Robert. Of course, he could have easily called me, but I didn't want to admit to Robert that I was having to feed a pay phone. We would talk about Priscilla. "Gosh, what do you think I should get her for her birthday?" he would say. I would listen to his stories about her and he would listen to mine about American Airlines flight attendant school.

Before I knew it, six weeks had flown past. I had put my nose to the grindstone in flight attendant school, hoping to distract myself from what was going on with Robert. I tried to avoid the *National Enquirer*, because Robert and Priscilla were frequently inside—or even on the cover—together. Thank goodness we didn't have the Internet or TMZ during those days.

Flight attendant school kept me busy and distracted me from dwelling over whether or not my future would be with Robert Kardashian—until my graduation in August 1976. I had given American my preferences for my base city: Los Angeles was my first choice in the hopes I would be able to reconnect with Robert. San Diego was my second choice. San Francisco was third. American didn't tell you where you would be based until the last minute, so I still didn't know.

Then Robert called and said that he and Priscilla had broken up.

"When do you graduate?" he asked. "And where will you be based?"

I told him I wouldn't know for two more weeks. As the weeks went by, it became clear that Robert had decided he wanted to continue to pursue me, and he was antsy to know where the pursuit would take place. Well, I didn't get any of my choices. Instead,

I would be based in New York City. I was devastated ... and scared. I was twenty years old, one of the youngest people American had ever put through flight school, and I was leaving the state where I had spent my entire life to move all the way across the country to New York.

"Where did you get? Where did you end up?" Robert asked.

"New York," I said despondently.

"That's actually good news!" he said. "Because I'm going with O.J. Simpson to the games [the 1976 Olympics] in Montreal, and afterward we have to go straight to New York for O.J.'s job with ABC."

O.J. was going to work as a commentator at the Olympic Games that year, Robert said, and we were all going to meet in New York and pick up where we left off in L.A. "O.J.'s going to get rooms at the Plaza," Robert told me. "It will be great. You can meet us there."

As Robert had promised, it was exciting. Robert and O.J. met me at the airport and we all rode into the city together in a limo and checked into the Plaza. I had never really been in a limo before, and I certainly had never been to the Plaza, so I just felt like the luckiest girl in the world. First, we went shopping. Then, dinner at '21' and dancing at Studio 54. But it was more than just where we went and what we did; it was how it felt. I could feel electricity in the air around us. From the moment I stepped off that airplane and met Robert at the gate, I could feel everything around me changing so fast. I knew my life would never be the same again.

The funniest moment happened on our New York City trip. Bruce Jenner had won the gold medal in the decathlon at the 1976 Olympics, so Robert and O.J. were all excited, saying, "Bruce Jenner won the gold medal!"

Bruce was, of course, the champion of the 1976 summer Olympic Games in Montreal, the symbol of athletic heroism in America.

Everybody remembered the huge moment when Bruce blazed across the finish line in the 1,500-meter run, his arms high over his head as the crowd went crazy, as he broke the world record and won the gold. Everybody remembered Bruce except me.

"Who's Bruce Jenner?" I asked.

O.J., on the other hand, was a star. He was crazy fun and incredibly famous. After running for touchdowns in his NFL career, a Heisman Trophy winner and a professional football superstar, he ran through airports in Hertz commercials, found fame as a network television sports commentator, and had endorsement deals for companies like Dingo boots. Fans followed O.J. wherever he went. And when he took us to the Dingo store on Fifty-Seventh Street and Fifth Avenue in Manhattan and bought us all boots, people gawked and asked for his autograph.

Even though everyone knew O.J. was married, he brought along Maud Adams, the famous model and James Bond girl. I thought, *My, he has pretty friends!* But we were having way too much fun to dwell on it, and after all, I wasn't his babysitter.

O.J. loved to dance, and we all loved to drink. We never got crazy drunk, but we all liked to have a good time.

I was on cloud nine all of that week. Then Robert and O.J. went home. The week American Airlines was giving me to find my sea legs in New York City was over. Talk about a cold-water moment. I went from living the high life in the Plaza to sharing an apartment way up on Ninety-Ninth Street and First Avenue with four flight attendant roommates. It was the only way I could afford the rent. The four of us were crammed into a tiny two-bedroom apartment, two women to a room, sleeping on twin beds. I remember pushing my little bed on its frame up against the wall beneath a window. Wow. I had a view of a brick wall across an alley. I felt so impatient knowing I was stuck in New York alone. *Wait, this isn't part of my plan!* I thought.

Still, New York was exciting—at least at first. Having grown up in San Diego, I was living a life I had never lived before. I had never lived in a high-rise, never ridden in a cab, never really used public transportation. Now I was taking a subway to get to work at LaGuardia, because that was the hub for most of my flights.

My life as a flight attendant was like something out of a movie. I had a blue blazer with wings on my lapel, and I was very professional. American was very strict about the dress code, and my hair was always picture-perfect. I had my skirt just the right length, I had just the right jacket. I took it all very seriously.

Ultimately, there was always some character on the airplane who wanted to reach out and touch someone—literally. "Hey, baby," the wolves would leer. "What are you doing tonight?" I was an airline attendant, not a hooker. So I kept my hot, very steamy pot of coffee with me at all times. It's amazing how a guy's attitude would change when I held a hot pot of coffee over his crotch.

I was flying everywhere. To and from all of the places American flies all over the country—Cincinnati, Cleveland, Columbus. After a few months of that, a seasoned flight attendant took me under her wing and told me that if I really wanted to go home more, I should sign up to be an "Extra." The senior flight attendants all got to do the L.A.–New York and New York–L.A. routes, she told me. But because they had so much seniority, they also took time off for vacation whenever they wanted. "Extras" were the girls who filled their slots. I signed up to be an Extra.

It saved my relationship with Robert. All I did from that point on was fly New York to L.A., L.A. to New York, and back and forth again and again and again, all on overnight trips. Robert would pick me up at the airport and we would go straight to lunch and spend the day together. We did that for several months. We were getting closer and closer.

But when the weekend was over, I was still stuck in New York.

started lighting candles.

Whenever I could, I would go to St. Patrick's Cathedral on Fifth Avenue and pray. I would light a candle—yes, a candle—because candles have always been lucky for me. I would light candles in that ancient church and pray to God that I would get transferred to Los Angeles.

"You'll *never* get transferred to Los Angeles," every flight attendant told me. "You have to have so much seniority. Only ten-year veterans get a sought-after city like L.A."

I kept praying, praying, praying, and lighting candle after candle, buckling down for the long, hard winter and coming to the realization about how unhappy I would be if I had to stay in New York, especially through the holidays. Christmas has always been my thing. To this day, I am still like a big kid on Christmas. I get *so* excited to decorate my house and spend time with my friends and family and have people over and plan my big Christmas Eve. I am famous for my over-the-top Christmas Eves now, complete with Santas and elves and reindeer and carolers. Back then, though, my Christmases were on a smaller scale. I was alone in New York, without family or friends during my very favorite holidays because of . . . this *job*. Again, I was so young. But I kept lighting candles, praying and believing that something good would happen.

Lo and behold, one day I got a call from the American Airlines corporate office. "I hope this is good news," said the voice on the other end of the line. "You applied for a transfer to Los Angeles, and your transfer was granted."

I fell to my knees and thanked God. I was bawling, literally crying, over this miracle. I called Robert. I called my parents. I called everybody. *"I'm coming back to L.A.! I'm coming back to L.A.!"* My mom and Harry flew to New York and helped me move. In those days you could check as much stuff as you wanted on airplanes, so we packed everything, even my TV, and checked it all.

I got off the plane in L.A., *my* city, the city of the man I loved—or at least, the man I thought I loved—wearing a pair of cream gabardine wool slacks tucked into brown riding boots and a matching blazer. I had a button-down shirt underneath and I wore a big hat. I collected my luggage and walked outside. Waiting for me at the curb at LAX in his new black Rolls-Royce was my prince, Robert Kardashian. I *ran* to him, literally flew into his arms. "Oh my God, oh my God! I'm finally here!" I cried.

We kissed, long, deep, passionately, and I knew—*This is the one.*

We piled everything into the Rolls and drove to his house.

The next morning I immediately started looking for an apartment. It didn't even occur to me to live with Robert; that just didn't seem cool. At that time, he was living with both his brother, Tommy, and his best friend O.J. It was a big boys' club. I called a couple of my flight attendant friends and the three of us found an apartment in Brentwood, close enough to both Robert in Beverly Hills and the Los Angeles International Airport.

Those were magical times. I would work two or three days a week, LAX to New York. I loved doing L.A.–New York because there were no stops. It was just back and forth, and back to Robert and our lovely life together again. Between the flights, Robert and I would play. Every night, it was someplace fabulous for dinner, which in 1977 meant Trader Vic's, Daisy, and Luau.

Luau was the first place Robert ever took me to dinner in Beverly Hills. Joe Stellini was the maître d', and Robert ordered this entire dinner for us.

"These are coconut rolls," Robert told me when a dish of snowy white rolls arrived at our table. I took him at his word, of course, and bit into one. It was a *hand towel*. Robert told that story for years. He thought it was the funniest thing. He was such a funny guy, and he was always playing practical jokes on everyone. The coconut roll/hand towel bit ranked among his best.

When I moved to Los Angeles, O.J. had been separated from his wife, Marguerite. They tried to work things out and had gotten back together, and when they did, she got pregnant with their daughter Erin. So now, after living with Robert for a time, O.J. was back at home with Marguerite. Then, one day, Robert's brother surprised us by announcing that he had bought a house in Beverly Hills right across the street from Sammy Davis Jr.

Now Robert and I had the house in Beverly Hills to ourselves, and I soon left the apartment I'd been sharing with the flight attendants. It was a relief to have some space alone with Robert, because when I first moved back to L.A., O.J. and Tommy and all of their friends were always there. The guys would play tennis at one another's houses, because tennis was the big thing back then. On Saturdays everyone would be at Robert's house playing tennis. On Sundays we would all be at O.J.'s house playing tennis.

My time living alone with Robert in his big, beautiful house on Deep Canyon Drive would turn out to be short-lived. Robert was a born-again Christian. He prayed before every meal and before each and every business meeting. He even carried a Bible with him. I had grown up going to a Presbyterian church on Sundays and holidays, but I was never really devout, especially not as devout as Robert.

When I went to see Robert for the first time in L.A., I realized that he was actually not only really fun (and funny) but he was also very spiritual. The first thing I noticed was that he had a Bible on his desk and another next to his bed. It was impressive to me that Robert seemed to be such a religious man. *Wow,* I thought, *what an amazing guy.* He wore his Christianity on his sleeve.

"That's a beautiful Bible," I said about the Bible beside the bed. It was covered in a special leather cover, hand tooled with his initials engraved on the front. (I have that Bible to this day.)

Through the years I would discover that Robert's family members were all very devoted Christians and often gave one another beautiful gifts that showed their love of God. When I went into Robert's kitchen, I saw an intricate three-dimensional sculpture made of clay hanging from a rawhide rope in his kitchen. On the pieces of clay were inscriptions from the famous John 3:16 Bible verse: "For God so loved the world that he gave his only begotten Son, that whosoever believes in him shall not perish but have everlasting life."

"It was a gift from my sister, Barbara," Robert told me.

The love of the Lord would be the thread that ran deep in our family for many years to come. The artwork bearing the Bible verse in Robert's kitchen became something that meant a lot to me. Last year, when I was with Robert's sister, Barbara, I mentioned how much the John 3:16 verse in the clay artwork she had given her brother had meant to me. "Whatever happened to it?" I asked. She told me she didn't know but would try to find out. Shortly afterward, she drove all the way to L.A. with her daughter, Cheryle, and gave me my own copy for my house. It almost brought me to tears.

Robert's love of God and religion was one of the things that attracted me the most. He wanted me to share in that love. One day he told me he wanted to take me to a Bible study at Pat Boone's house. Pat was, of course, the pop singer turned motivational speaker who hosted these big Bible studies at his house every week, and over the years, celebrities like Zsa Zsa Gabor, Doris Day, Priscilla Presley (thanks to Robert), and Glenn Ford were just some of the people who attended. Robert went every week and he really wanted me to come. Of course, I agreed, and I was glad

I did. The minute I walked into Pat Boone's big, beautiful, sprawling house in Beverly Hills, I met the most welcoming, wonderful, magical group of people I'd ever known in my whole life.

Pat Boone hosted, but others often led the studies, particularly our pastor, Kenn Gulliksen. Pat couldn't have been nicer, and his wife, Shirley, was so sweet. I met his daughters, too, and I was especially excited to meet his daughter Debbie, who would become a popular singer just like her dad. We would meet in Pat's big family room with all his friends and extended family members and talk about faith and Christianity, stories from the Bible, what they meant, and our interpretations. The speakers always gave us something to really think about all week. I had a wonderful time going to the meetings and I really became closer to Jesus Christ because of them.

Robert and I started attending Pat Boone's Bible study groups regularly. I met a group of friends there that I would keep for years afterward. Robert introduced me to religion in a whole new light. He really taught me the importance of Christianity and how making it more of a focus in my life could make me feel whole. It felt so right to be dating someone who felt the same way I did. I accepted Christ through those Bible studies at Pat Boone's house, and I became a born-again Christian.

Soon after that, Robert decided I should move out because it was against God's plan for us to live together. Not long after that, because of the Bible studies, Robert decided that it wasn't a good idea for us to even have sex anymore. We were full-on dating, with full-on sex, and all of a sudden, mid-relationship, he decided that we were not going to sleep together anymore, because it was not God's will. I agreed, since that *is* what the Bible says. But Robert wanted me to move out *altogether*. So I found myself sitting there, packing up all my clothes, thinking, *What the hell is going on here?*

A. C. Cowlings, one of Robert's and O.J.'s friends, who would later gain fame for driving O.J.'s Bronco after the murder of Nicole Brown Simpson, helped me move. I went from Robert's big, grand house in Beverly Hills into a tiny little apartment in Sherman Oaks, right behind a Marie Callender's pie shop. So there I am in my apartment, and one night Robert came to take me out in his spanking-new white Rolls-Royce. By then he had a black Rolls and a white Rolls, and he parked in the garage underneath my apartment to pick me up. He took me out to dinner and then he walked me back upstairs. We would still kiss and make out, but otherwise nothing, because we were living this clean, Christian relationship.

One night, after we kissed, he left as he always did. But a few minutes later he was knocking on the door. When I opened it, he was shaking, and I could tell he was about to cry.

"What's wrong?"

"I banged my new Rolls-Royce into a pillar in your garage," he said.

We went downstairs, and there was a huge dent in the back of his car.

"I'm so sorry," I said.

I don't know why he came back to tell me. I think he was just shaken up. He just needed a hug. But in my head, as I watched him drive off, I thought, *Serves him right for kicking me out!*

Restlessness is my nature. And I was restless about my relationship with Robert. *This is a guy who asked me to marry him three weeks after we started dating, and now . . . nothing. What's the problem?* I thought. *Ask me AGAIN!* I waited and I waited.

Then, in August of 1977, Elvis Presley died. We got the news while we were at dinner at the house of our best friends, Joyce and Larry Kraines. The first thing Robert wanted to do was call Priscilla. He was close to her and Lisa Marie, and he wanted to check on them. He got her on the phone right away and asked her if she was okay.

Oh, boy, I thought. *They've reconnected.* I never really understood why they broke up, so I didn't know what this meant. Maybe now Priscilla would have more emotional space? Maybe now Robert would want her back? Over the following months, I was apprehensive that Robert would start thinking about Priscilla again.

Then, suddenly, it was the holidays, my favorite season. Robert and I had so much fun and spent the holidays with each other's families. We drove down to San Diego in his white Rolls and had Christmas Eve with my mom and dad, and the next morning we drove back to L.A. to spend Christmas with his family. In January, I went back to work flying and Robert, as always, was working hard in his law practice.

That winter, we went on a couple of ski trips. I got the ski bug bad, so I decided to plan a girls' trip to Switzerland in the winter of 1978. Robert decided to go to Rio at the same time I was on my ski trip. He had a lifelong desire to go to Carnival, so he went with a buddy. By the time we both got home, I had sort of had it. I missed Robert so much when I was on my trip. I decided I didn't want to do girls' trips anymore. I didn't want to be by myself anymore. I didn't want to live in an apartment. I was ready to live out my dream of becoming a wife and a mother with six kids of my own. The calling was so strong that I decided, *If Robert doesn't ask me to marry him, I am just going to have to move on.* I didn't want to, but I thought I might have to. I felt like I was on the slow boat to China with Robert Kardashian.

Right before I left for my girls' trip to Switzerland with one of my best girlfriends, Cindy Spallino, a fellow flight attendant, I went to get my nails done on Rodeo Drive for my big trip. I had wedding rings on my brain. On the way to the salon, we walked by Van Cleef & Arpels. In the window was a beautiful, five-rows-deep, pavé diamond wedding band. *Wouldn't it be cool to have a wedding band like that?* I thought.

That ring became my dream. I didn't tell anybody. I just kept it to myself and thought, *Someday when I get married, I would love to have that ring*.

Unbeknownst to me, while I was in Switzerland, Robert went ring shopping with my girlfriend Joyce Kraines. I came home with my arms full of European fashion magazines: European *Vogue* and others. They were so beautiful and the photography was just stunning. I love to read fashion magazines. I had them on my coffee table, and for some reason some of them ended up at Robert's house.

On Easter Sunday, 1978, I spent the night at Robert's house so that we could get up early and go to church. We made little Easter baskets, which we gave to each other on Easter Sunday morning. We were getting ready to leave. I was in the dining room when Robert came in and took a folded piece of paper out of his back pocket and suddenly dropped to one knee.

"I love you so much and I want to spend the rest of my life with you," he said. "I'd like you to be my wife . . . *Will you marry me?*"

I started to bawl right there in the dining room. He unfolded the piece of paper, and it was a page out of my European *Vogue* with a picture of a big gorgeous diamond.

"I would love for you to have this ring someday," he said. "But until then, I'm going to find you the perfect thing, and I'll do it next week."

Of course, Robert could have bought me anything he wanted. But he was a frugal guy; in those days, it was one thing to buy a Rolls-Royce; it was quite another to spend hundreds of thousands of dollars on a diamond.

Oh my God. He was so sweet and so scared. He was quivering, and I thought he was going to cry. Of course I said: "YES!" We were both crying and laughing.

We decided to go straight to San Diego to tell my parents. "Mom, we're coming down to have lunch with you," I said on the phone.

We hopped a flight on PSA and my mom picked us up at the airport. We all went out to lunch and Robert and I told my mom, Harry, and my sister, Karen, the big news. Everyone was so happy. We flew home right after lunch and went over to Robert's parents' house. We told his mom and dad and they were so happy too. His mom, Helen, even cried, and she was not the crying type. His dad was hugging us and said he wanted to take the whole family for dinner at the Beverly Hills Hotel. So we all met up at the Beverly Hills Hotel for dinner—Robert's mom and dad and Tommy Kardashian and Joan Esposito and his uncle Bobby and aunt Jean—and we had an amazing engagement dinner.

The next day Robert went ring shopping. When he came home at noon, he was so excited. "I have a surprise for you!" he practically sang. "I found the perfect, perfect ring!"

He pulled out a bag from—oh my God!—Van Cleef & Arpels, and inside was the exact same ring I had seen in the window that day before my trip to Switzerland!

"Someday I am going to buy you that big diamond, but for now . . ."

I gasped. I was literally shaking. "Who told you about this ring?!" I asked. I was in a state of shock. This was *my ring*.

"Nobody!" he insisted. "I just saw it and I thought it was amazing."

Another amazing coincidence. He had chosen the same ring I had picked out that day I went window-shopping with Cindy Spallino. There have been many moments in my life when things have happened just as I imagined, just as I had dreamed and hoped they would, and this was one of them. I was floored. I already knew Robert was The One for Me, but the fact that he had walked into that store and come out with the ring that was exactly my vision still amazes me to this day.

I didn't wear it until we were married—it was my wedding ring and I never had an engagement ring—and it, like Robert Kardashian, was my dream come true.

CHAPTER FOUR

Heaven in Beverly Hills

ne day in 1978, before we got married, I went to Robert's house to find O.J. Simpson sitting at the desk in Robert's den.

"You gotta make this call for me, Kris," he told me. "I'll dial the number, and when somebody answers, ask if Nicole is there."

"Why don't you do it yourself?" I asked O.J.

"Because she lives with her parents and they are going to answer."

"How old is this girl?"

He said she was several years younger than me at the time. I was twenty-one, so Nicole must have been eighteen. I called the number. The woman who answered, who I now know well was Nicole's mother, Judi, asked me, "Who's calling?"

"Kris," I said.

Then I handed the phone to O.J. That was the beginning. O.J. had gone to the Daisy with his friends, most likely including

Robert, where they had met a beautiful young blond waitress who worked there. Her name was Nicole Brown.

"Hi, baby!" O.J. said after grabbing the phone from me.

When they hung up, he told me that he and Nicole were full-fledged dating.

"I really don't agree with this," I told him, because he was still married and Nicole was apparently so young. I began to get really angry. But O.J. just said I was young and didn't understand. He was a smart guy who knew right from wrong, he told me, and it was love at first sight with Nicole. He was so smitten, so taken with her. He couldn't help himself. He was not going to take no for an answer. O.J. *never* took no for an answer.

Soon after that, O.J. brought his young, blond, and beautiful girlfriend over to the house where I was living with Robert. O.J. had built her up as the most beautiful girl he had ever seen, so I was excited to meet her and see what all this infatuation was about. When Nicole finally came over, she seemed extremely shy and quiet. But O.J. was right: her beauty took my breath away. She was tall, tanned, fit, and gorgeous, the ultimate California girl.

I fell in love with Nicole Brown immediately. We were destined to become best friends.

Robert and I were married on July 8, 1978. It was a fairy-tale wedding from start to finish. Joyce Kraines threw me a bridal shower at Hotel Bel-Air. We were married at the Westwood United Methodist Church on Wilshire Boulevard, and no expense was spared. We had over three hundred guests, and the former florist to the Nixon White House did the flowers. We hosted our reception at the Bel-Air Country Club, and all of our friends were there. It was an elegant, beautiful affair, a storybook romance consummated at the altar. Kenn Gulliksen, our pastor from the Bible studies at Pat Boone's house, officiated the wedding.

Tommy was Robert's best man, O.J. was a groomsman, and A. C. Cowlings was the ring bearer. I can still see him walking down the aisle, the big, burly professional football player carrying a huge, gorgeous white satin pillow my grandmother had made for the ring. He was such a big guy that everyone laughed. My best friend, Joyce Kraines, was my bridesmaid, nine months pregnant. My sister, Karen, was my maid of honor.

On our wedding night, Robert and I stayed at Hotel Bel-Air. In bed together, he told me things nobody had ever said to me before.

"You are my dream come true," he said. "I'll never forget seeing you at the racetrack on the day we met. I knew then that you were going to be my wife, my future, my love."

For our honeymoon, I had put in for miles, and Robert and I got two free tickets to Paris on American Airlines. We flew to France, where we rented a car and drove all through Paris and then down to the South of France, where we spent a night on the beach in Deauville.

That night was magical. I had never been to Paris before. We just took it slow and enjoyed each day and each other to the fullest. We spent lots of time sightseeing together and exploring all the little places we went. We were able to just get to know each other even better and relax.

He made everything magical for me. He told me that he couldn't wait for us to begin our life together. He wanted to take care of me, to create for me the best, sweetest life possible.

Everyone loved Robert. He had a great sense of humor, an incredible work ethic, and a ton of grateful clients and loyal friends. He was honest and funny and a wonderful husband and family man. He would have done *anything* for me. He was all about class and elegance and hard work. He loved the nice things in life, yet he had the simplest heart and was so generous in spirit. If somebody needed help, he gave it. I always thought I would grow up and get married and have six kids, but I never knew I would get more than a girl could ever dream of in Robert Kardashian.

He was so happy that I was his wife. But he didn't want me to be spoiled. He wanted me to appreciate the things we had. He wanted me to learn and grow slowly into my role as his wife and the life of privilege and success that we enjoyed together. Within limits.

"I can give you a lot of material things," he said. "But I'm not going to give them to you all at once, because too much, too soon is not a good thing, either."

Still, he would do things like wrap a Barbie doll up for my Christmas present, and when I unwrapped the doll, I would gasp when I saw she had a diamond wristwatch around her waist. Or he would put onyx-and-diamond earrings under my pillow for my birthday. There wasn't one thing that I wanted that Robert didn't eventually give me. He was the most thoughtful, generous, amazing guy I had ever met. He was my prince.

The greatest gift he gave me was a child.

While we were honeymooning in Europe, Robert's first cousin Cynthia Shahian, whom everyone calls "Cici," stayed at our house, watched our dogs, and answered the phone. Many of the calls were from American Airlines.

"Where's Kris?" they would ask. "She's not checking in. She needs to get back to work." I had planned to go back to work, but Robert and I were having so much fun spending time together and having the greatest honeymoon in the world, I just knew

I wouldn't. As much fun as I had working for American, and as grateful as I was for my fabulous job, my life had changed.

One day, Cici called me in Europe. "Kris! American is looking for you to come back to work," she said. "What should I tell them?"

I turned to Robert. "Tell them you're retiring," he said.

"Tell them I'm retiring," I told Cici.

Cici, of course, handled the call to American Airlines. Cici, I would soon discover, could handle anything. From the moment we met, Cici and I became fast friends and cohorts in crime. It's funny how life gives you anchors along the way. Cici was such a gift to me, and soon became a powerful thread that would run through every stage of my life. She has the most amazing, remarkable personality, and is always the life of the party while being the wisest voice of reason in any situation. Cici was the one I would soon always turn to for anything and everything.

It was good that I retired from the airline on my honeymoon, because two weeks later I discovered I was pregnant. Nine months, two weeks, and two days after our wedding, I gave birth to our first baby. It was a girl.

She was born in the middle of the night, and the next day, as soon as we were transferred to a room, O.J. came to see us. He was *so* excited for Robert and me, so excited about the birth of our first baby.

"This is such great news!" he boomed when he walked into the hospital room. Then he added with a wink, because maybe he knew that Robert maybe had hoped it was going to be a boy, "All great, macho guys have girls first."

It was so cute and, again, so was O.J. I absolutely loved O.J. He was like a brother to me. It meant so much to have one of Robert's dearest friends come to the hospital when we had our first child.

When you are young, you think of silly names, I guess, but

I loved the name "Courtney." I thought it was *so* pretty, and I wanted it to be really different and amazing and unique, so I named her Kourtney Kardashian with a *K*. I kept writing it down to make sure I was okay with it, because it looked so strange to me at first. "Kourtney" with a *K* might have seemed odd, but I knew if I had a girl that had to be the name. If I had a boy, I was going to name him Sarkis, which is an Armenian boy's name. But I ended up getting Robert a dog for his birthday before we had Kourtney and we named him Sarkis. So it all worked out.

Robert *loved* the name Kourtney and absolutely adored the little girl who went with it. He would have been okay with a girl or a boy, though. He was just that kind of guy. He was a really calm, good guy, and, yes, he had his limits and could put his foot down firmly. But not when it came to his daughter. Kourtney had her daddy wrapped around her little finger.

I was equally smitten. Kourtney brought us both so much joy. There were times when I would carry her around all day long. She was so little and petite and cute and such a good baby; we just couldn't take our eyes off of her. I couldn't get over the realization that I could love someone that much. I thought that I was so much in love with Robert, but I didn't even know what love was until I had Kourtney.

Kourtney became our entire world. We took her everywhere we went. I remember the first time I left Kourtney with a baby-sitter. There were some family friends with girls across the street from us, the Masons, and I asked the girls to come over and watch Kourtney one day. I was only going one mile up the street to go to the market, but halfway there, I had to turn around and go back. I couldn't stand the thought that someone else was watching Kourtney and that maybe they would drop her or something. I was so young, and I was so scared she might break.

My parents offered to watch Kourtney for us while we went to

Hawaii for our first wedding anniversary that year, but even then I couldn't stand it. I cried myself to sleep the first night, and finally, we had to come home early. I just missed Kourtney too much.

I was so happy to be able to concentrate full-time on my dream of being a mother and wife. My first nine months of motherhood were spent in the Deep Canyon Drive house. I had a baby nurse for the first ten days, at Robert's insistence, and it was such a treat. I wasn't nursing Kourtney, so I was able to sleep at night, which was such a good start. She was on a schedule right away and that worked out really well. After the baby nurse, I didn't really have any help, but still we did great. We were a happy little family.

One funny moment in Kourtney's babyhood happened one afternoon when O.J. was over to play tennis with Robert. O.J. was in his tennis whites, and we were out in front of the house saying hello before they went down to the courts. O.J. picked Kourtney up and lifted her up in the air. "Hi, Kourtney. You're so cute!" he cooed at her.

But Kourtney was allergic to her milk, and she was a frequent barfer. She took a breath and exploded, like the little girl in *The Exorcist*, hurling barf all over O.J., literally covering him and his tennis whites in baby vomit.

"Oh my God, Robert, take your baby!" O.J. screamed.

He had to come inside and take all his clothes off, because he reeked! We found a pair of shorts for him, which were huge, and a T-shirt that didn't fit. He eventually just went home, shaking his head.

When Kourtney was about nine months old, we bought a house on Tower Lane in Beverly Hills. O.J. and Nicole rented our Deep Canyon Drive house when we moved. They were much more serious now than they had been before and they wanted to live together. O.J.'s wife, Marguerite, remained in the big house on Rockingham Drive in Brentwood.

Tower Lane, as we called it, became the touchstone for the Kardashians. It was a big, two-story Cape Cod–style house, around seven thousand square feet. It had these levels in the back that led down to a pool house and a tennis court. We had a big grill out back and everyone came over on Sundays for barbecues and tennis.

That house on Tower Lane was where my adult life really began. The foggy time before, when we lived on Deep Canyon, where I was a newlywed and a new mother for about five minutes, were behind us. On Tower Lane, I really came up for air and found my sea legs as a wife and mother. I quickly lost the fifty pounds I had gained in my pregnancy with Kourtney and I felt good about myself again. I just had such joy and excitement for life then. Life on Tower Lane was nothing short of idyllic.

We decided to go ahead and have another baby because we were having so much fun. From the day we met, Robert and I talked about how we wanted to have a big family, so we never expected to have anything less. We couldn't wait to have another baby. My pregnancy was so easy the first time, and we were beyond happy with Kourtney. So I just couldn't wait to do it all again. Giving birth had been the most powerful and amazing experience I had ever had. All I talked about for months after having Kourtney was the whole birthing experience. I would sit and talk about it to anyone who would listen. The thought of doing it again and again just thrilled me—and the site of our next conception was perfect for the baby that would result from it: the glamorous ski town of Aspen, Colorado.

It was the winter of 1980, and O.J. had just retired from professional football. He was finally able to go skiing. Under his football contracts, he was never allowed to do certain things like ski, so he wanted to learn how to ski. Robert, O.J., Nicole, and I went on a ski vacation to Aspen.

We shared an Aspen town house that winter week and had *so*

much fun. Michael Jackson's *Off the Wall* album had just come out and we had it blasting, shaking the town house walls. We spent our days trying to teach O.J. to ski, which was really funny, and we would go down the mountain and meet for lunch and drink hot toddies.

We really bonded and I got to know Nicole. At first, I didn't think she and I would have much in common. I had a new baby and she was younger and single. She and O.J. spent their nights out having fun and Robert and I stayed in, watching TV, and going to bed at nine p.m.

It turned out that Nicole and I really had fun together. She had really fallen for O.J. by then. The two of them were madly in love and had this obvious chemistry that you could feel when you were in the same room with them. They were constantly kissing and touching—they absolutely could not keep their hands off each other. He was already incredibly possessive of Nicole. Even when she would go to the bathroom, O.J. would wonder out loud when she was going to come back. "O.J., she'll be back in just a minute. Just relax," I would laugh.

We went to the movies that week and we saw a movie called *Silent Scream*. The tagline was "Terror so sudden there is no time to scream." Kind of creepy, considering how things turned out. In any case, I hated scary movies, but O.J. and Nicole loved them. I had my hands over my eyes most of the movie, and O.J. and Nicole thought that was so funny. From then on, every time we played charades—and we played a lot over the years—whenever O.J. and Nicole had to act out a movie, they always pretended like they were screaming. It was a private joke for the rest of our relationship.

In Aspen, O.J. and Nicole would go out after a fun dinner most nights, and Robert and I would go back to our room because we were the old married couple. We made very good use of that time in the condominium by ourselves. Kimberly was definitely born out of a night of passion. Robert and I always had our best sex on vacation, when we could relax and have fun, and the child who would come next was definitely a product of that.

When I came home from Aspen, it took about a month for me to realize I hadn't had a period. I bought a pregnancy test, but when I took it, it turned out a little fuzzy. It wasn't positive right away, but it wasn't negative, either. I called my doctor, Paul Crane, and asked if I could come in and take a urine test. Within minutes, Dr. Crane said, "Kris, you're pregnant." I was beyond thrilled.

When I had found out I was pregnant with Kourtney, I had gone to Saks Fifth Avenue in Beverly Hills and bought a fuzzy little lamb with a music box inside, and I wrapped it up and took it to Robert's office. "What are you doing here in the middle of the day?" he asked. "I just came by to say hi and to give you a little present," I said. So when I found out I was pregnant again, I ran to Saks and bought a little bunny with a music box in it. I had it wrapped up and I headed to Robert's office.

When I showed up at his office in the middle of the day and said, "I have a little present for you," Robert looked stunned. "No," he said, unwrapping the bunny. He was so excited. I ran up to him and gave him a big hug. "We're going to have another baby!" I cried. "Oh my God, we have to celebrate!" he said. Every time I found out I was pregnant, I told him the same way.

The pregnancy was an absolute joy. I was spending all my days with Kourtney, who was of course still an infant. On October 21, 1980, our second daughter was born. Naming her was easy, because I had a girlfriend named Kimberly, and she was so beautiful. I loved how "Kourtney" and "Kimberly" sounded together. And, of course, I loved the letter *K*.

From the moment she was born, Kimberly Kardashian was

absolutely breathtakingly beautiful. In the first weeks that she was home from the hospital, I remember walking downstairs to find Robert and Kimberly, who was lying in her bassinet. Robert had her dressed in Baby Dior with a pink satin bonnet. I looked at her face and thought, *She is so beautiful!* She was just stunning from the beginning and had the most adorable personality—curious, sunny, playful, *adorable*—and she was a gift from heaven for Kourtney, who thought Kimberly was born solely as a friend for her. It was love at first sight between Kourtney and Kimberly—just as it was love at first sight with Kimberly for all of us.

Now I was twenty-four and had two babies, and I had no idea it would be so hard. Everyone told me that life would change with a second baby. Let me tell you: change it did! I tell new moms now that one is like one, but two is like twenty. I was overwhelmed, but life went on. My mom and dad came up to visit as much as possible, and Robert's parents, Helen and Arthur, and his extended family were a huge part of our lives.

The definition of happiness for me is spending time with family, and we did so much of it back then. Robert's aunt Dorothy and her husband, Jack—who we always called Auntie Dorothy and Uncle Jack—would come and take Kimberly and Kourtney to Douglas Park in Santa Monica while everyone else made dinner. Robert's cousin Cici, who was by now one of my closest friends and confidantes, was always the first one in the kitchen. We had this huge Armenian family, and everyone helped with the cooking and the kids. Those years were fabulous.

From 1980 to 1983, I was all about being the perfect wife and mother: raising babies, forming traditions, and settling into my life's dream. I found so much joy in creating routines—especially holidays and special occasions—and keeping my house the way I loved it. I loved potting plants. I loved creating the schedules. I loved everything about the life I had with Robert and our two children.

Every morning, after Robert went to work, I would have the whole house to myself. We had amazing people working for us, and I would make sure the house was picture-perfect. I made breakfast for the babies, I played tennis with my friends, I met friends for lunch. I went shopping for the most adorable clothes for our two girls, who were always perfectly groomed, with big bows in their hair. Then I would come home and play with the babies some more.

I obsessively cleaned my house, straightened the drawers, swept the floors, and threw loads and loads of laundry in the washing machine, even though I had a housekeeper. If I walked past a table and it was dirty or dusty, I had to grab a bottle of Windex or Pledge and make it shine. It gave me great satisfaction just to clean out the refrigerator. If you opened my refrigerator door, everything was pristine and perfect inside. (Funny enough, all my kids today do the same thing. The inside of Kimberly's refrigerator looks exactly like mine did thirty years ago, everything perfectly clean and organized.)

As you surely know by now, I've always been a perfectionist, type A personality. Everything has to be a certain way, and the world around me has to be in perfect order if I am to be relaxed and move on to do something new, different, or fun. That's just who I am. I find joy in buying something new for my house, decorating, and dressing my kids. Back in the beginning years of my marriage to Robert, it was a good day if it ended with me bathing the babies in a bubble bath, filled with the cutest bath toys, and afterward dressing them in their pink satin Baby Dior nightgowns. I loved brushing their hair, turning on a movie, or reading them to sleep with a book. The biggest joy in my life was taking care of those babies. I knew I'd been blessed.

On some nights, once the babies were in bed and the nanny

was on the watch, Robert and I were able to have date nights. With babies tucked in, everybody safe and sound in our gorgeous house on Tower Lane, we'd tiptoe downstairs, where we would dress up and head out for a night in Beverly Hills. We were living *la vida loca*!

Robert was quite the dresser. He would put on a gorgeous sports coat, great slacks, and beautiful Gucci loafers. His hair was always swept back perfectly and his nails were always manicured. Again, the perfect guy in every way. We'd get into one of his Rolls-Royces and hit the town. It was quite the life: everything was perfect, perfect, perfect . . . until imperfections began creeping in.

It began with something strange. In 1982, for some odd reason my body broke out in this crazy, horrendous episode of psoriasis from head to toe. The rash was so bad, I looked like a burn victim. It was the first time I experienced any kind of physical disorder, and it was really life-changing.

I was very lucky to be healthy and athletic. I just loved to be out in the sun in my bikini, swimming with my kids. Now I had this rash erupting all over my body with huge, red, angry sores. I panicked. I thought I had some obscure disease and was dying. I went to my doctor, the Beverly Hills cosmetic dermatologist Arnie Klein, and he took one look at me and said, "Wow, I think you have psoriasis!"

"Psoriasis?! What is that?"

"Haven't you ever heard of the 'heartbreak of psoriasis'?" he said.

"Hell no, but I definitely have now!"

I would soon learn that psoriasis can be caused by emotional stress. What stress did I have? Living a perfect life in a perfect house with a perfect husband and two perfect children? I wasn't sure—at least, not yet. Arnie Klein sent me to his colleague Dr. David Rish, who specialized in the care of psoriasis. Dr. Rish put me on a regimen that involved pills and spending time in a sun bed every other day. Gradually, after a year and a half of treatment, my psoriasis healed. I still suffer from outbreaks from time to time and now use medication to help control it, but nothing as severe as I experienced then.

After my psoriasis treatment was over, Robert and I decided to take a trip. My parents drove up and watched the kids, and we had the time of our lives traveling to Europe in 1983. We started in Rome and then went to Capri, Venice, and Florence. It was on the trip to Europe that Robert and I decided it was time to have another baby. We conceived again in Italy.

Nine months later, in 1984, four years after the birth of Kimberly, our third daughter was born on June 27.

I loved the name Chloe, but I didn't know if I could change the *C* to a *K*. Sure, it would be easy to do, but would it be fair to the child? I wondered about it, because I had never seen "Chloe" spelled "Khloé" before. But of all the names I came up with, nothing else fit. From the moment I saw her, Khloé just looked like a Khloé.

Like her name, Khloé looked different. Different from everyone else in the family, from the moment she was born. She had blond hair and these greenish eyes. She looked a lot like my maternal grandmother, Lou Ethel, and Robert's mother, Helen. Kourtney and Kimberly came out dark and Armenian looking, and Khloé arrived looking nothing like them.

Khloé learned really fast that it isn't easy to be the third daughter. She was instantly funny; she knew how to get attention. She wasn't going to be left in the dust. Growing up, Khloé always found a way to carve out space for herself, usually through humor. There was a time in Khloé's life when she really thought she was a dog, and when people came over, she would bark and lick them and sometimes bite their legs. This was a standing gig for her; it was her form of stand-up comedy. It was so damn funny. She developed the most amazing personality and learned how to be strong and take care of herself.

Our friends loved our three girls. They were always entertaining, doing little skits and dances. They would show off and they were never shy. We had a loud, excitable, fun family. We had such an amazing group of friends, so my social life was really rich and full, but the family life was equally as wonderful. Again, I felt really lucky—and blessed.

Yet, something was missing.

A boy.

From the first time I gave birth, Robert's parents and all of his Armenian family members were praying for a boy. But first I had Kourtney. Everyone was excited about Kourtney. Then I had Kimberly, and everyone thought, *Oh, so cute to have two little girls!* Meanwhile, they all kept praying for a boy. Then came Khloé, another girl, and of course everyone was still happy. But it felt like something was still missing. Robert and I talked about it for a really long time, and we decided to give it one more try. We wanted another child, and we decided that if it was a fourth girl, it would still be great, but we really wanted to go for that boy.

I started reading up on how to conceive a boy. There was no Internet at that time, so I read a lot of books on the subject. I became this expert on how, when, and where to have sex to achieve a baby boy.

"Oh my God, we have to have sex *right now!*" I would tell Robert over the phone. "This is it, this is the boy! *This is the boy!*"

Robert would race home and it was wham, bam, thank you, ma'am. We didn't have sex frequently, but just enough, because sex had become all about conceiving the boy. You had only one shot at it. You had to do it just the right way. We tried all these crazy positions: upside down and sideways, me lying there with my feet in the air, drinking special juice or tons of iced tea.

It was pretty funny and we would laugh about it. Sure enough, I got pregnant. We tried to stay calm, because we wouldn't know what sex the baby was until I gave birth.

I went into labor the night before St. Patrick's Day, 1987. All of my girlfriends showed up at the hospital. Shelli Azoff brought Fatburgers for everyone. It was a huge party at two a.m. in the waiting room with all my friends and family and Robert's family there, everyone thinking and praying, *Let it be a boy! Let it be a boy!*

If it was a girl, we would name her Kelly—with a *K*, of course. If it was a boy, we were going to name him Robert Arthur Kardashian after Robert and his father, Arthur, in the Armenian tradition.

In the delivery room, my doctor, Paul Crane, who delivered all my kids, warned me, "I don't want you to be upset, but I am pretty sure this is a girl. I'm just saying that because when the baby comes out, I don't want you to freak out on me if it is a girl."

"I'm going to be fine," I said.

I screamed when the baby came out and Dr. Crane said, "Oh my God, it's a boy!" I think he was as shocked as I was. But lo and behold, it was a boy—Robert Arthur, although we would come to call him Rob—followed by a celebration like no other. My best friend, Joyce Kraines, heard the commotion. She had her ear up against the door the entire time I was giving birth. I was staring up at the big metal operating room fixtures when I heard Dr. Crane yell to Joyce, "Put on some scrubs!" Joyce came running into the operating room, a mask thrown over her face, and she came to me and started kissing my face and giving me huge hugs.

My mother-in-law came in with jewelry—the most beautiful diamond and sapphire brooch you have ever seen in your life, which had been handed down for generations—and a thank-you note for me. *It's a boy, it's a boy, it's a boy!* When I gave birth to Kourtney and Kimberly and Khloé, I didn't get anything, but I have this boy and she's suddenly giving me her jewelry! There were flowers everywhere. *God, I should have had four sons!* I thought, kidding, of course. But it was a day I'll never forget. In those days, a mother would spend a few days in the hospital after giving birth, and I really enjoyed it, with friends and family stopping by constantly.

Now we had four children and no worries when it came to our lifestyle. Robert's career was booming. He had kept his bar membership active, but was working on a company he owned called *Radio & Records*, or *R&R*. It was the newspaper for the music industry, and it was huge. He had sold the company to an even bigger company in Dallas, but he had stayed on to run it for another five years. Once that contract expired, he wasn't sure what he wanted to do next. He ended up working with our good friend Irving Azoff at one of the companies he was running, MCA Radio Network, and Robert went to work at Universal Studios, where the company was based.

Life was great and getting greater all the time.

On February 2, 1985, our friends O.J. Simpson and Nicole Brown were married. Before the wedding, O.J.'s buddies—Robert, his brother, Tommy, A. C. Cowlings, football great Marcus Allen, and Donald Moomaw, pastor of Bel Air Presbyterian, who was going to perform the ceremony—decided that O.J. could use a little marriage Bible study to prepare for the major step of matrimony. They thought that O.J. needed a little counseling, just to talk about what it meant to be in a monogamous relationship and how to be a good husband. They wanted O.J. to give this, his second marriage, a really good shot.

He had been married to an amazing lady, Marguerite. She was beautiful and they had gone to school together. He walked away from that relationship when he fell in love with Nicole, and I think all of us were afraid of his wandering eye. We were hoping for the best. We were hoping this would be a solid relationship and that they would be together forever, because they were so much fun to be around as a couple.

O.J. and Nicole were married in a tent in the backyard of O.J.'s house on Rockingham Drive. OJ was thirty-seven; Nicole, pregnant with their first child, was twenty-five and never looked lovelier. I remember being so happy for her. I felt like they had both been through a lot, and sacrificed so much for each other to be together. I thought Nicole was finally going to have her happily-ever-after.

The years passed quickly, almost in a blur. Robert and I continued in our strong faith and religious practice, both in our home and at church. We both loved the Lord. We went to church on Sundays. We had all our kids christened and took them every Sunday to Sunday school. Our home was filled with faith and love, and I was really proud of that. I started going to the Tuesday community Bible study in Santa Monica, which I loved. In Bible study, I met two of my closest friends: Candace Garvey and Dru Hammer. Dru was married to Michael Hammer, grandson of Armand Hammer, and Candace eventually married the baseball great Steve Garvey. Through Bible study, I met these two lifelong friends and many others.

I had an amazing social circle at the time. We had girl luncheons for everyone's birthdays, celebrations for *everything*. Joyce Kraines, Sheila Kolker, Shelli Azoff, Cici, Candace Garvey, Lisa Miles, and me—old friends and new. We were always having tennis parties, barbecues, concerts, dinners at Morton's, Chasen's and L'Orangerie. We were all having babies at the same time too. Our kids grew up together. It was like they had a whole bunch of cousins—the families were that close—and we all did the same things—like getting our boobs done.

It was 1988 by then, and a few of my Bible study girlfriends were having their boobs done. Pretty soon, *everybody* was having boob jobs. Of course, I decided I needed a boob job too. I had four kids and the boobs were looking like they could use some perking up. So I scheduled the surgery.

I will never forget waking up a few hours later. My eyes opened and I could see my girlfriend Sheila Kolker hovering over my bed squealing, "You look like a supermodel!" I was so groggy. *I do?* I thought. But I couldn't tell. I was still covered in bandages. After I healed, I realized that because my doctor had put the implants *under* the muscle, it didn't even look like I had my boobs done at all. In those days, under the muscle was safer, but that didn't give you those high, perky, fabulous boobs that you see on Playboy bunnies, which was what I was seeking. Staring in the mirror, I was like, *Hello? Where are my boobs?*

I started talking to Nicole Simpson about it. "Well, I want to get my boobs done too," she told me. By then, she and O.J. had had their two children, Sydney and Justin, so she was ready to perk up her boobs, just as I had been.

"Have him do your boobs first, and I will see how yours look and then I'll do mine all over again," I told Nicole.

Nicole went to see Dr. Harry Glassman and the surgery was scheduled. Of course, Nicole's boobs were 2die4. I went by her house after the surgery and she took off her shirt and said, "Kris, look!"

My mouth fell open. They were *gorgeous.* I thought, *I want two of those, please!*

O.J. was of course *so* excited about Nicole's new boobs, because Nicole had that tall, lanky, gorgeous, athletic body. She was *so* beautiful. Looking back on it now, we both probably should've just kept our boobs the way they were. But in those years—the late eighties—everyone wanted to have big, enormous boobs. We were all obsessed, and after Nicole had hers done, I went to the same

Dr. Harry Glassman and had mine done all over again. This time I was very, very happy with the results.

Robert and I were having so much fun with O.J. and Nicole back then.

We were always together, having dinner, playing tennis, having parties. By now, they had moved back into O.J.'s house on Rockingham Drive. They loved to have scavenger hunt parties. One time, they told us all to show up at their house wearing white. Everyone showed up in tennis whites, and O.J. lined us up in couples and handcuffed us to our partners. Then he gave us a list of household items, the craziest stuff: a toothpick, a mousetrap, yesterday's newspaper, a steak, a pack of matches from the Beverly Hills Hotel. The prize would be an amazing piece of Lalique crystal. Everybody ran to their cars, and we had to all get in the same door and climb over the steering wheels because we were handcuffed together. Everyone was squealing and laughing. Robert and I drove to Uncle Jack and Auntie Dorothy's house down the street, and we were able to get every single item. It was one-stop shopping. We won that year. It was so much fun.

O.J. and Nicole had tennis parties, too, and they would give all their guests new tennis racquets and tennis balls. O.J. *loved* giving parties and he was always extremely generous. Nicole loved to put together barbecues, and every Fourth of July they had a huge one. The Fourth of July was O.J.'s holiday. They would have people over from the entertainment industry, everyone from the Jackson brothers to the singer Bill Withers. And there were women. Young women everywhere. All of the girls would come to O.J.'s Fourth of July parties dressed to the nines in their little dresses and high heels with their hair and makeup done. It was a big joke between O.J. and his buddies A. C. Cowlings and Marcus Allen. They would get all the pretty, perfectly coiffed young women to the party, where they would throw them in the pool. They thought that was really funny.

Nicole would have people barbecuing ribs and steak and chicken, and her mom and dad, Judi and Lou, would come with all of her sisters. Nicole was really close to her parents. They were always at the house on Rockingham, helping with their kids, Sydney and Justin. I always took Kourtney, Kimberly, Khloé, and Robert to the barbecues too.

It was 1988 and everything was still right with the world. I had a wonderful husband and four gorgeous children. Everything was perfect. I was blessed in so many ways; even my psoriasis was gone. But something was growing inside of me—something worse than the heartbreak of psoriasis.

I had no idea that within a year I would come close to losing everything—including my mind—in what can only be described as my year from hell.

CHAPTER FIVE

Unfulfilled

Feelings are interesting things. You can't control them, or at least I can't control mine. You feel what you feel, and usually I understand why. If I'm feeling sad, I know why. If I'm feeling bored, I know why. If I'm feeling excited or blessed or thankful, I know why. But in 1989 I started to feel really gloomy and really depressed and really unhappy. And I couldn't figure out why.

My son was almost two. I had the best life in the world. I didn't work and I thought that it was a gift from God to have my babies and be able to raise my kids and give all of my attention to my family. I had the best friends a girl could ever want: supportive, beautiful, smart, independent, strong women who were great mothers, great friends, and a great support system. As always, Robert's cousin Cici was a really important friend in my life. She was around for all the Armenian parties, and the wedding showers, and through the whole process of our marriage. I had parents who adored me. I had in-laws who loved me and would do anything for me. I had a husband who was absolutely devoted to me and four adorable children who loved me.

Yet, I was *unhappy*.

I was selfish and restless and bored.

My feelings for Robert had changed. I still loved him after ten years of marriage, but I soon began to realize that I wasn't *in love* with him. I struggled with this for months and months. I would sit there and ask myself, *Why am I feeling this way? Why aren't I feeling frisky toward my wonderful husband? Why aren't I more lovey-dovey?* I had an amazing guy who everyone loved and admired. *Why don't I feel attracted to him? Why don't I feel in love with him anymore? What's happened?*

Nothing—and everything. Our emotional bond, which had once been so tight, had loosened and seemed to be slipping away. I had started to change inside, and I felt extremely troubled about it. I would cry myself to sleep at night trying to figure out what was happening to me. I was more than just unhappy; I was miserable. I would struggle to get through my day without breaking down in front of Robert or the kids.

We would often go to Palm Springs for the weekend, where Robert's parents, Helen and Arthur, had a house. I remember being in Palm Springs and being with Robert watching a movie called *The Thorn Birds*, the famously romantic TV miniseries starring Richard Chamberlain and Rachel Ward. It turned out to be a monumental movie for me. At the end of the movie I just broke down and cried because it was so passionate and sexy and so all these things that you're supposed to feel when you're really in love. We all have cold-water or "Aha!" moments in our lives. For me, it was watching *The Thorn Birds* and feeling like: *Wow. That's how I want to feel about somebody. That's how I want to be for the rest of my life. That passionate, that romantic . . .* All of those feelings that I didn't have with Robert anymore.

As my feelings toward Robert began to rapidly decline, I think O.J. and Nicole could sense what was happening. We were spending a lot of time together. Every year on my birthday, November 5, Robert, O.J., Nicole, and I would go back to New York City. O.J. was working for NBC and he and Nicole bought a beautiful apartment right on Central Park, where the four of us would stay together.

The weekend of the New York Marathon of 1989 was significant for a couple of reasons. Number one, it was the year that I noticed a tremendous change in O.J. and Nicole, or at least in Nicole. O.J. remained the same, always. But Nicole really started to change. She became more withdrawn and private and seemed anxious. She was biting her fingernails down to the quick and just seemed to be on edge all the time.

Second, there was my deepening sense of distance from Robert. On our first night in New York, I had a really hard time being intimate with him. I just wasn't feeling it. It was just like somebody had turned off a switch. I knew on that trip that it was going to be difficult for me to continue in the marriage. I wanted so much more . . . *passion*! I had four kids, but I was only thirty, and I was craving passion. Looking back on it now, I was only just coming into my own sexuality. I felt like I was married to my best friend, who, like any friend, I was happy to see and spend time with some days, but other days too much was too much. I'd had these four kids and had been a good wife, and I was feeling, *It's my turn. I need to have somebody be there for me.* I wanted to be madly, passionately in love with somebody. Again, I was really young . . . and really bored. Not with my life, because I had a lot going on, but it had become monotonous. Of course, I didn't breathe a word about any of this to Robert, who didn't seem to notice that my feelings toward him had changed. Or at least he didn't tell me he noticed anything.

———

While I was struggling with my relationship with Robert in New York that weekend, Nicole was struggling with her relationship with O.J. One day she asked me to join her for a long walk through Central Park, which was filled with runners training for the marathon. We must have walked for two hours. All the while, she talked about how she was really struggling with O.J. and her stepson, Jason. Jason and Arnelle were O.J.'s kids with Marguerite, and Nicole and Jason were having a really hard time getting along.

What Nicole was really struggling with, though, was that she had discovered O.J.'s infidelities. She was also having a hard time with the way O.J. treated her, and she told me about him getting physical and roughing her up. She didn't go into much detail, but she was just really having a hard time. She never came out and said "I'm being abused by O.J." I so wish I would have asked her for specifics. But I didn't want to cross a line if she didn't want to talk about something, which would become one of my biggest regrets. All she told me on our walk was "I want to leave him, but I don't know how. I don't know if I can stay. He's really hard to live with."

She told me about four incidents on four different occasions. Here is one of them: She was going through one of O.J.'s underwear drawers, and she found a jewelry box with gorgeous diamond earrings and a diamond necklace inside. She didn't say anything to him because she thought she had found a surprise gift meant for *her*. Months passed. She had an anniversary and a birthday. No jewelry. When she went back to look again, the jewelry box was gone. Then she saw a picture of an actress—I won't mention her name—in a magazine and the actress was wearing the jewelry. Nicole was devastated and said she needed to talk about it.

The next day was my birthday. Nicole and I got up early, had breakfast at the apartment, and then went shopping at Bloomingdale's. We were on a mission: Nicole wanted to buy O.J. a pair of leather gloves. No occasion: she just wanted to bring him home a present and thought a pair of gloves would be the perfect gift. We went to the glove counter and she picked out a pair of beautiful leather gloves, bought them, and had them wrapped. I've often wondered: *Were these the same leather gloves found bloodied at the crime scene after Nicole was murdered years later?*

After she bought the gloves, Nicole told me, "Go off and do some shopping and let's meet up a little later on the first floor." She went to the lingerie department and bought me this entire beautiful Christian Dior lingerie extravaganza. She was so beautiful and sweet, thinking that this would spice up my sex life with Robert because I'd given her this whole "I don't feel sexy" sob story. I still have that lingerie to this day. I don't have the heart to ever put any of it on, but it was just so special that I saved it. It was just who Nicole was. She was always thinking about everybody else.

Nicole looked so beautiful that day. After we finished shopping, O.J., Nicole, Robert, and I went out for lunch. Then we returned to the apartment for a quick nap before going out that night. We had big plans: a fabulous new restaurant for my birthday, then out dancing at a nightclub. We were so excited. Nicole had even bought a new dress.

That evening, when I was all ready and dressed, I walked out into the living room. O.J. came out of the bedroom and shut the bedroom door behind him.

"Nicole's not feeling well," he said. "She's got the flu. She's not going."

"What?" I asked.

"She's not going," he repeated. "Let's just go."

"Well, let me go in and see how she's doing," I said. "Maybe she needs some soup or something."

I turned and started toward the bedroom, but O.J. stopped me in my tracks.

"Oh, no, no, no, no!" he said. "She doesn't want to see you."

He was so adamant. At that time, I couldn't figure out why. O.J. and I had been friends forever, and Robert had known him even longer. Now, suddenly, he was acting very private. It wouldn't dawn on me until several years later that Nicole had been threatened or abused by him. In hindsight, I should have gone into that room to find out what was going on. But you don't imagine in a million years that your friend is in danger or trouble. Not like that. Not back then.

It was 1988, and that was one of the first signs, a sign I should have noticed.

Six years later, Nicole would be dead.

Later, she told me that she and O.J. had had a terrible fight. But she didn't say that he had hit her. I guess she wasn't ready or willing to tell me that. Not yet. Apparently, they had been arguing a lot at that point, which was why she had wanted to go on that long walk with me in Central Park. Every time she tried to leave O.J., he wouldn't let her go. That same year, on New Year's Eve, she had the pictures taken with the bruises on her neck and face, pictures that would be circulated far and wide. But we wouldn't know anything about it then, and we wouldn't see them until it was too late.

About a month after that trip to New York, O.J. beat the shit out of Nicole, and she finally had the nerve to call the police. The problem was that most of the policemen who patrolled O.J.'s neighborhood were O.J.'s friends.

It was a strange dynamic: even though Nicole and I were extraordinarily close, she was ashamed or embarrassed to tell me what was really going on. Thinking back on it now, I realize that there were so many signs. I was with her once at my son Robert's first birthday, in March of 1988, at a kids' gym in Santa Monica. When she walked in, I looked past her and saw a brand-new white convertible Ferrari. "What is that parked out front?!" I said. "Oh my God!"

"Oh, yeah," she said. "That just means O.J. slept with God-knows-who this time. That's my 'I'm sorry' present."

"Wow!" I said, focusing on the Ferrari and not the heartache behind it.

There was no more joy in the fun foursome we had once had.

When couples start going through these funky things, it really causes a lot of separation issues. All of us went off into our own corners. We had all tried to do the same things we had always done, but it just wasn't the same. Around this time, the end of 1989, Nicole had started to think about a real separation from O.J.

At the same time, I was still feeling one of the most destructive of emotions with Robert Kardashian: boredom.

One day I told Robert, "I think we should be separated."

"What?!" he said. I believe this came as a shock to him.

"You know and I know that things have been different between us," I said. "I'm not feeling the same way I used to feel. I'm confused, and I think a separation could be great for us. You love to go to Palm Springs . . ."

He had been going to Palm Springs often and staying at his parents' house. He loved to go down there.

"Why don't you just take a minute," I said. "Let's take a breath. Give me a break. I just need to figure out why I am having these feelings. I don't think it is fair to you for me to feel like this."

"Feel like what?" he asked.

"Just different," I said, trying to hold in my emotions and not hurt him with the whole truth.

I was really asking him to buy some time, for permission to breathe. I knew Robert was used to controlling me—in a nice way, but he was always the boss of everything—because he was twelve years older than I was. We married when I was very, very young.

He had been the only man in my life since I was eighteen, and now I was thirty. I had been on this journey with him. We had four kids together, and I just needed a break for a second. I needed him to just give me time to figure myself out. I don't know why I was having a midlife crisis at thirty, but I was. I knew that my marriage had not been okay for a while. I knew I had not been okay for a long time. I knew I needed help. I didn't even realize how much help I needed at the time.

"Armenians don't get separated," Robert said. "It's either marriage or divorce."

I think he was trying to scare me, but it didn't work. It just made me mad.

"Well, this is what I need to do," I said. "I need a separation."

Finally, he faltered. "Okay," he said. "I'll give you a break."

He left that night for Palm Springs. For two days I felt relief that he was gone. I needed my independence. I had gone from being a teenager to being the mother of four children. I now had my fourth baby. I had lost the pregnancy weight, I had had a boob job, and I was finally feeling good about myself again. I wanted to have some fun. Just a little. I had never really dated. I certainly never went out to bars or clubs at night, *ever.* I wasn't the girl who hung out with her friends and partied. I finally realized that for some reason I wanted some of that. And Robert was not going to give it to me. It was very clear that the guy was not going to leave me alone, especially when, unexpectedly and unannounced, he drove back through the gates of our home two days after he left for Palm Springs.

"What are you doing here?" I said.

"I decided I don't want a separation," he said.

I believe today that if Robert had let me have a break and left me alone to get through whatever I was going through—if he had given me the break I'd asked for—I probably would have been over it in a week and back on track. But because he fought me so hard and would not let me have the time to myself to figure it out, I felt trapped.

What happened next was really odd. A good girl was about to go bad, *really* bad. I felt on some level like Satan had just taken over my body and said, *"You're mine."*

I have a picture of me with a group of friends together at dinner at the Hillcrest Country Club. When I look at that picture today, I can remember exactly what I was thinking. I was trying to smile and look happy, to act like I was okay and that my marriage and my family—my most precious things—were going to be okay. But I *wasn't* okay. I was going crazy inside. I remember thinking that night, *How I am I going to get through the next minute without breaking down?*

Two weeks after that picture was taken, I stopped by a friend's house on the way home from a dinner out. Our kids were with our live-in babysitter. Robert was on a boys' ski vacation. All I could think was: *Thank you, God, for giving me a couple of days to myself.* I desperately needed breathing room.

I walked into my friend's house alone. There was a party in progress. I met a guy there. I had seen him around. He was part of a group of people who were always at this one friend's house. He had been at all of the barbecues and parties, but I hadn't paid him much attention. I actually had thought he was really arrogant, and I'm sure he knew I was married.

When you're married, you send out signals: *Married, not interested, stay away.* On the night I walked into my friend's house, though, I must have been sending out an *I'm single, searching, available, come closer* signal, because this guy came on crazy strong. We had an instant attraction.

His name was Ryan, and he was a producer. He looked like Rob Lowe. For a second, I thought he *was* Rob Lowe. He was so cute: young, dark hair, great body. We started talking. We talked and talked, laughed and laughed. Fun, fun, fun. No one had paid that much attention to me in *forever.* I remember my girlfriend asking me, "Hey, Kris, can you go upstairs and get me the music player from the hall closet?"

I went running upstairs to get it, because I knew the house really well. Ryan followed, running right upstairs behind me. I turned around. "Oh, hey, Ryan," I said, grabbing the music player. Then BOOM. He kissed me . . . and I kissed him back.

What the fuck? I thought.

That kiss was more than amazing; it was like a revival, a resuscitation, an awakening from some long, deep, unconscious sleep. I hadn't been kissed like that in ten years. It made me feel young, attractive, sexy, and alive. Along with these feelings came a wave of nausea. I actually wanted to throw up at the same time. Because it dawned on me that I had not felt that way with Robert for years.

I ran downstairs. Nothing else happened that night. But I started thinking about it. About him. I doubted myself. I didn't want to cheat on anyone. I was a Christian girl who loved the Lord and had four beautiful children and a perfect husband and a perfect home and family. I had a lifestyle that nobody would ever dream of throwing away. More important, I was married to one of the best guys in the entire world.

I couldn't see the forest for the trees. I had these feelings inside that had been brewing for a long time. I didn't know what was wrong with me. I felt like a fuckup because I couldn't get my marriage together . . . *and for absolutely no good reason.* I wasn't married to an ax murderer. I wasn't married to a cheater. A lot of people had a lot of problems in their marriages, and I did not have a single one except for my own feelings of being unfulfilled.

There wasn't anyone I felt I could turn to; I didn't think anyone would understand. I was too embarrassed to go to any of my friends and tell them what was going on. Instead, I lied to them, lied to my best friends in the whole world. I felt like a freak, like something had to be wrong with me. I didn't think anybody would understand what I was feeling.

Except maybe Ryan.

It wasn't long before he called me and I said I would see him. He had an apartment in Studio City. One thing led to another, and before I knew it, we were kissing again and not stopping this time. The next thing I knew I was in his bed with the sheets flying. As it had been with the first kiss, I felt like I was being awakened from a long and deep sleep. The difference between the kiss at the party and this one was that the next time I opened my eyes, I was in the middle of a raging affair. Wild crazy sex all the time, sex everywhere we could think of. We had sex in cars, sex on the tennis court, sex in the pool house, sex in the garage when we got home, sex up and down the stairs, sex everywhere, all the time. It was out of control, crazy, dangerous. Wild. Just like that movie with Diane Lane and Richard Gere and Olivier Martinez, *Unfaithful*.

Or in my case, *Unfulfilled*.

Until now.

All I wanted to do was spend my time with Ryan.

Again, it was as if I'd been abducted and thrust into another world. I had spent my entire life so proud, especially of having what I've always considered to be the best job in the world: being a mom. I was the Brownie leader, the soccer coach. I was the one who always had the pool parties, the *everything* parties. I couldn't wait for Easter, when we would take all the kids down to Palm Springs and have a huge Easter egg hunt, the Christmas parties, the *Snow White*–themed birthday extravaganzas, and the endless trips to Disneyland. One time, I was the Brownie leader and instead of camping, I decided to take the whole troop of Brownies down to SeaWorld.

I wanted my kids to have a fantasy childhood. It was just so much fun being their mom. I would spend way too much time shopping for my girls and making sure they had matching dresses with big bows in their hair. Every time a new show came to the Forum—*Sesame Street On Ice* or the *Ice Capades*—we would all go. I was always taking my kids to little kiddie places like Six Flags Magic Mountain or the zoo. We took countless trips to San Diego, and the famous zoo there, and to see my mom. *Everything about me was all about family*.

Now it was all about sex. One minute I was making brownies for my friends and having a family barbecue, the next I was in the middle of an insanely intense affair. I would tell Robert I was going to lunch and I would end up at Ryan's apartment having crazy, fabulous sex for hours in the middle of the day. I felt like I was in a movie, and I kept thinking it was so seductive; he was so seductive. He really was this artistic, passionate guy.

I constantly lied to Robert. I had a breakfast, I was going to meet a friend, I was going shopping. I didn't work. I was a housewife. I was raising my kids. I had a baby son at school who needed me. But I would drop Kourtney, Kimberly, and Khloé off at school and rush straight to Ryan. Breakfast, lunch, and dinner with Ryan. Ryan, Ryan, Ryan. I could not control myself. It was crazy, and every time I did it, I told myself it was the last time. Isn't that what happens when someone is caught up in an affair? You keep getting sucked back in. *I'm just going to go back this one more time,* you tell yourself. That's why they call it seduction. It's like trying to quit smoking: you say, *This is my last cigarette,* and it's never anyone's last cigarette, unless they really get help. I wasn't willing to get help, because I was having too much fun.

Robert wasn't the only one I lied to. My girlfriends had always known where I was and how to find me. So when I began disappearing and had lost fifteen pounds and started tanning and getting bikini waxes every other day, they knew something was up. I would look my girlfriends in the eye—even Joyce Kraines and Shelli Azoff—and lie that I was going to the car wash. I figured the car wash took about an hour, and I would hightail it to Ryan's house. Joyce finally asked, "How many times can you go to the car wash?"

As time went on, Robert obviously realized that I was changing. Everything about me was different, and he was panicking and angry. He was trying to figure out what was wrong with me. He tried harder to be a better husband. But the bond between us was broken because I had already slept with someone else and I was obsessed with the guy. I didn't have that feeling for Robert—I hadn't had that feeling for Robert for years, even before I met Ryan. Now that I had connected emotionally and physically with someone else, I had checked out of the marriage, and on some level he knew it.

Robert started paying more attention to my movements. When I would go downstairs at night to call Ryan, he'd follow me and try to listen to my conversation. It got ugly. "Who are you talking to?" he would demand. "Oh, just a friend," I would lie.

I was out of control and selfish. Robert would leave town to go on a business trip, and I would have Ryan and a couple of his friends come over in the middle of the day or late at night for drinks. Nothing too crazy was going on, but he started coming around, and I would explain him away as a friend of a friend or just a guy coming by to play tennis—because I always had instructors or friends coming by to play tennis. I thought he might just blend into the woodwork. But Robert knew something was up, and I began making a lot of mistakes. I just didn't care anymore. One morning I left the house early to meet Ryan, and Robert had me followed. He found out we were at a restaurant in Beverly Hills, Ryan and I alone in a booth, having breakfast.

I was sitting in the booth, facing out, when the door opened and Robert came walking toward me. My world started spinning. I thought I might faint.

"Well, I caught you, *I caught you!*" he said.

I was shell-shocked. *Oh my God, oh my God.*

He ran out of the restaurant. I ran after him. He jumped in his car and drove away. I got into my car and followed him. We went back to the house, where we had a huge fight. The worst part was, I cared more about how Ryan was feeling after that scene than I did about Robert. I met back up with Ryan later that afternoon at his apartment. When I walked out of his apartment an hour or two later, Robert was standing out front. I think he had had me followed by a private detective.

"Now I know where you spend your time," he said.

One thing led to another. Robert kept catching me with Ryan. I kept thinking, *Surely Robert won't come back to Ryan's apartment,* but he did. Again and again and again. He caught us three different times. I just could not quit Ryan. It was like being sucked into a vacuum cleaner. I don't know what happened to me; I just lost my mind. Those were the darkest days of my life, because I was slowly realizing the sadness of the situation and the grief and pain I was causing everyone else. And I couldn't change it.

This went on for three months, at which point Robert filed for divorce. I was served with divorce papers at my house. I called my girlfriend Candace Garvey, crying my eyes out. "What do I do? What do I do?"

"We're going to call Dennis Wasser," she said. "He's the best divorce attorney in town." I called Dennis and he agreed to accept the case, but I didn't know how to pay his retainer, because I didn't have access to any money. I had never paid a bill. I didn't even know how much we paid the gardener. I couldn't tell you what we owed on the house. I had a credit card and even a Gelson's charge card for buying groceries, but I never wrote a check, *ever*. My husband paid the bills, he wrote the checks, he handled the money. I had no money—not one dollar—to my name. He controlled everything. I had to take Candace Garvey's offer to loan me $10,000 to pay the attorney's retainer. It never occurred to me before that moment in this dark time that I had no power. Later in life, I would decide that was a situation I would *never be in again*.

My friends were so confused and devastated when they found out about the affair—especially O.J.

"I need to talk to you, Kris," he said. "Get over here *now*."

I drove over to Rockingham, where O.J. was waiting for me in the kitchen.

"I want this guy's phone number," he said, meaning Ryan's. "I'm calling him *now*."

I gave him the number, knowing he was going to scream at Ryan.

"You just fucked Snow White," O.J. told Ryan. "You got that? You just fucked Snow White. Do you know what you've done to this entire universe, you asshole? You motherfucker. Now you're going to have to deal with me."

He slammed down the phone, and glared at me.

"What is the problem with you, Kris?"

"I don't know, I don't know, I don't know," I said. "I don't know why I don't have the same feelings for Robert."

He cut me off. "All you had to do is get a vibrator," he said. "What'd you need this guy for?"

He was trying to make some sense of it. Of course, later I would realize that O.J. was the biggest player of them all, and here he was scolding *me* for my infidelity. Everybody had a talk with me eventually. Robert's best friend from high school, Larry Kraines, even tried to talk some sense into me, as did all of my friends. Some of them were upset that I had lied to them about going to the car wash so many times. Others just couldn't deal with it, and they just stopped talking to me because they were so upset. I totally understood, but it hurt.

"Snap out of it!" a lot of them said. "You're being a bad girl. Now just cut it out!"

The only person who seemed to understand that I was really troubled and couldn't control what I was feeling was Anka, the mother of one of my best friends, Lisa Miles. I have now known Lisa for thirty-five years; Anka is in her eighties and one of the dear loves of my life. One day she sat me down on the stairs of our house on Tower Lane.

"I understand what you are going through," she told me. "Why can't you just go through it? Get it out of your system and go back to your husband. Don't get divorced. You will regret it one day."

She was right, of course, but I couldn't see it then.

Robert had moved out and I was living in the house on Tower Lane with the kids. We decided that every other weekend Robert would come stay at the house and I would leave and go to a friend's house. That way, the kids would never have to be disrupted.

We decided that we would tell our kids about the divorce together. The kids were young: Kourtney, eleven; Kimberly, ten; Khloé, six; and Robert, two. We sat the girls down and said that we wanted to have a little family meeting, which they surely thought odd because we had never had a family meeting before.

"We're getting a divorce," I think I said.

I don't even remember exactly what else we told them. I was completely in a fog; I was so devastated and shocked that this was actually happening that I don't remember parts of it today at all. I think I have blocked the things that are too crazy and painful to remember.

They stared at us, unbelieving at first, then the waterworks. They cried, cried, cried, cried, cried. It was horrible. Khloé didn't really understand what it was all about, and of course Robert wasn't in the family meeting because he was only two. But it was awful, and doing that to them is the single biggest regret of my life to this day. I know it was just devastating for them. I know Kourtney and Kimberly took it the hardest because they were the oldest. When I look back on it, they were really good kids for not being more rebellious, because I really spun their world out of control.

After Robert moved out, I stayed at Ryan's place a few times on the weekends when Robert had the kids. By then I was well on my way to deciding that life with Ryan wasn't all it was cracked up to be. He lived in a tiny, dumpy apartment in the Valley, and I had just left my seven-thousand-square-foot mansion with gates and Dobermans and Rolls-Royces. I had thought there was this special connection and a future between Ryan and me, but now I know that the affair was more about running *away* from Robert than running *to* Ryan.

It was physically excruciating to even go through the motions of being a mom, the role I've always loved most. It was difficult to even wake up, pull myself out of bed, and take care of my kids. Even feeding them breakfast was tough. I would cry all day. I would get them to school or camp, then spend all day crying, struggling. It was an effort to tie my shoes.

Then I got some terrible news. My mother, my best friend and mentor, had cancer. I was going through a horrible divorce and my mother was very, very sick. I can't remember ever feeling as devastated. My mom, who was a pillar of strength and energy, and certainly my support system, was diagnosed with colon cancer. She is one amazing woman who had already battled breast cancer. And now this. She didn't deserve this. I felt helpless . . . and selfish. Selfish for what I was putting everyone through, and now my mom was sick. At a time when she needed me the most, I needed her the most.

Just when I thought it couldn't get any worse, it went from dark to black, and I wasn't emotionally stable enough to handle it. I needed to get it together. I was supposed to be the strong one now. I was supposed to be there to get my dad and my kids and my family through this. And I was lost.

My dad Harry said, "Kris, you really need to come and see your mom."

She was going through chemotherapy, and Harry asked me to drive down to San Diego because she was having radiation that day. It was such a WOW. It was a sign, somebody literally saying, SNAP THE FUCK OUT OF IT, KRIS!

I remember thinking, *How am I going to drive to San Diego? I can't even put my shoes on.*

I asked Ryan to drive down with me. So there I was, driving down to San Diego with this guy, who had just helped me tear apart my family, and I was fighting with him all the way. I can't even remember about what. I do remember thinking, *My mom needs me. I don't know if she's going to make it. My marriage has fallen apart. My kids are angry because I've hurt their dad. My son is a toddler and he needs me. My house is falling apart because I'm emotionally vacant. My body is breaking down; all I want to do is sleep.* I wasn't present, emotionally or physically. Now here I was in this car, trying to absorb the fact that my mother had cancer. It was just a lightbulb moment, but the lightbulb didn't turn on—not yet, anyway.

We pulled up to the hospital. I parked my car. And Ryan said, "What do you want me to do?"

"Just wait in the car," I said, which was so odd. I had to hide my boyfriend in the car. I kept thinking, through the fog, *What are you doing? Why is this guy even with you? Your mother has cancer.*

I walked into the hospital lobby, where my dad Harry was

waiting. I could tell he was very upset. My mother had just been through a round of radiation. I walked into her room completely numb. She didn't look well at all, and it dawned on me: *She's so ill and suffering, and doesn't know whether she is going to live or die, and I've got this kid sitting in my car, waiting for me.* It was so wrong on so many levels. I thought: *I may lose my mother, my best friend, and I have been so consumed with my own nonsense.*

Wake up! Your mom needs you. I visited with her for a very long time and at long last began to take stock of what was happening around me. Several hours passed, all with Ryan still in my car. When I went back out to the car, I realized I needed to get it together. I was going to let everybody down. My mother went on to survive breast and colon cancer. She's a survivor, and I knew I was too. I knew that I came from some damn strong stock. My mother taught me—both through her life and the illness she conquered—that we both have great strength and courage.

I would need my mother's brand of courage for the journey that lay ahead.

One weekend when Robert had taken the kids to Palm Springs and I was alone, I couldn't find Ryan. *That's really weird,* I thought. So I drove to his apartment, even though it was midnight. I had a key. When I got there, I saw a strange car parked in his driveway. I thought that was weird, too, but I guessed that maybe he had a friend over. I walked upstairs and used my key to let myself in.

The minute I walked in, I felt something was wrong. I opened the bedroom door and stepped inside. Ryan leaped out of bed, *naked*.

"Hey, why aren't you answering your phone?" I said.

Then, from behind him, a girl got out of the bed.

"What's going on?" she asked.

"You fucking son of a bitch!" I screamed.

The joke was on me. Suddenly it all came crashing down. I had just ruined my entire life and my whole family and given up everything I knew and loved for this guy, thinking I was going to be with him. I had thought this guy was in love with me. Part of me had thought I was going to *marry* Ryan.

What else did I expect? I was thirty-two by then, and Ryan was ten years younger than I was. I was devastated, and I didn't know what to do. I screamed and cursed at Ryan, and the girl went flying into the bathroom and locked the door. I stormed out, slamming the door behind me, and Ryan threw on his pants and came running downstairs after me.

"Don't ever call me again," I said.

He was bawling. "Don't leave me!" he cried. "Don't leave me! Don't leave me! Don't leave me! She's *nothing*! It was a one-night stand! I met her in a bar!"

I got in my car and squealed off, Ryan calling and calling and calling me all the way. When I was halfway home, I picked up the phone. After a long conversation, he eventually convinced me to turn around. I drove back and we sat there talking in my car.

"I just can't do this anymore," I said. "I have given up too much. It's over."

But it wasn't over. Not yet.

That's how crazy I was.

Soon after that, my dear friends Candace and Steve Garvey invited me to go on a ski vacation with them in Deer Valley. They were doing a television show around this ski event.

"Oh, you can invite your friend if you want," Candace added, meaning Ryan.

I thought that was incredibly gracious and generous. Steve and

Candace weren't as much friends with Robert as they were with me, and Candace knew I was going through a horrible time. When you are in a situation like I was, your friends don't know what to do, because they don't want to take sides. Robert and I had the same friends. They were in a really uncomfortable position and didn't want to upset Robert by siding with me. After all, I was the problem. It was really bad, but Candace was always there for me, and honestly, it meant the world to me. She was willing to show me love while I tried to figure my life out.

"C'mon, Kris, let's go on vacation," she told me.

I wanted Ryan to come along. It would be the make-or-break trip for our relationship. This was going to be the guy or I had to move on. But there were problems—and not just catching him in bed with someone else. As passionate as our relationship was when we were in bed, it was even more passionate in the opposite direction when we were trying to get along. He was difficult and moody, and I had four kids to worry about.

On the morning we were to leave for the ski trip, Ryan and I got into a fight, and he threatened to cancel. We were fighting about something stupid, but he was ready to bail, with only twenty minutes before we had to leave for the airport.

"I'm not going to go, I'm not going to go," he kept repeating.

"Please go, please go," I pleaded, hating myself for having to talk him into a ski trip. "I don't have anybody to go with. We planned this trip together."

Finally he relented and we headed to the airport. I should have known how awkward it was going to be.

We arrived in Deer Valley and stayed at one of the most beautiful resorts. We had a three-story town house to ourselves, complete with an outdoor Jacuzzi and a swimming pool. There was a fireplace in every room. It was heaven. We had the fireplaces crackling, the champagne poured, and the Jacuzzi hot.

The next day I watched Ryan gravitating toward the Hawaiian Tropic girls that were swarming around the resort. And I knew: When your boyfriend is paying more attention to the Hawaiian Tropic girls than you, you have a problem. At the end of the trip I thought, *This guy is a lot of fun, and it's definitely been a roller-coaster ride: fun, wild, exciting, and a little scary. But this is not the guy for me. I have to end it and I have to end it now.* I felt like I always had to babysit him, not to mention worry about who he was sleeping with when I wasn't around. The trip was a very sobering end to a very passionate relationship.

After we got home, I went over to Ryan's house to pick up some things I had left there and to say good-bye. I was crying, but I tried to be calm.

"You know what? You have been really amazing to get to know, but I just can't do this," I told him. "You're not ready." Meaning he was so young and so not ready for the responsibility of someone like me and my four children. I mean, can you imagine?

I knew I had made a *ginormous* mistake, but it was too late.

I had lost Robert.

Suddenly, I realized everything that was great about my marriage. Robert was the greatest guy in the world. He would never cheat on me. He only wanted the best for me. He encouraged me to find things to do for myself and have new interests. He took me on vacation, bought me anything I wanted, and let me be the best mother I could be. He nurtured our relationship.

Robert made me a better person. He introduced me to a life I would have never known otherwise and encouraged me to be a good Christian. When I lost him, I lost friends, I lost respect, and I lost love.

He adored me, and I treated him so badly. To this day, I still cannot tell you why. Again, it was as if my body had been taken over by demons or aliens. I was really ashamed of myself. But I didn't try to get Robert back. I didn't want to insult him like that. I had been *so* wrong. I had so embarrassed him, humiliated him, destroyed him. Not only that, but my bad behavior had taken a serious toll on our kids, and they certainly didn't deserve that.

The divorce got ugly. Robert canceled my credit cards and revoked my Gelson's grocery charge privileges.

"What do you think I'm going to do, charge too many tomatoes?" I asked.

I mean, my kids had to eat. I was paralyzed. One night I took my kids out for pizza with Candace and another friend, and I didn't have money to pay for pizza. That might have been my lowest moment, when I realized I couldn't buy my children pizza. If Robert wanted to show me that I was nothing without him, it worked.

I spent the next couple of weeks mourning and taking stock of what I had done. I had been on a kamikaze mission and imploded my entire family along with myself. I was so embarrassed. I had disappointed so many people. These were people who had once respected me, and admired me, and I let them all down.

I continued down this path of emotional instability for the longest time. I couldn't even perform the simplest tasks or do my errands. I wanted to just shut down, not think, go to sleep. But I wasn't eating, wasn't sleeping. I was *so* tired. I never saw myself ever in a million years being divorced. I always thought I would live happily ever after and raise this wonderful family with a loving husband and house full of loving kids.

What I put my family through during this time will always be my biggest regret. What it taught me—and what I tell young women going through something similar—is that there are ups and downs and changes in life, but you have to have self-control. You have to understand that relationships have their ebbs and flows, and that life just evolves. It is about love and friendship. It's not always about passion and heat. I just didn't understand that. My feeling unfulfilled was valid, but the way I had responded to it wasn't fair. I struggled through very dark days, accepting what I had done, before I began to see a light at the end of my tunnel.

Eventually, there was light. I knew that I was at a crossroads in my life and I knew that I was not at peace with myself. I was devastated that I had broken up my marriage. I had great guilt. I felt ashamed and disgusted with myself. I had always imagined myself as someone who would only be strong and committed and passionate about my family, my husband, my children. Yet, somehow, this horrific situation had taken over my life, and I had let it happen. I definitely had let God slip out of my life, and I needed to snap out of it and get things back on track.

I was sitting in my backyard one day, and it felt so empty because my husband was gone, my friends were gone, the laughter was gone, the music was gone, the happiness was gone, the peace was gone, and the contentment was gone. So much was gone. My house had become a shell. I was stripped of every emotion I had always relished. I was the one who was always excited or passionate about everything, but my impulsive search for passion had, ironically, stripped me of the passion I once had. You could feel it in our house. I had let everything I loved slip away in exchange for an insane affair.

As I sat there looking at my four kids playing in the pool with all their friends over, I had one of those "Aha!" moments. We had had the fairy-tale life, and suddenly it was over. My kids were living on a battlefield, and that wasn't fair. That wasn't what they signed up for, and it was certainly not the way I thought my life would go. I thought, *That's it. This is my life! I am not going to let this destroy my children for one more moment.* I made a declaration to myself: *You know what, I'm going to wake up tomorrow morning and I'm going to be a whole new girl. I'm going to get up, I'm going to pick up my dry cleaning and get my car washed and get my house cleaned and get my drawers organized and get my kids' lunches made.* I was going to throw every ounce of my being into my kids and our home. I was going to be the best mother and housekeeper and carpool driver. *I'm going to do it all, and I'm going to do it really well, because that's what my kids deserve.*

I stood up and went upstairs to my bathroom, and I remember I was so drained. I started splashing cold water on my face, and I remember thinking that this was a cold-water moment, no pun intended. I was going to get back on track. I was going to go to church. I was going to pray about my situation, and I was going to pray for my children, and one day I hoped I would live long enough to make it all up to them.

That day, I decided from that moment on I was going to be the best Kris possible. I was going to be a woman who always tries to live the truth.

CHAPTER SIX

Meeting My Match

My attorney, Dennis Wasser, was indeed the best in Los Angeles. He had everything under control. "You'll probably get your house," he said. "Stick to the plan. Everything's going to be okay."

In June of 1990, Dennis went into court for some emergency relief, and soon I was getting a monthly allowance. I was able to pay my bills. I was far from being whole again, but everything was going along okay. Robert and I shared visitation with the kids. I don't think they fully grasped what had happened, and Robert and I both tried very hard to keep things as normal as possible for them. We stuck to their routines: school, lessons, summer camp, and summer school. We kept things moving. I think because we kept them busy, they were kind of okay. We put on a happy face, and I don't think they understood everything going on at the time.

Finally, I went on a blind date, a really lousy date that a friend talked me into. I came home that night and began thinking about what to do next. It sure didn't include dating. The regret and remorse of what I had done had begun to subside, and I was getting back to the hard work of making things better. I went back to the business of being the best mom that I could be. That was my priority. I had destroyed my marriage, but I didn't want to lose my kids. I didn't want my kids to have *that* as their memory of me.

The next morning I vowed to forget about dating and spend all of my time and energy on my new life with my children. I made my kids lunches, I took them to school, I went to the dry cleaners, I did my errands. By the time eleven o'clock rolled around, I got a call from Candace Garvey.

"How's it going?" she asked.

"It's going fine."

"Well, I'm up here in Alaska, and the greatest thing happened. I'm here with a guy named Bruce Jenner. Do you know who Bruce Jenner is?"

Candace and Steve were shooting an outdoors television show up there, and Bruce was one of their guests. He was up in Ketchikan alone for a small celebrity fishing tournament. Candace noticed that Bruce wore sweats pretty much every day; she had first thought of asking me to help him spruce up his style. Candace always dressed like a Ralph Lauren model. In Alaska, she was sporting the kind of vest with all the little pockets that fishermen wear, khaki pants, and a really cute shirt, her hair perfect and her face gorgeous. Bruce remarked on how great she looked.

"If you think *I* look great, you should see my friend Kris," she said. "Kris really knows how to dress; she *really* knows how to shop," she told him. Then she stopped mid-sentence, struck by an idea. "Oh, wait a minute, Bruce," Candace continued. "This is perfect! Kris would be great for you to go out with!"

Candace immediately switched from the personal-shopper idea

to being utterly convinced that Bruce and I would make a perfect match. That's Candace for you. Bruce, of course, who wasn't into shopping, especially when it came to clothes, didn't immediately warm to the idea, to say the least.

"Oh, yeah, that's just what I need, Candace," Bruce replied. "A professional shopper."

When Candace called me, I was hesitant from the start. "Yeah, I know who Bruce Jenner is," I said.

"Don't you think he's adorable?"

"Yeah, he's all right. Why?"

"Well, I want to set you guys up on a blind date."

"What?"

We talked for thirty minutes about why I should go on this blind date with Bruce Jenner.

"Candace, I don't want to ever look at another guy for as long as I live," I said. "I've given up guys. I just want to be a mom. The last thing I want to do is to go out on a blind date." She went on and on and on about all of the reasons why I should go out on a date with Bruce Jenner. I just repeated, "Hell no." I didn't want to go out with *anybody*, especially somebody whom any of my friends knew. It would just be too much. But Candace wouldn't give up.

"Come on, Kris, come on, Kris, come on, Kris," she said.

If you know anything about Candace Garvey, you know that she is persistent. I knew she was never going to give up unless I agreed to go on the blind date.

"Okay, okay, okay, I'll go out with your friend Bruce when you guys get back from Alaska," I told her.

I figured she'd call me in two weeks and then I could get out of it. Candace came home a few days later, and the minute they landed at the airport she called me. I was minding my own business, trying to be Mother of the Year, when the phone rang: a conference call with Candace, Steve, and me.

"Let's all go to dinner together tomorrow night!" they shouted in unison.

"Tomorrow night?"

"Yes! Steve and Bruce are playing in the Michael Jordan Golf Tournament at the Riviera Country Club," said Candace. "Meet us there and we'll all go out to dinner afterward."

"Oh my God, Candace, please—"

She cut me off in the middle of my excuses. Again, nobody says no to Candace Garvey.

"Okay, okay, all right, I'll meet you there."

I hung up and immediately found a babysitter for the next night, doubting everything all along the way.

The next morning Candace called.

"Are you excited about tonight?"

"Not really. I really don't want to do this. I'm doing this for you."

"You're perfect for each other," she said. "He's got four kids, you've got four kids. It's going to be great. You could really use a good guy. And Bruce is a *great* guy. He's not dating anybody. It's perfect timing. Where do you want to go?"

"I'll meet you at the country club, because I'm not going out with this guy by myself. Let's go to the Ivy at the Shore."

"Okay, great," said Candace.

I brought my nanny, Tracy, with me on the blind date. My housekeeper was staying with my kids, and I told Tracy that I wanted her to come with me so that I didn't have to get into Bruce's car with him alone. I never wanted to be put in the position on a blind date where I was in the guy's car by myself. I don't know why I felt like that, but I did. So Tracy came with me to the Riviera Country Club.

As I walked inside the clubhouse, Bruce Jenner was walking out. He was wearing golf clothes—red golf shirt, khaki pants—and he had long, shaggy hair and a big smile on his face. He looked adorable.

"You must be Kris," said Bruce.

"And you must be Bruce," I replied.

"Oh my God!" he exclaimed, and he came running over and he threw his arms around me and picked me up into this big bear hug.

"Finally, I'm in the arms of a real woman!" he said.

"What?" I asked.

"You have four kids, I have four kids. This is amazing!" he said.

It was *way* forward, but I had to admit: he was so cute. He was an adult. After dating somebody ten years younger than I was, it was nice to see an adult who was happy and really thrilled that I had a brood of kids and that I was a mom and a family girl.

"Come on, let's go inside and find Steve and Candace," he said after putting me down.

I turned around, looked at Tracy, and tossed her my car keys.

"Bye, Tracy, see you later," I said.

We went inside. It was really strange, because I knew so many people there. Everybody was like, *"Hi, Kris. Hi, Kris.* What are you doing here?"

"Everybody knows who you are," Bruce said.

We had a lovely thirty minutes in the clubhouse, having a drink at the cocktail party after the golf tournament. Then Bruce, Candace, Steve, and I drove in two separate cars to Ivy at the Shore for dinner. Me and Bruce went in one car, talking all the way. At the restaurant, I ordered swordfish and Bruce ordered meat loaf. (Now, every time we go to Ivy at the Shore, we have to order the same things. Sweet, right?)

After dinner, we went to Candace's house. I was going to spend the night there so nobody would have to drive me home. The last thing I wanted was for Bruce to drive me home. I just didn't want any awkwardness between us. I still felt very vulnerable. So Bruce drove me back to Candace's house and we sat and talked for the longest time there. We had one thing in common: we had both gone off track with our lives. We talked about me and we talked about him, especially about how his life had derailed after his huge success in the Olympics, with two divorces and various disappointments in starting his business career. I couldn't help but feel compassion for him. I also found myself thinking that I might want to be the person to help Bruce find his way again.

"I had the best time tonight," he told me before he left. "I'd love to see you again. I'm leaving town tomorrow, but can I call you when I get home?"

"Sure," I said. "Call me when you get home."

He called the next morning. "I have to go to Florida," he said. "Do you want to meet me there if I send you a ticket?"

"What for?" I asked.

"I'm in this boat race, and then I have a golf tournament, and I'm giving a speech, and I have three or four days in Florida," he said. "Would you like to visit me there? No hanky-panky. I'll get you your own room."

It took me a second to say, "Sure."

We had a great time. Bruce was such an exciting guy. He never seemed to sit still. On our first morning in Florida, he hopped into a Cigarette speedboat, racing at 100-plus miles an hour in a professional boat for a major sponsor. It was intense and dangerous. The next day he jumped into a race car at a NASCAR race, again at 100-plus miles an hour. A day or two after that, he was playing professional golf in a major tournament. I kept thinking, *WOW! This is someone who grabs life by the tail with such an incredible level of energy*. Like me, he got out of bed running, going a million miles an hour with an agenda that would frighten most people. I had finally met my match.

From then on, Bruce and I became inseparable.

The first time Bruce ever picked me up for a date when my children were home, a couple of weeks after our trip to Florida, he was taking me to a private cocktail party for Ronald and Nancy Reagan. He was wearing a jacket that was as old as he was, with a huge hole in the shoulder. I thought, *Oh, boy, this guy needs a little help! He needs someone to love on him a little bit and get him back in the game*. He had been living alone too long, and he was depressed and didn't care about his appearance.

At the same time, Bruce was absolutely endearing. I loved how honest and sincere he was, and we had something huge in common: we both loved our children more than anything else. Before we went to the cocktail party for the Reagans that night, Bruce went straight upstairs to where my son, Rob, was going to bed. All the kids were in Rob's room, hanging all over the bunk beds and watching Bruce say good night to Rob.

"Hey, kids," he said. "I'm Bruce, and I'm here to get your mom for a date. Is it okay if I borrow her and take her out for a little while?"

Except for Kourtney, who stood off to the side and gave Bruce a skeptical look, they all started giggling with delight. It was very endearing.

He was so into the kids and how they felt about him. I thought that was amazing. *Here's a guy who's sensitive to what is going on here*, I thought. I had such a great love for him just for that, and I loved the fact that he had four kids too. This was definitely a fabulous, serious, real kind of love, different from the secret, shady relationship I had just been through with Ryan. We just loved each other from the start. I loved everything about Bruce. I loved his sense of adventure, his spirit, and his love of kids, especially *my* kids. I loved that he loved me, and he let me be me.

The courtship was fast and furious. Bruce and I were having *so* much fun, and it was so unexpected. As I mentioned before, I had given up guys. Right? Forever. Right? Until this big surprise named Bruce Jenner came along. After the Reagan event, Bruce was called out of town, and each time he went somewhere he invited me to go with him. Sometimes I went; sometimes I didn't.

After he left on one trip, I told Bruce I was having a tenth birthday party for Kim at the Tower Lane house. He was playing in a golf tournament in which O.J. Simpson was also playing, but he made a point to fly home for Kimberly's birthday party, which really meant a lot to me. There was more to it than that: his coming home for my daughter's birthday was a milestone. I realized this guy was serious. I wasn't dating a twenty-year-old; I was dating an adult. He made me feel special, and he made sure that I knew that my kids mattered to him.

That was October 1990. The holidays were approaching, in a fast and furious rollout: first Kim's birthday, then Halloween, Thanksgiving, and then Christmas, my favorite of all seasons. As always, we had the most amazing Christmas. Bruce got so caught up in it that he got the Ninja Turtles dressed up as Santas to come over and entertain the kids. Bruce was as excited to have me in his life as I was to have him in mine.

After New Year's, we were invited on a celebrity ski trip with Candace and Steve Garvey. All of our kids—four on each side—went along, and it was a true test of our relationship. It's a big deal to take eight kids skiing, especially when half of them aren't even ten yet. From the moment we arrived at the airport, I realized this was going to be a blast, because the kids had so much fun and Bruce was so great with them. He took everybody under his wing, teaching all of them—even Rob, then only three—how to ski. I just knew that this guy was a great dad.

I also knew I was falling in love with him. I had only known him a few months, but I was in love with him. It was magnetic. Physically, sexually, emotionally. He was the best friend, best lover, best dad, best pal. Bruce was *everything* to me and we started doing everything together. If I went shopping or went to get my nails done, Bruce would go with me. All of a sudden I had a shadow. It was fun. I never wanted to be apart from Bruce. We just loved each other.

I had been lacking the self-esteem to just really be myself, in my own skin, in my own home. Bruce had been lacking his own version of the same thing. It was as if we were meant to meet exactly when we did. I just felt really free with Bruce. I felt like he gave me new breath. I felt like I was safe again. I felt like I was where I belonged.

Everything in my life has been God's plan. I really do believe that. My faith is strong, and it always remained strong through my entire life. Through all these ups and downs and horrible things, I always kept a strong connection to God. I would pray about the things that were going on in my life, as wrong or as right as they were. I can't tell you how many times I prayed for forgiveness for the whole Ryan thing. I regretted that so much, and I will always love Robert Kardashian, but I knew I had met Bruce for a reason. We had that same sense of adventure and the same sense of what we wanted out of life. Like me, Bruce had been through some emotionally draining relationships. He had been through a couple of divorces. So he had some experience in that department, and he obviously knew I was going through a divorce, and I was struggling. He was very patient with me and really understood that I was having a hard time ending my relationship with Robert. Still, our relationship moved very, very fast. He would bring his own kids over, and his kids and my kids all got along, and everything was *so* good.

I don't know if I deserved it, but I do know that God is a loving and compassionate God, and that he is a forgiving God. And God answered my prayers by sending me Bruce Jenner.

Then something horrible happened: Ryan resurfaced.

There were pictures of Bruce and me in some of the weekly magazines, just reporting that we were dating. One night when, thankfully, Bruce was not spending the night at my house, who came ringing my bell? Ryan. On a wild and drunken binge, screaming at the top of his lungs outside of the house. I wouldn't let him in, so he climbed over my wall and started banging on my door. My kids were asleep, so I let him in before he woke them up.

"Bruce Jenner!" he screamed. "Fucking Bruce Jenner???! This is horrible. I want you back!"

"No, no, no," I said. "You have to go home, Ryan. You have to sober up and calm down."

I calmed him down and sent him home. He called me a few times after that when Bruce was in the car with me. Nothing ever threatened Bruce, but he quickly had enough of the calls.

"Let me talk to that asshole," he demanded, grabbing the phone.

"You're dating my girl," Ryan told him.

I thought, *Now you are going to fight for me, dude? After cheating on me?!*

Bruce grabbed the phone. "This is Bruce Jenner," he said in a calm, even, controlled tone. "I'm going out with Kris. I would appreciate it if you would never dial this number again. You got that? Good." And he hung up.

That was the end of it. Finally, I was able to close the door forever on Ryan. When Bruce did that, it gave me the power to move forward in peace.

After a couple of weeks of our relationship moving fast and furiously, Bruce said, "I would like to go to dinner with Robert. How do you feel about that?"

"Sounds good," I said. "What are you going to talk about?"

"I think that if you and I are going to end up together, I want him to know that I can certainly take care of you," he said. "We don't need his money, and you are fighting over things that shouldn't be fought over. Why don't we just start over?"

I was so raw that year, and it sounded like a good idea. My joke with Robert had always been that I came into the marriage with only one thing to my name—an antique desk—and that I would leave the marriage with only the desk. We would laugh about it, like, *Oh my God, if I ever leave, I'll take my desk and run,* you know? Now it was about to really happen.

"You know what? I came into that marriage with nothing, I'll leave with nothing," I told Bruce.

Lo and behold, Bruce calls Robert and says, "Let's go to dinner." They went to dinner at Hamburger Hamlet on Sunset Boulevard.

"I'm in love with Kris and I'd like to marry her," Bruce told him. "We'd like your blessing."

Bruce had not asked me to marry him yet, by the way.

"We don't want to be in this nightmare of a divorce with you anymore, so let's just call it off," Bruce continued. "You take your house. We don't want your money. Pay your child support, because that's fair, and let's call it a day."

Of course, Robert said, "Okay."

So the two of them, in one short dinner, worked out my whole divorce. The next day I called up Dennis Wasser and I said, "It's all worked out. We're going to give Robert the house—" He stopped me mid-sentence. *"But you would've gotten your house!"* he said.

KRIS JENNER

"You know what? I'm done," I said. "It's emotionally too stress-ful for me. I'm about to lose my mind."

The meetings with the attorneys, going to court, the incredible stress, along with my own sense of guilt over what I had done to Robert—it was all just too much for me to handle. I was the one who messed up the marriage. I felt like I should be the one to end it peacefully. It was the right thing to do. That Bruce was offering to take care of me and my whole family helped me in my decision, of course.

Bruce Jenner was not exactly rolling in dough. He was no Rock-efeller. Bruce was renting a modest little house in Malibu at that time—barely better than the bachelor apartment where I had had my affair in Ryanville—which we determined was unacceptable for the six of us. I was obviously going to have to leave the house on Tower Lane. But we were able to negotiate a deal with Robert to let us stay in Tower Lane for six months before Robert would take it over. In the meantime, I was able to get organized.

One night Bruce had to give a speech to the Boy Scouts of America at the Century Plaza Hotel in Los Angeles. I remember looking up at him as he gave his motivational speech. Each time he gave it, it brought me to tears. He had so much to offer as a human being, friend, and lover. I was really so in awe of him and attracted to him, and I thought, *This could really work*. After he was finished speaking, Bruce grabbed my hand and we walked across the room to the meet and greet. He introduced me to somebody saying, "This is my girlfriend, Kris Kardashian." As we walked away, he said, "We've got to do something about changing that last name."

"What did you have in mind?" I asked.

" 'Jenner' sounds good," he said.

That's when I knew: we were going to be together forever. I had already put my kids through this horrendous divorce. Who-ever was going to come into my life to fill that role would have to be a very special guy, and I just knew: Bruce Jenner was it. Bruce loved them—and me—from the start.

Bruce and I decided to move to a house in Malibu, which was a nice transition for me at the time. It got me out of Beverly Hills, where I was uncomfortable anyway, with all my girlfriends still seemingly mad at me and where I was still ashamed of what I'd done. I was so happy to start a new life with Bruce, and I needed a fresh start. It felt good and clean to move to Malibu.

We leased a beautiful house right on Malibu Road and the Pacific Coast Highway. We signed the papers. I remember being quiet that afternoon on the way home as the enormity of the new life I was launching for me and my kids began to sink in. Bruce and I had dinner plans at Saddle Peak Lodge in the Santa Monica Mountains, right off Canyon Road in Malibu, with Candace and Steve and our girlfriend Mary Frann. We were driving back to Tower Lane to change clothes.

"You're awfully quiet," Bruce said.

"I know," I said. "I'm taking my kids on this journey with me and it scares me a little bit. We've leased this house together. We're not married, I've got four kids. It's a little bit weird. I love you, but this feels a little crazy. I've got a big responsibility to my kids."

That night, February 10, 1991, at dinner at the Saddle Peak Lodge high up in the hills of the Malibu Canyon, Bruce ordered a bottle of champagne while waiting for our friends to arrive. I thought that was a little strange, since Bruce always drank beer. After the champagne was poured, Bruce suddenly got down on one knee in the middle of the Saddle Peak Lodge. Everyone was watching us; I could feel the weight of a hundred stares.

Bruce looked at me as if I were the only one in the room, even though he must have known everyone was staring at us too. "Kris, will you marry me?"

"Are you serious?!" I said.

"Yes, of course I am serious. I have already told your ex-husband I am going to marry you. I want to marry you. Let's get married. Let's just do it. Why not? What are we waiting for?"

"Oh my God," I said, and I started to cry. "This is crazy. Yes, okay, yes."

All of a sudden, we were engaged.

Now we had the job of telling everybody we were going to get married, and it was really exciting. I remember our friends got to the table—Steve and Candace and Mary—and we shouted, "We're engaged!" And they were like, "Oh my God!"

We went home that night and told the kids. Bruce's four kids were having a sleepover with my four kids, and we walked into the living room and there were eight kids there waiting for us. We told them the news, and they were all happy—even Kourtney—and jumped up and down, yelling and screaming, hugging one another.

We started to tell my parents and his family, and our friends, and except for a few people who were really Robert's closest friends (and those still unhappy with me), everybody was really, really excited. I was on top of the world. The commitment alone felt good. It was so crazy how things fell into place in such a short amount of time. I was still so young, and I had four small children, and this was crazy and perfect all at the time same.

The next day, Bruce had to play in a golf tournament in Los Angeles. He did a lot of the celebrity tournaments. It was so much fun to be there and to tell everybody, including the reporters at the tournament. The press got excited, and it was a really fun day. That afternoon we flew up to Bruce's house in Lake Tahoe in his small private plane, which Bruce piloted himself. I was in the copilot's seat, and I had the headset on. I still felt horrible for what I had done to Robert, but happy that I was able to make peace with him on some level. All I really cared about anymore was that Robert thought I was a good mom. After all, I was still the mother of his children. I had told him a million times how sorry I was for what I'd done, and in my prayers I apologized to God and to my family. Now I had done all I could do. Now I had to start my life over.

Up in the air, I looked out the window at the clouds and I remember thinking, *Thank you, God. Thank you for taking me through that storm of craziness and having me come out the other side as a whole, happy girl without too much damage.*

Bruce and I were engaged five months after we met. Our wedding came two months after that. So from "Hello" to "I do" was exactly seven months. Quick, yes, but as Bruce told me on the night of our engagement, what were we waiting for?

Our dear friends Terry Semel, then chairman and CEO of Warner Bros., and Jane, his wife, hosted our wedding in the backyard of their Bel Air home on April 21, 1991. We had the most amazing ceremony. Both of our families were there and it was the most glorious setting. Jane had gorgeous white tables out on her veranda with beautiful white flowers and a white berry cake from Sweet Lady Jane.

Everybody was thrilled, especially our kids. All eight of them lined up and performed this little skit, which they had written themselves, and I couldn't believe they all got along so well and could pull that off without a single one of them getting shy. Even my little boy, Rob, was really good in it, and he was now four. They were all so cute and sweet. The girls had on white dresses and party shoes, and the boys had suits.

Everybody we loved was there. It was the perfect day. All that had happened in the preceding years had really stressed out my mom and my stepdad and my grandmother. They were such a huge part of my life, and I'm sure they, like everyone else, thought I had gone more than a little crazy. It's hard to tell your adult daughter what to do. (Believe me, I know that now.) And I can only imagine the pain that they were all in after I basically torpedoed my marriage and my family in the process. I think my parents were so happy that I was able to put it all back together and that my kids felt good again.

After the wedding, Kourtney had a really hard time with Bruce for the first five years or so. She didn't want anybody to take the place of her father. She felt this anger toward Bruce and was a little confused. She even dressed in black during those days whenever Bruce was around. But once she realized that Bruce wasn't going anywhere and that he really did love her and all of us, Kourtney came around. Bruce is smart: he didn't come in as this authoritative-crazy dad figure. He just came in and showed them that he would be there because he loved me. Bruce's idea of raising kids is like a day at summer camp. He took the time to play with each of my kids and teach them things, especially sports—tennis, golf, water and snow skiing— and sometimes help them in school. Like the time he suggested that Kim do her school research project on *him*.

"Who are *you*?" she asked.

"Let me tell you," said Bruce. Kim wrote her paper on Bruce. Of course her female teachers had a crush on Bruce, and of course Kim got an A.

Eventually my kids came to love Bruce as much as I did. Rob was so young, he didn't know the difference. Khloé was young as well when Bruce and I were married. As for Bruce's kids, their dad had been single for ten years, so it wasn't like he was in the middle of any nonsense by the time we got married. They were happy to see him happy.

We settled into married life in Malibu, and Robert moved back into the big house on Tower Lane. We shared visitation 50 percent each, and pretty soon Robert was coming to dinner with me, Bruce, and the kids once a week. Robert wanted to be with the kids as much as he could be. He loved seeing them and he was the greatest dad. "It's the upside of divorce," I would tell people. I had the kids every other weekend, and Bruce and I didn't have any kids of our own. So every other weekend we had all this time to ourselves.

Our first job, though, was making a living. We went to work rebuilding Bruce's career, with me as his manager by default. Suddenly, I went from being a housewife to having a job. It wasn't just any job, either: I had to buckle down and figure out a way to make a life for Bruce and me. I had walked away from any substantial money from Robert, and although Bruce was doing motivational speeches and product endorsements, I could see that his work wasn't going to be enough to keep our life afloat.

The best symbol of where Bruce's career was at that time was in his sock drawer.

That's where he kept the gold medal he had won for the decathlon in the 1976 Bicentennial Olympic Games. Granted, there's only so much juice you can pump out of one Olympic career. Two great days in July 1976 were not going to get us through the rest of our lives. But there was far more to Bruce's talent and success than those two days in 1976. He was an ordinary kid with dyslexia who worked his ass off and became someone to look up to after winning the Olympics.

I knew we had to tell his story to a world that had forgotten it. We took Bruce's gold medal out of his sock drawer and dusted it off and framed it in his office, and that became our motivation. We wanted to be champions again.

"We're going to take the moment that you shined brightest in your life and make sure no one will forget it," I told Bruce. "There should be Bruce Jenner clothing, Bruce Jenner exercise products, Bruce Jenner endorsement deals, Bruce Jenner vitamin supplements," I said. "We'll build this house one speech and one endorsement at a time."

Bruce didn't have a press kit, a business card, or even a piece of stationery with his name on it. He didn't really have an office or a proper business system set up to support what should have been a thriving enterprise. Along the way, somebody missed the boat on an opportunity that could have had legs and longevity and given Bruce a life of more stability.

He was living paycheck to paycheck from his personal appearances and speeches. I had to roll up my sleeves and figure out a better way. I had been around businesspeople my whole life, from my mother and grandmother in their candle shops to Robert Kardashian, and I had ideas about how to improve Bruce's business. I hired a young woman who had once worked as Robert Kardashian's assistant, Lisa Frias, and together we set up an office that was very quickly rockin' and rollin'. We brought in a new computer system to replace Bruce's twenty-year-old typewriter and hired a production company to assemble a highlight reel of some of his greatest moments as an athlete, speaker, and product endorser. Soon we had a press kit and gorgeous business cards. We put the iconic images of Bruce crossing the finish line in a flash of red, white, and blue at the 1976 Olympic Games on everything. We knew Bruce was good at what he did; we just had to make sure everyone else realized that too.

I sent his press kit to every speakers' bureau in the United States. It was a huge undertaking, but with my little team of elves, including Lisa, my girlfriend Stephanie Schiller, and a few others, we made Bruce a superstar again. Bruce really knows how to motivate people. He really has a story to tell. He's great at meet and greets. Everybody loves him. We just had to get him out there in front of the world again. That became my primary focus, eighteen hours a day. Lo and behold, it worked. The speech requests started rolling in, the business changed, we upped his fees, and we got him back on the road again.

At one of Bruce's speeches, David Heil, who worked for a men's clothing company called David Rickey & Company, came up to us and said, "I would like to treat your husband to a whole new wardrobe." He had seen Bruce in a really bad tuxedo and decided we needed help. "Thank you, God!" I said.

David came over to the house and, sure enough, gave Bruce a whole new wardrobe. He spent hours designing a new look for Bruce, complete with really amazing ties that set his new suits apart from anything I had ever seen before. Soon, Bruce looked the part of the superstar that he truly was. He was an icon, an Olympic champion, a motivational speaker, a dad, and now he was a husband—my husband—and we needed to get to work and get him going again. One day at a time, we did.

We did a lot of traveling. Bruce was working for companies like Coca-Cola and Visa and all these major organizations that required him to travel. We would do corporate entertaining for Coca-Cola and travel to different parts of the world: the Olympics in Barcelona, Spain, or Lillehammer, Norway. We just ran around the world doing different things for different companies and having a blast. Soon, we had solid endorsement deals with different companies. We were on our way as a couple, both in love and in business.

After living in Malibu for a year and a half, I decided it required too much driving. My girls were going to Marymount, the private all-girls school right on Sunset Boulevard, and it was a little silly to live so far away. So, in the middle of 1992, we leased a house in Beverly Hills. That way the kids were closer to their dad in Beverly Hills, and the whole transition and custody switches were a lot easier. When we were gone, Robert would take care of the kids. He was dating an amazing woman, Denice Halicki, whom I'm sure he was in love with. She was really, really cool, but especially amazing to my kids.

Our business continued to thrive. We started doing info-mercials. We got a call from Jack Kirby, who ran an infomercial company. "How would you like Bruce to do an infomercial about sunglasses?" he asked.

Bruce flew to Catalina and did that infomercial for Eagle Eyes, and it ended up running on television for ten years. Next, Bruce and I did an infomercial for the Super Step, a home aerobic step program. This one was different because we were going to shoot the infomercial together—and I had never been on television before.

It was the first time we had ever been asked to do a project together, and I really wanted to do a good job. I stood next to Bruce in my little turquoise spandex shorts and a matching turquoise sports bra. Bruce was cool and collected as always, the seasoned pro; I was shaking like a leaf, so nervous I could barely get my name out.

"Hi, everybody, I'm Bruce Jenner," he said.

My line was supposed to be "And I'm Kris Jenner," which I must have said fifteen thousand times before I got it right. I was so scared. I wanted to be perfect. I was so excited to be on TV. I was trying really hard. As the shoot went on—for hours, thanks to my verbal missteps—I became a little more comfortable but still so stiff. Poor Jack Kirby, the producer, was like, *Oh my God, how are we ever going to get her comfortable on camera?* Eventually they did, through trial and error on my part. When the infomercial aired, it shot to number one and stayed on the air for almost two years, making a ton of money for the company and for us.

One after another, we had more offers for fitness infomercials. We created a series, *Super Fit with Kris and Bruce Jenner*, for which we filmed even more infomercials together. We were soon on the media circuit, doing interview after interview. We felt so blessed. Everything was going so well: our careers, our kids. Everybody was happy. It was still a little rough around the edges with Robert, but we were working it out.

Then O.J. and Nicole came back into our lives.

CHAPTER SEVEN

June 12, 1994

They were separated, then back together, then separated, then back together, O.J. and Nicole, then O.J. without Nicole, back and forth and back and forth again. Which was really hard on all of us who were their friends.

When Bruce and I were first dating, one of our first trips together was to Hyannis Port, Massachusetts, to Ethel Kennedy's house for the Robert F. Kennedy Center for Justice & Human Rights Golf Tournament. Bruce played in that tournament every year. He was very close with Ethel and her kids, all of whom had gone to the Olympic Games in Montreal, where they watched Bruce win his gold medal in 1976. Since then, Bruce and Ethel had been supportive of each other and were great friends.

At the tournament in Hyannis Port, Bruce ran into his old friend in the locker room: O.J. Simpson. O.J. had been an on-air reporter for ABC at the Montreal Olympic Games in '76, and he and

Bruce had been friends ever since. That day in the locker room, Bruce said to O.J., "I think I am dating a friend of yours."

"Who?" asked O.J.

"Kris Kardashian," said Bruce.

"No way," O.J. said, picking up a phone and calling me on the spot.

"I think you have something to tell me, Kris," O.J. said in his deep, melodic, instantly recognizable voice.

"What?" I asked.

"I'm here in Hyannis Port at Ethel's tournament, and I'm sitting here next to Bruce Jenner, who says he is going out with you," he said. "What's going on, Kris? Why didn't you tell me you were dating Bruce Jenner?!"

It was a significant phone call. O.J. was like a big brother to me at that point in time. Instead of never speaking to me again after what I did to his best friend Robert, he was now calling me and basically giving me his blessing to date Bruce. He was saying, "Bruce is a great guy. I'm happy for you."

"Why don't we all get together when we all get back home?" O.J. said.

We did. I hadn't really seen Nicole and O.J. very much since the beginning stages of my divorce. I didn't know it then, but Nicole had still been struggling with O.J.'s infidelities, and my unfaithfulness to Robert and our subsequent divorce was very hard on her. She was quite angry with me for throwing away what she considered an awesome marriage to a great guy. She would have done anything to have a husband who was as loyal to her as Robert had been to me. But when we saw each other again, we fell seamlessly back into place. I think Nicole knew how sorry I was about what I had done to Robert and that I had beaten myself up as much as I could, and now I needed to move forward.

From our first moment together as a foursome, O.J., Nicole,

Bruce, and I became very close. It was great to be with Nicole and O.J. again. But by 1993, things were very tricky with them as a couple. They became separated again and were having a really rough time, although I didn't know the half of it. Not yet, anyway.

What are you doing for Cinco de Mayo?" Nicole asked me on the phone one day.

"Nothing," I said.

"I need to get out of here," she said. "Let's go to Mexico."

I told Bruce about it and he said, "Great." He had a small private plane at that point, which he piloted himself as a commercially rated pilot. "I'll get the plane and we'll fly down and stay at my friend Jerry's house," he said.

I invited Robert's cousin and my very close friend Cici and my friend Ayshea, and Nicole, Bruce, and I, along with all four of my kids, all flew down to Mexico. My friend Faye Resnick, whom I met when Khloé was in preschool with Faye's daughter, Francesca, at Beverly Hills Presbyterian, decided to come with Francesca, too. They had a house there, so when they heard we were going down to Cabo San Lucas, they decided to make it one big party. Francesca was Khloé's best friend, and Faye had been a rock for me throughout my affair with Ryan. She and Nicole were just getting to know each other through me.

A friend of mine had dated a guy named Joseph, who had become a good friend to all of us. Bruce called Joseph "God's Gift to Women," because he was *so* good looking. We had known Joseph for a long time and really liked him, so at the last minute I invited him too. But he couldn't ride with us on Bruce's plane, which was full. "If you can fly all the bags down, I'll get you a ticket and you'll stay with us at the house," I told Joseph, who said he'd love to do it.

We had this huge group of people at Bruce's friend Jerry's

enormous estate, right on the water in Cabo. We arrived on May 2, spent the week down there, and had the best time. We all wanted to be home for Mother's Day, especially Nicole, who would never miss a Mother's Day with her two kids. Before we left, though, O.J. caught wind that we were down in Cabo, and he got really upset. He started doing some digging and somehow he found out that Joseph, God's Gift to Women, was down there with us.

Jealous? Oh my God! O.J. went crazy with phone calls. He could be pretty persistent when he wanted to be, and he started calling, calling, calling, calling, calling the house and all of our cell phones. Because it was Mexico, it was hard to get calls in and out during that time. Still, enough of his calls got through, and it was absolutely nutty.

Finally, Mother's Day arrived, a sunny Sunday morning, and we all got back on the plane to fly home. Back then, private planes coming internationally couldn't fly straight to L.A. You had to land at Brown Field in San Diego to clear customs. So we flew to Brown Field, and the minute we landed, my phone started blowing up: O.J., O.J., and more O.J. He had already left me a dozen messages, which all sounded the same: "Where is she? I know Joseph's down there! You guys better tell me what the fuck is going on!" He sounded insane, so jealous that she was on this trip and that Joseph was there too.

Now he was ranting at me: *Where were you? When are you getting back? What's going on? Who is Nicole with? What's this I hear about JOSEPH being down there?!!*

Joseph was fabulous, and there was absolutely nothing going on between him and Nicole. When we landed at Brown Field, Nicole rented a car to drive herself to her mother's home in Laguna, where her kids were staying. I don't think she had told O.J. what her plans were that Mother's Day.

That night Bruce and I had Mother's Day dinner with our kids and settled in for the night. Soon the calls from O.J. started coming fast and furious again. He called me at least fifteen times before I went to bed. He wanted to know *everything* about the trip, what we had done every second we were there, and what Nicole's mood had been like. He wanted her back, he said, and how dare she leave him, and who was this guy Joseph? It got so bad that we were more than a little concerned about his state of mind. I think he felt that Nicole had slipped away from him, and he was incensed and angry at the prospect of her being attracted to anyone else or having fun with other people. He wanted to control her, and he wanted to control that trip, even after the fact.

I have to admit, I felt really bad for O.J. then. Obviously, I didn't have a crystal ball to see what was coming, but I could tell O.J. was in panic mode and that he needed someone to help calm him down. He was way out of control, and when someone shows you that side of their personality, you can't just explain it away. We could tell there was a true problem there. But we didn't know what to do about it—and we never knew where it would eventually lead.

It was 1992. I think Nicole was at a place in her life where she was finally getting strong enough to be on her own, and she was trying to build up that strength in order to be a good mom and at the same time tell O.J. the one word he didn't want to hear: "No."

She wanted out of her marriage; she had just had enough. But none of us really knew how much "enough" meant. Nicole was extremely private about what she was going through with him. I thought that most of her problem with O.J. was that he wasn't faithful and he cheated on her, and that that's what made Nicole so crazy. She didn't share the abusive side of him with anybody for a really long time. I feel like she finally got the nerve to walk away, and her first step was our trip to Mexico.

After the trip she began going on about her plans. First, she had to find a place to live. O.J. stayed in the house on Rockingham, while Nicole moved into a small house at 325 Gretna Green Way. O.J.'s house on Rockingham was a gorgeous English Tudor. It was such a beautiful, spacious home where we spent a lot of time and had a lot of memories: we had had a lot of celebrations, we had played a lot of tennis, and we had gone to a lot of dinner parties there.

I think in the beginning it was a very emotional struggle for Nicole to move out of O.J.'s house on Rockingham and into the house she rented on Gretna Green Way. In moving out, she was finally doing what she felt she needed to do all along. This had great significance for her; she was growing up and being strong, which I wouldn't learn until after she was gone, because she didn't tell me she was being abused, and I didn't recognize the signs of domestic abuse until much later. Now I try to understand what she was going through. I realize how much inner strength she had to muster to be able to do move out on her own without really telling anyone why.

I went over to see Nicole as she was preparing to leave Rockingham. We went upstairs. On the right was Sydney's bedroom, and then the next bedroom was Justin's, and then the last one was O.J. and Nicole's. We walked into her master bathroom—they had his-and-hers bathrooms, so she had her own—and we stood there talking. She was picking things up to pack and trying to explain to me why she was leaving O.J.'s house, using as little detail as possible, which I now understand.

We were both standing in front of the sink, looking at each other in the mirror. For some reason we were having this conversation in the mirror, speaking to our reflections instead of face-to-face.

"This is just something I really need to do," she said. "You're just going to have to trust me."

"This is so sad," I said. "I feel so bad."

"This is something I really need to do," she said.

They had always had a very volatile relationship, with very high highs and very low lows. I was used to the breaking up and making up, but this seemed very final, and I didn't understand why.

"Okay," I said. I just knew that she was serious and committed to making this move, and there was no turning back at that point. "Okay, I'm your friend. No matter what, I'm here for you."

Once Nicole decided that the separation was going to be permanent, she bought her town house at 875 South Bundy. I helped Nicole move in. I went over when she was unpacking. Our mutual friend, Faye Resnick, was there too. I walked inside, looked around, and went WOW. Her new home was so beautiful. Nicole loved to decorate and she loved design, and she had transformed the town house in no time at all.

"Hey, it's me!" I yelled when I walked in.

"We're upstairs!" said Faye.

I went upstairs, and they were unpacking her closet. I started helping in the closet, and Nicole took out a black Donna Karan sweater with gold buttons and handed it to me.

"You always loved this sweater, Kris," she said. "You can have it. I don't want it anymore."

I threw it on immediately, and I still have that sweater to this day.

Nicole was trying so hard to start anew. She had lived this life with O.J. and she was still in love with him, but the dark side of him outweighed the good side of him, and she had finally had enough. We began going on walks and runs, talking about what was going on in her life.

Bruce and I had rented a fabulous house in Benedict Canyon in Beverly Hills, in the same neighborhood where I had begun my married life with Robert Kardashian. I was finally back in a place where I felt safe and comfortable. I had a new beginning in my life too. I felt that finally everything was going to be okay.

I felt sure that Nicole was going to have a new life as well. I remember one day specifically: she said she was going to go to Mexico and buy some patio furniture for her place.

"It's really cheap and really fabulous down there, and I'm going to get O.J. some too," she said.

That kind of showed me that they were still friends and things would probably work out for her, the same way that they really worked out for Robert and me: we could still be a part of each other's lives, still be friends. After all, we had kids together.

O.J. and Nicole's kids, Justin and Sydney, were little, and Nicole was such a good mom. A mom who wanted to decorate her own Christmas tree and put all the lights on the house herself. A mom who would go to the flower market once a week and always have fresh flowers everywhere. A mom who had this really nurturing, domestic side. That's all Nicole wanted out of her life: to be happy and content, and to have peace. That's what she talked about. She talked about just having that peace.

Once, when we were walking together, Nicole told me about a woman who she had become attached to who was having domestic violence problems. She was troubled that this woman was living in a shelter and couldn't afford things for her children. Nicole was trying to raise money for her and her kids. I thought, *How did she even hook up with this lady?* To this day that conversation haunts me, because on later reflection I realized that Nicole was trying to raise money for a woman she had clearly met in a domestic abuse shelter. I don't know if Nicole left in the middle of the night one time and ended up at one of those places or what happened, but I would soon be thinking of this conversation often. It haunted me, because I thought, *Wow, she was in that much trouble*.

At the time, though, I just thought the women's shelter was just another charity she was involved with, because as a celebrity wife you get asked to do things from time to time. I thought she was still working with contacts that she had met when she was married to O.J., and now that they were separated, she was going to continue her charitable work, which I thought was really admirable.

It seemed that O.J. was in a calm place. Then he would return to the ugly place. Of course, I wouldn't ever know when he would go to the ugly place until after the fact. After Nicole and my walks down San Vicente Boulevard, I would get into my car in front of her town house and say good-bye to her. I wouldn't know what would happen in the next twenty-four hours. Some mornings she would be really agitated and really, really upset. Once she told me something that would be seared forever into my memory:

"He's going to kill me," she said. "And he's going to get away with it."

She said this on several occasions, always during one of our walks or runs along San Vicente Boulevard after we'd dropped off our kids at school. She went on to say that he just wouldn't accept the fact that she no longer wanted to be with him. Wouldn't accept that they were divorcing. Wouldn't accept that she would have custody of their kids. Wouldn't accept that Nicole had her own house and that the kids were happy. Sydney was really into dance and Justin was doing his thing in school. After their divorce in October 1992, Justin and Sydney were getting adjusted to a different life, without their father, away from his big house on Rockingham.

And because he wouldn't accept it, Nicole was soon drawn back into O.J.'s orbit.

In the course of their separation and divorce in 1992, Nicole and O.J. started dating again. Not living together, just dating. They became more and more friendly, and before we knew it, they were kind of together. I was surprised, and because I didn't know the full extent of things at that point, I was also excited.

O.J. and Nicole soon began entertaining as a couple again and having parties the way they had when we were all younger. For some reason, we were all obsessed with the Newlywed Game, and we liked to play the game at their parties. At one party I recall talking to O.J. about how he had become totally immersed in golf. All he could talk about was how his golf game was improving, who he played with, and which celebrity tournaments he was playing in. He was practically married to golf. That night we had dinner early. After dinner O.J. said, "I've got to go to bed early to get up at five o'clock and play a round of golf before I do anything else."

We all went home early: Bruce and I back to our house, Nicole back to her town house. The next morning, when I talked to Nicole, she was a wreck. She was convinced that someone was looking in her windows and climbing through her bushes in the middle of the night. She was especially sure someone was looking in her kitchen window downstairs. Nicole was very careful about security. She never went in and out of her front door, because her town house was on a busy street. She always drove into her back alley and straight into her garage, which was attached to her house, and then went into the house from there. The only time she ever used the front entrance was when she and I went on our runs and walks. When we left, she would put her key under a pot, and then we would pick it up when we got back.

She was shaken up and certain that someone was spying on her. This went on for weeks. Then she became convinced that the person spying on her was either O.J. or someone sent by O.J., who was obsessed with what she was doing when he wasn't with her. Nicole wasn't the kind of person who was spooked by just anything. She was a very strong girl. She wasn't typically scared of things. But this really concerned her.

Otherwise, she was doing well. She looked better than I had

ever seen her. She was in shape, she was healthy, she felt good. When she had been married to O.J., she used to bite her nails so much that her fingers would bleed. Now, after the divorce in October of 1992, she had long nails again. Her hair was thick. She was tanned and gorgeous. Being away from him was obviously much healthier for her. The stress of being with him had taken such a toll on her body, and now she was in such a better place.

After their brief stint of post-divorce dating, Nicole started pulling away from O.J. again. It just wasn't working out. Then, before I knew it, it was March of 1994. I had been trying to have a baby with Bruce for the longest time, and I had just suffered a miscarriage, so I was really down and depressed. Nicole decided she was going to find a way to cheer me up.

"I've got the best idea," Nicole told me on the phone one day. "Let's take all the kids and go to Cabo." She wanted to take Bruce, me, all of our kids, her sister Minnie, and our friend Faye Resnick to Cabo San Lucas, Mexico, for Easter weekend.

And oh, yes, she was going to invite O.J. too.

"I'll be in charge of renting a house down there," she said. "And I'll make sure we have the most incredible place ever. I'm going to take care of everything."

Of course, that was usually my job: taking care of everything, especially on vacations. Now I wasn't in the best place, and Nicole knew it. For her to take charge and rent a place for us really took a lot of weight off my shoulders.

"Great," I said. "All I want is something on the water with a great sound system so we can have music and a place to have the kids and hang out."

A few days later she called me back, all excited.

"Oh my God, I found the perfect place! I rented two houses together, right on the beach at Palmilla."

Again, I was in the dark about her on-again, off-again relationship with O.J., a game that must have been a lot more devastating for her than I ever could have imagined. At the time I was happy to see Nicole with him, because it seemed to make her happy. If I had known then what I know now, of course I would have never encouraged her to allow herself to return to that kind of hell. But at that time, she seemed so full of life. It seemed they were always trying to make their relationship work.

So we all flew off to Mexico for a few days, which we had done so many times before. Nicole and O.J. went first. Then Bruce and I, along with Kourtney, Kimberly, Khloé, and Rob a day or two later. I remember arriving at Palmilla and being driven over to the house that Nicole had rented. Nicole was in our house, standing at the front door, so excited to see the look on my face when I saw the house she had rented for us. She was so proud of herself.

"Are you ready?!" she said.

"YES!" I screamed.

She opened the front door.

"I got your favorite music!" she said. All I could hear was Luther Vandross music blasting from inside. There was a chef who had just made fresh guacamole and chips and was serving margaritas, and Nicole was just beaming. I'll never forget that smile on her face that said: *Look how great I did!* We were squealing like little schoolgirls. We were jumping up and down, so excited to be there, so excited to kick our heels up and just relax.

Nicole and O.J. were staying in the house next door with her sister Minnie and her guest, and also our friend Faye, her boyfriend, Christian, and her daughter, Francesca. In the house that she had rented for us, my kids scattered, looking for their bedrooms. It was Easter weekend, and I had gone out and bought Easter baskets for all the kids. I brought Easter plates, Easter napkins, and supplies to have a big Easter egg hunt on the beach.

1973: My high school graduation.

Starting my life as a flight attendant. College wasn't for me.

1977: First ski trip with Robert, Aspen.

Robert with his *two* Rolls-Royces. He was pretty extravagant. And I loved him.

1978: At my engagement party.

Robert's and my wedding party.

Cutting the cake at our
Big Fat Armenian Wedding.

1978: Honeymoon
in Auberge de
Noves, France.

Pregnant with Kourtney.

I just gave birth to our first baby, Kourtney.

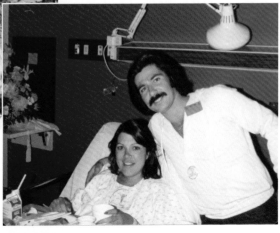

Proud Grandma! My mom with Kourtney at her first birthday party.

Kim's first Christmas with big sister Kourtney.

Kim's first birthday.

1981, Christmas. Robert playing Santa and Kim putting up a fuss.

Robert and his parents.

Mom and stepdad Harry.

1985, Christmas. Kim, baby Khloé, and Kourtney (left to right). Khloé's first Christmas.

Me and Robert with Kim and Khloé (in Robert's arm) in the play area near the tennis court.

Khloé at age 2.

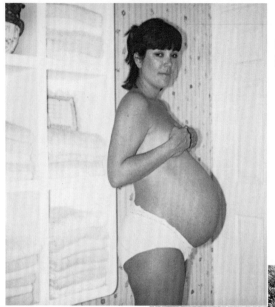

Pregnant with Rob, my first boy.

My two Roberts at baby Rob's second birthday party.

Rob and family friend, baseball Hall of Famer Steve Garvey.

ABOVE: Power couples. Me and Robert, O.J. and Nicole.

RIGHT: Nicole, O.J., me, and Robert. For a while, we were inseparable.

BELOW: On the slopes with O.J. and Nicole. It was O.J.'s first ski trip.

RIGHT: Robert's 40th birthday bash. This is me with then "big brother" O.J.

Taco Night. You know how I love to cook. That's Nicole feeding me a chip.

Me and my parents.

Grandma, grandpa, and me with the kids.

The family wedding portrait.

Bruce loves being daddy!

Our Brady Bunch on steroids. Bruce with his four and me with my four, Christmas 1990.

Me and Bruce with Candace and Steve Garvey.

Me and Bruce with our friends Kathie Lee and Frank Gifford.

Me, Bruce, and O.J. (and Steve Garvey, far left). Ironically, O.J. is friends with Bruce, too.

1991: Me and my man.

Me and the love of my life, Bruce Jenner.

ABOVE: Easter 1994: After one of my famous Easter egg hunts. This was our last vacation with O.J. and Nicole.

LEFT: Me and Nicole. If I only knew the pain behind that smile . . .

BELOW: Me, Bruce, Nicole, and O.J. with our kids.

Family Fitness—one of our business ventures takes off.

Khloé, Bruce, Me, and Rob at an event in front of Bruce's Olympic Gold medal *Sports Illustrated* cover.

Keepin' Up with the Kardashians—this is how it started.

Keepin' Up with the Kardashians—our family keeps growing.

I must have had four hundred plastic eggs filled with jelly beans. We were all so, so excited.

We were listening to the music, eating the chef's delicious guacamole, and drinking our margaritas. The kids were running around in their bathing suits. I remember that Nicole brought the tape of the movie *Pretty Woman* with her, and every day we had *Pretty Woman* on the TV. Every time I walked into her house, she was back in her kids' room, watching *Pretty Woman* over and over again.

My kids were still pretty young. Kourtney was thirteen, Kimberly was twelve, Khloé was ten, and Rob was seven. The girls were old enough to take care of themselves. They could all run up and down the beach and play with one another. Of course, they had all grown up with Nicole and O.J.'s kids and Faye's daughter, Francesca, so everyone got along and had a great time playing together.

It was one of those glorious trips, for the most part. Then one night we all decided to go into town and have dinner at a local restaurant. We were having a drink at the bar before we sat down at the table. I was sitting next to O.J, and I remember thinking how fabulous everything was. Then, five seconds later, right after Nicole left to go to the bathroom, O.J. started majorly *flirting* with two girls at the bar.

It infuriated me that the second Nicole went to the ladies' room, he was immediately putting the moves on the closest targets.

"Stop it!" I snapped.

That took him aback. "What?" he asked.

As far as I knew at that point, this wandering eye was O.J.'s only real problem. I didn't really realize that abuse was going on at the time or how bad it was. Still, I wasn't going to let him get away with flirting.

"Cut it out, O.J.," I said, practically screaming. "What's wrong with you? We're on vacation as a family, your kids are sitting right over here, Nicole's in the bathroom, and you can't handle being here for five seconds while she is gone without doing this?"

He knew I was really upset. After screaming at him, I walked away and joined Nicole in the ladies' room. I just had to breathe for a minute because what O.J. had done was so obnoxious.

"What's wrong, what's wrong?" Bruce kept asking when I came back to the bar.

"I'll tell you later," I said.

That night I realized that Nicole and O.J.'s relationship was over, because O.J. just couldn't help himself. He felt almost entitled to flirt. It was just so stupid, and I felt so bad for Nicole. I felt like he was never going to get past this, and she was just going to continue to be disappointed and upset over and over again. I knew O.J. wasn't going to change. I knew she had to cut him off, to end it forever. It was a powerful night for me. I didn't tell Nicole about O.J.'s blatant flirting, but I did tell my other girlfriends who were there.

After that night, the trip went dark. We did have a good time on Easter Sunday, when we had the big Easter egg hunt. For our kids, O.J. and Nicole were still, as they called them, Uncle O.J. and Aunt Nicole. We were that close. That vacation, as always, all of our kids had a ball. They watched movies, they went swimming, and they went into town and had dinners together. Sydney and Khloé were close friends, and Justin got along with everybody. It was like one big happy family.

Our Easter egg hunt was done in the backyard, around the swimming pool, and in the sand. Nicole had stuffed all the eggs with candy, and she and I prepared the whole scene and gathered Easter baskets for everyone. Bruce and O.J. hid all the Easter eggs. Once we hid all the eggs, we got the kids all together.

"All right, guys, one, two, three . . . go!"

It was so much fun. But on Monday morning, O.J. got up and announced that he was going to leave. He was going to go play in a golf tournament. He left by himself, leaving the rest of us to continue our vacation. A few days later, it was time for us to leave. On our way to the airport we stopped for a bite to eat. It was cool that day, and the little restaurant we went to was on a hill. Nicole got so cold that she took a tablecloth from the next table and, joking around, put it around her shoulders. I took a picture of her that way, smiling, standing in the wind with a tablecloth around her shoulders.

Later, somehow, that became the first picture of Nicole that was released to the media after she was murdered.

Back at home, Nicole turned quiet. There wasn't much communication for a few days. Then she called and said, "Kris, it's over. I just can't do it anymore."

We started taking our walks again, and she once again expressed her fears that somebody had been looking into her kitchen window, crawling through her bushes, and following her as she went about her day. She told me that she thought she was being stalked. And she believed it was O.J. She felt like he was angry that she no longer wanted to try and make things work between the two of them. Soon it became clear: O.J. was indeed stalking her. He was calling her and trying to find out where she was all the time.

A month after we got home from Cabo, Nicole gave me an album with pictures of all of us from the trip. It was the nicest thing, so sweet. She was always like that. She loved her photo albums, and she always kept track of everything.

Just after that, Nicole suddenly got really sick, which was unusual for her. She was always healthy and strong and athletic and beautiful, always took care of herself, always exercised. But she got really, really sick. It turned out to be pneumonia. She was at home, stuck in bed with this horrible sickness. I would drop soup off at her house, but she just could not seem to get well for the longest time. She was sick for about six weeks. Finally she started to come out of it a little bit. By that time we hadn't seen each other to hang out or anything for a while, so we talked mostly on the phone. Eventually, we were able to start our walks again.

Suddenly it was summer. My kids were in camp, Nicole's daughter, Sydney, was in a dance camp and Justin was doing summer activities too. Bruce and I were still trying really hard to get pregnant again, but we were having trouble for some reason. Nicole was always so supportive of our unending and thus far unsuccessful attempts to have a child.

"Come over to my house, we're going for a walk," she would say. "We're going to get you in shape because you're going to get pregnant!"

One day she came over and brought me a huge box of clothes.

"What's this?" I asked.

"My maternity clothes from when I had Justin," she said, explaining that our friend Allen Schwartz from ABS had made all of these maternity dresses for her. "I want you to have them, because I *know* you're going to get pregnant. I know you're not pregnant yet, but you are going to get pregnant and you are going to wear these dresses."

Late one night Nicole called around ten. Bruce and I were already in bed.

"We've got a problem," she said. "Faye is getting really bad with the drugs, and I want to have an intervention."

She wanted to do it that night. Immediately. That was Nicole. No time to wait when it came to helping someone out.

"Get your ass out of bed and get over here," she said.

"Okay, great, I'll bring the coffee," said Bruce.

We all met at Faye's boyfriend Christian's house. And while we waited for Faye to arrive, Nicole asked me, "Do you have my key?"

"What do you mean, do I have your key?" I asked.

She was missing the key she always left under the pot during our early morning walks.

"Somebody's taken my key," she said. "I think it was O.J."

"Let's go through your bag," I said, and we took every last thing out of her purse and rummaged through it, looking for her missing key. Nicole was in a panic while we were waiting for Faye. We couldn't find that damned key anywhere. When Faye walked through the door to find all of her friends waiting in an intervention, she was, of course, shocked, then scared. We wanted her to go to rehab. After Nicole promised Faye that she and I would take turns visiting her every day so she wouldn't be alone during visiting hours, Faye finally agreed to go. Her boyfriend, Christian, immediately took her to rehab and we all went home. The next couple of days Nicole and I called each other and met at the rehab facility to visit Faye, just as we had promised.

One day Nicole said she needed to switch visiting days. Sydney's dance recital was that weekend and, of course, she would never skip that. I said certainly we could switch days, and we changed the schedule. There was something else, Nicole said.

"I really have something important to talk to you about," she said.

"Okay," I said.

"Can you come over today after rehab?"

"Sure."

At the rehab facility, Faye and I decided to call Nicole. I couldn't attend Sydney's recital because Bruce had to fly to

Chicago and I had to take care of the kids that night. Faye and I wanted to say hi and tell Sydney good luck at the recital.

"I have to go to Sydney's rehearsal in two hours," Nicole told me. "Can you get over here before then? I need to talk to you. It's really important."

I told Nicole that I had to go to the market and knew I couldn't get there in time.

"That's okay," said Nicole. "Can you meet me tomorrow for lunch? I really have to talk to you about something really, really important."

"Of course," I said, and she said, "Great."

Then Nicole told Faye that she was sorry she couldn't be with her that day, due to the recital, but she was looking forward to seeing her the very next day.

After I left the rehab facility I went to the market, because all of the going back and forth to the rehab facility was taking a toll on our family life. We needed groceries. But Nicole needed me to come over right then and there, and I couldn't. She said she needed a couple of hours to talk to me, and I just couldn't pull it together that day. That decision would haunt me forever.

It was June 12, 1994, and it would be the last time I would ever speak to Nicole.

I woke up early the morning after Sydney's dance recital. Bruce had gone to Chicago to play in a celebrity golf tournament, so I took the kids to school down the hill. On my way to the school, I called Nicole and got her answering machine.

"Where are you?" I asked. "See you at noon! Can't wait. Bye!"

When I got back to the house at around 8:30, my assistant, Lisa, came in and told me that Judi, Nicole's mother, was on the phone. Bruce and I had been planning a trip and we were using Judi as our travel agent, and I thought she was calling about flights or some other travel detail.

"Can you tell her I'll call her right back?" I asked.

I heard Lisa tell Judi I would call her right back, but then Lisa walked right back into the kitchen, her face ashen.

"I think you want to take this call," she said.

"Why?" I asked.

"Kris, get on the damn phone!" Lisa exclaimed. "It's an emergency!"

Oh, shit. I picked up the phone.

"Hello?"

Judi was hysterical.

"Nicole's been shot," she said. "Nicole's been *shot!*"

I was instantly numb. *"What?"*

"She's been shot! She's been shot!"

"Oh, my God!! Where is she? I'm on my way."

"No, she didn't make it."

"What!!?"

All I could think of in that split second was that it was a drive-by shooting on her street.

"Well, where was she??!!"

"She was in front of her house."

My mind was racing, and I was thinking, *Shot?* Somebody just drove by and shot her? It didn't make any sense. When you hear something that shocking, you can't process it. I still hadn't processed the fact that Judi had told me that Nicole hadn't made it.

I just kept saying, "Well, what hospital is she at?"

And Judi kept answering, "No, you're not listening, Kris. She's *gone.*"

Everything became a blur. We had just been with Nicole a few nights ago. And now she was *dead*? Everything just started spinning. The room was spinning. My mind was spinning. I was hysterically crying. Lisa, my assistant, didn't know what to do with me. I was just inconsolable. Finally, I realized it wasn't about me: Nicole's mother was still on the phone.

"Judi, should I come down there?"

She told me not to, not yet. "Let me get some more information," she said, because nobody had any information. Judi had just heard it herself, I guess, and had called me. Everybody was just waking up and getting this news, and I'm not sure what time Judi found out, but she was just so upset, obviously. She was just a mess.

"Where are the kids?" I asked.

She said they had been taken to the police station.

"Stand by," she told me.

Eventually someone picked up Sydney and Justin and brought them to Judi's house. I turned on the television, and all that was on was news about Nicole Brown Simpson being murdered in front of her house, on her steps on South Bundy. Hours later, it was revealed that she had been stabbed to death, and that her friend Ron Goldman, who was in front of the house with her, was dead too.

I didn't know Ron Goldman, but Nicole and I had a very close friend whose name was Ron Hardy, and at first I thought it was that Ron who was killed. So I was even more hysterical, because Ron Hardy was also one of my dear friends. However, I got ahold of my Ron and realized it was another Ron who had been with Nicole.

That same morning, after I hung up the phone with Judi, I called the Chicago golf club where Bruce was playing in this tournament, not realizing that O.J. was also in Chicago playing in a golf tournament. Wow. To this day, I don't even know for sure if they were playing in the same tournament. (Bruce doesn't remember, either.)

"I need to speak to Bruce Jenner. It's an emergency. Please go get him," I said.

The director of the golf course found Bruce on the ninth hole and told him that his wife was on the phone, saying it was an emergency. Bruce's first thought was that my grandmother had passed away. When Bruce said, "Hello?" I blurted, "You've got to come home. Nicole's been murdered!!"

Bruce had the golf course director drive him straight to the airport with a police escort. By then everyone had heard about the murder of Nicole Brown Simpson. When he arrived at the airline check-in counter and the attendants realized who he was (a friend of O.J.'s) and where he was going (back to the scene of the crime of the century), they bumped somebody out of a first-class seat to get Bruce home.

What was interesting was that one of the airline gate agents told Bruce, "That's really odd. We just did the same thing with O.J."

Meaning O.J. had also left Chicago and somebody had to be bumped off the plane to give him a seat.

While Bruce was flying home, all hell was breaking loose. I had called my girlfriend Shelli Azoff and told her about Nicole.

"Oh my God! Oh my God!" she said.

Shelli called my ex-husband, Robert, all within minutes after Judi's call to me. Robert called me, and he said something strange: "See, you better be nicer to me." He was kidding. It was his way of joking, but it was just such a stupid comment. He was always a practical joker, but that went too far.

"That's not funny," I said.

Then I asked, "What do you think happened?"

"I don't know," Robert replied.

The next thing I knew, I was watching the news and seeing Robert Kardashian picking up O.J. Simpson from the airport. It already felt like years had passed since I had taken the kids to school that morning. It was so odd and surreal. I was in my kitchen, paralyzed, because I was watching O.J. arriving at his house on the television and Robert was driving the car. Robert was holding a Louis

Vuitton bag, O.J.'s garment bag—*the* garment bag—and walking onto O.J.'s property. There to greet them was Howard Weitzman, our longtime friend and now O.J.'s criminal attorney. As this surreal scene was unfolding, all I could think was: *What the fuck is going on here?*

I had a crack addict's need for information, so I called Robert, asking what was going on and begging him to call me back. He eventually called me when he got home and said, "Everything's fine. I'm going to help him through this."

I didn't know what to think, didn't know what to believe, didn't know what to do. None of us could really believe what was happening. One night we went to bed, and life was pretty normal, and the next day we woke up and our entire universe had changed forever.

O.J. and Nicole were two of my best friends. Now Nicole was gone and life as I knew it was over. I grew up very fast that day. It was life changing. Heartbreaking. Devastating. Tragic. Surreal. Emotional. Paralyzing. I couldn't even find the energy to take care of my kids. Everyone was paralyzed—from Nicole's parents to her family to all of our friends. Everybody was calling one another, saying, "What happened?" "Oh my God!" "What's going on?"

I was distraught and there was nowhere to go and nothing to do. No action to take. No way to help Nicole's parents, or her children, or, most important, Nicole herself. It wasn't like she was injured; I couldn't go visit her at the hospital. I was going crazy with grief. Then I remembered the lasagna. A few days before the murder, on one of our walks, Nicole and I had been talking about lasagna. Nicole had told me that there was a way to make lasagna without cooking the noodles first. We both made our lasagna from scratch, and she said there was a way to make it where you would put the noodles in raw and then they would just cook themselves while the lasagna was cooking. I thought that was just crazy.

"Nicole, that's impossible, you can't do that," I said.

But she insisted that it wasn't just doable, it was great.

I asked my assistant to go to the grocery store and get all the ingredients for lasagna. I would've gone to the market myself, but I knew I couldn't hold it together.

I could not get over the feelings of anguish and pain I had about the way Nicole died. I instinctively knew that in some way O.J. had something to do with her death, and I truly couldn't believe she had been so betrayed by the person who she had once loved most. That O.J. would be so destructive and selfish and jealous that he would do that to her was just mind-blowing to me. All these thoughts were running through my mind: *This can't be true. This can't be true.*

That's when I started cooking lasagna, which would take three hours to make. In the kitchen I had the TV on, and the only thing on every channel across the country was this story about the Nicole Brown Simpson and Ron Goldman murders. I would listen to it over and over and over and over, just hanging on to every little piece of information that came across the screen. As I made the lasagna, I was just bawling over the stove, crying, crying, and crying, using the lasagna recipe Nicole had just told me how to make. The weekend before, we had thrown a barbecue at my house, and Nicole had brought a salad in this big, gorgeous Lucite salad bowl. I pulled out the salad bowl and made a salad in it in some sad little attempt to be closer to her.

It's silly how you behave when somebody passes away. You just don't know how you're going to react. My reaction was to cook. So I made this big lasagna, Nicole's way—and, as with everything Nicole had done, it was great. Soon my friends started to come over. Candace Garvey came over, and Cici came over. One by one, everybody showed up.

Nicole's parents were in Laguna, trying to figure what to do and to get the kids organized, and I couldn't get ahold of A. C. Cowlings, one of Nicole and O.J.'s best friends and O.J.'s former teammate, who we had all known forever. I couldn't find anybody. I felt like we had this big group of friends, but suddenly I was on this isolated island, and no one was talking to one another. It was almost as if immediately the line in the sand had been drawn, and it was Nicole's side against O.J.'s side, but subliminally.

Not so subliminally, I discovered that my ex-husband, Robert Kardashian, was on O.J.'s side.

Very quietly, as the day and the phone calls and the news reports wore on, we realized she had been stabbed. All of a sudden my head was reeling, because being stabbed, repeatedly and angrily and brutally, is much different than being shot.

The police came to my house and started asking us questions, because my voice and my messages were on Nicole's answering machine, since we were supposed to have lunch at noon on the day after her murder. The police knew about our plans and wanted to question me immediately to find out what our meeting was all about. I couldn't give them much information, because Nicole had left me a pretty cryptic message about why she had wanted to have lunch. She needed to talk to me and wanted it to be very private, just her and me, and it had to be out of her house. She had stressed that *nobody* could be around, and my house was full of people, and her house was full of people, which was why she wanted to meet at a restaurant where we could wear our sweats, be alone, and hopefully be anonymous.

Later on the day after the murder, Nicole's sister Denise called me.

"It's really important we talk," she said. "I need to know what you know."

I wasn't sure what she meant.

"Nicole said she was going to see you yesterday," she said.

"No, we made it for lunch today because I couldn't go yesterday," I said.

"Well, she had something really important to talk to you about," she said. "She wanted to show you the pictures."

"What pictures?"

"The pictures in her safety-deposit box."

"What are you talking about?"

Denise explained that Nicole had been beaten up by O.J., and she had been keeping this physical proof in the form of photographs and, it would turn out, other evidence, in which she had documented seventeen years of abuse. Nicole really wanted someone close to her to know what was going on, so that somebody— namely me—could be a witness. I could tell from my conversation with Denise that she had talked to Nicole about sharing the photographs with me. Apparently, Nicole thought this was a good idea. Denise had seen the pictures and she was hoping I had seen them too.

"Oh my God! It's too late! It's too late!" I cried.

The realization that she had wanted to confide in me like that hit so hard. Right before I was divorced, O.J. and Nicole had asked Robert and me to be Justin's godparents. I knew that Nicole looked up to me a little bit; I felt she thought that I was somebody in her life who was stable, somebody who went to church and loved God. Somebody who she could depend on. Somebody with four kids who was a good mom. She apparently felt like she could finally tell me what was going on behind closed doors with her and O.J.

And I let her down.

The news from Denise devastated me. I felt that if Nicole and I had talked on the day when she wanted me to meet her, things might have been different. I'll never be able to change what happened that night when she went to Sydney's recital and then went to dinner with her family and then went home to be so brutally murdered. But at least I would have known the truth, and I would have learned it firsthand from her. Maybe I could have at least been more helpful to the prosecution during the trial.

In the end, Nicole wasn't able to tell anybody about the abuse she had suffered. She took those pictures of her battered and bruised face and neck and put them in that safety-deposit box for a reason, and thank God she did. They would turn out to be very helpful, especially in the civil trial against O.J.

Still, it haunts me that she wasn't able to tell me about the pictures—and that I wasn't there to allow her to tell me. One thing I learned from this horrendous experience is something I would tell anybody going through something like this: Act on your feelings and share your thoughts rather than hold back, even if it means crossing a privacy line. When you feel like something is really wrong, it's usually wrong. Follow your instincts; you might just change someone's life.

CHAPTER EIGHT

Backstage at the Trial of the Century

We were beginning to see the trial of the century take shape, with talk of evidence, attorneys, gossip, and innuendo. It was "a modern tragedy and drama of Shakespearean proportions being played out live on television," as Tom Brokaw described the trial on NBC. Soon, everything was Nicole and O.J. all the time, 24/7. If I turned on the television, it was all I saw. If I stepped outside, there were packs of paparazzi in front of our house.

The media figured out quickly who Nicole's friends were. The most famous newscasters and journalists in the world were calling us for interviews, and people were sitting in front of our house, screaming out questions to us whenever we left. We were followed everywhere. It was a media frenzy.

That time was incredibly horrible for multiple reasons, one of which was that my ex-husband was in the O.J. camp and I was in the Nicole camp, and my kids were stuck in the middle. My kids were old enough, by this point, to know what was going on. Kourtney was fifteen when Nicole was killed, Kim was fourteen, and Khloé was ten. They went from being teenagers to young adults overnight as a result of this murder and the ensuing trial. This was Uncle O.J. and Auntie Nicole. These were people they had known their entire lives. When Kourtney was born, O.J. came to the hospital the next morning to see her. O.J. was always part of our life. Now they were hearing horrible stories about Nicole and horrible stories about O.J., and they were devastated. I decided that I would have a long talk with Robert about doing what was best for the kids. He agreed.

"We have to try to keep it together for the kids," he said.

I agreed, but soon things got difficult. As the two sides were clearly drawn in the sand with a big white line, it became tougher for me to see Robert's point of view. It became tough for me to be nice to him. Because I couldn't understand in a million years how Robert couldn't see what I was seeing, how he didn't seem to even bother to look at the evidence.

Of course, O.J. Simpson as a murder suspect was tough for most people to grasp. It was just unbelievable to anybody that O.J. Simpson—everybody's hero, the all-American athlete sprinting through the airport in the Hertz commercials, the wholesome hero selling Dingo boots, the smart sportscaster at all the football games and the Olympics, the superstar whom everybody had put up on this pedestal—could have committed capital murder.

I knew him as a bigger-than-life, amazing personality. A guy who could have a conversation with anybody. Someone outgoing and effervescent and savvy and seductive and manipulative and charismatic. Someone who loved to talk and was so good with people and great at capturing their attention. Someone who could have said anything and you would believe him because he was so captivating. He had this incredible, magnetic personality. That's why he was so good at being a spokesperson for different companies: people *wanted* to be around him. To quote a *Newsweek* story that was published just after the murders:

> *Simpson was more than another storybook American success . . . Orenthal James Simpson was the prototype of the modern athlete as total package—a record-shattering running back with a luminous personal charm that attracted advertisers and film producers by the limousine-full. Before Magic, before Bo, before Michael and the Shaq, there was The Juice. While other great players faded from view as memories of their competitive feats slipped into the past, O.J. Simpson sustained a lasting bond with his public . . . He was aging with an uncommon grace that seemed destined to place him in an elite circle of sports figures like Palmer and DiMaggio.*

People loved O.J., and, I would soon discover, people *believed* O.J.

O.J. told Robert that he didn't kill Nicole. O.J. told him that it was a horrible thing that had happened to Nicole. O.J. told Robert that he didn't know who had killed Nicole, but that it for sure wasn't him. Robert really wanted to believe the best of O.J. He was somebody he had known for most of his life.

So Robert believed O.J.'s story that he was innocent.

I didn't believe O.J., not for a second.

The morning after the murder, the police dusted Nicole's house for prints and dissected and searched the front lawn, the back garage, and everywhere else, over and over again. The whole process was captured on television, because the news crews were parked across the street from Nicole's town house, which faced the street. They captured every pathetic moment of the police gathering their evidence, which apparently didn't amount to much.

Watching all of this on television, I called up my dear friend and Nicole's neighbor Ron Hardy and told him, "Ron, get over there quick."

"Why?" he asked.

"I am watching TV, and the police are done with their investigation," I said. "The police have taken down the yellow caution tape, and nobody has washed Nicole's blood off of the steps.

"I'm sitting here watching this, and I can't take it anymore. Go over there and wash the blood off the steps!"

Again, I would have done it myself. Again, the media still had us surrounded.

"Okay, okay, I'm on my way," said Ron.

Today, I can't believe I asked him to do this. I really wasn't thinking clearly about his feelings, and I still feel badly about that. How could I have asked him to go wash someone's blood off the stairs? I just blurted it out: "Go over there and wash the blood off the steps!"

And, God bless him, he did it.

Like everyone else, I watched what happened next on television. I watched Ron Hardy drive up to Nicole's town house. I watched him park in the back alley and come out onto the front steps with a garden hose, where he started washing the steps. It was so surreal and horrific and devastating, as was everything.

The next day, I was driving in Brentwood with my dear friend Cici, Robert's first cousin. We were at a stoplight on San Vicente in

Brentwood when we turned and found ourselves sitting in traffic next to Robert's car, and in the passenger seat was O.J. Simpson.

"Oh my God, oh my God!" Cici cried out.

We looked at the two of them and they looked at the two of us, said nothing, and then just drove off.

We couldn't believe it. I mean, if one of your best friends had lost his wife to a terrible tragedy the day before and you hadn't talked to your friend yet, wouldn't you expect him to pull the car over and jump out and hug you? But O.J. and Robert were just cold. They didn't speak. They didn't smile. They didn't say a word. They just looked over at us as if we were two strangers and drove off. Cici and I were like, "What the hell is going on?" It was such a crazy moment that I would tell the prosecutor, Marcia Clark, about it during the trial.

That night I called Robert.

"What the hell was that all about?" I asked, meaning the silent treatment on the street.

"O.J. was really upset because we had to go to the airport to get his golf clubs," he said.

"What?" I asked.

"Well, Kris, he was at a golf tournament," Robert said, referring to O.J.'s supposed whereabouts in Chicago the day after the murder. "When the police came and took him to the airport and he got on the plane, his golf clubs didn't make it. They just arrived today."

I thought that sounded suspicious in any situation, especially on the day after O.J.'s wife had been brutally stabbed to death in her front yard.

"So you're trying to tell me that you guys needed to go to the airport to get golf clubs from the airline when we all know that the airline will deliver them to your house?" I asked Robert.

"Kris, he really needed his golf clubs," Robert said.

"His wife is fucking dead!" I screamed. "Why did O.J. need his golf clubs?"

The rumor that would soon circulate was that the murder weapon was in O.J.'s golf bag, a knife hidden among the metal clubs so that it wouldn't set off security alarms. If he had the knife in the golf bag, it would make total sense that O.J. and Robert *had* to drive to LAX to personally retrieve the bag. I've thought back to that moment beside them in the car on San Vicente many times since—about how odd and crazy it was for us to run into them on their way home from picking up these golf clubs.

The golf clubs were in the trunk of Robert's car that day. I'm not sure how he justified in his mind that this man needed to get his golf clubs from the airport himself. O.J. Simpson did not need to go to the airport himself. He had enough people to go to the airport for him. The airline would have sent the golf bag back to the house. That's what made no sense whatsoever.

Much later, Robert told me that one thing stood out to him about O.J. after the murders. It came to him soon after he took him to pick his golf clubs up at the airport. Robert and O.J. went back to Rockingham with the clubs, but the media were swarming around O.J.'s house. It was impossible for him to get into the house with those golf clubs, so they drove to Robert's house. They left the golf clubs in the garage there.

According to Robert, that night or shortly thereafter, O.J. said that he wanted to go for a walk, and he needed to go by himself. He said he needed to go "talk to Nicole." So he went on this really long walk in the dark in Robert's neighborhood in Encino, where Robert had leased a house. I'll always wonder what O.J. did on that walk. Did he take the knife out of the golf bag and throw it into a canyon or in somebody's trash can? That still haunts me.

Robert lived in Encino with his girlfriend, Denice. Things were going really well for Robert and Denice when all this happened. O.J. was living in the house on Rockingham, where the media constantly hounded him that day after the murder. The media could not figure out how he kept getting in and out of his house without seeing him. I knew he was coming and going through the tennis court in the backyard that connected to a neighbor's property. I wanted to scream at the television: *You can't see him go in and out because he's going out from behind his house! Figure it out, people!*

Finally, O.J. obviously couldn't take the pressure of sneaking in and out of his own house anymore. A few days after the murder, he moved into Robert's house in Encino. One day, I went over to Robert's to pick up my kids. I walked through the front door expecting to find everyone there. But the house was . . . empty. There was absolutely nobody home. No Robert. No Denice. No O.J. No kids.

One thought consumed me: *Search the place!* I didn't know if I had ten minutes, I didn't know if I had one minute. But however long I had, I wasn't going to waste it standing in the hallway. So I ran up to the room where O.J. was staying, and there was his damn Louis Vuitton garment bag. I went through it with a fine-tooth comb, trying to satisfy my own curiosity, my own doubts. If there was a piece of incriminating evidence anywhere, I was determined to find it and turn it over to the prosecution. It was torturing me that there had to be *something* somewhere, and I was determined to find it. There was nothing in the Louis Vuitton bag. So I began ransacking the entire room. I looked through every closet. Searched through every drawer. I went through all of O.J.'s stuff, but I didn't find much of anything.

Then I heard a car pull up outside: Robert and the kids. I ran downstairs and was standing nonchalantly in the entrance hall when they walked in. I took the kids and went home, the whole time just thinking, *What the hell is going on?*

The next time I saw Robert, a day or two later, I asked him, point-blank, "Where's the golf bag?"

"In my garage," he said.

"Didn't you look through it?" I scolded him.

"No," was all he said.

I forced myself to stay strong for my kids. I had to be an example to them while they tried to make sense of this whole situation. Their dad seemed to be siding with O.J., and their mom was obviously siding with Nicole's family.

A few days after the murder, Nicole's mom, Judi, called me, asking Bruce and me to go over to Nicole's town house. Sydney and Justin, O.J. and Nicole's kids, were staying with Judi and her husband, Lou. She wanted them to have all their belongings with them, because she felt that that would help make the transition easier for them. I thought it was remarkable of Judi to even think of that. She is so caring, and she's such a good mom. She just wanted to be a good grandmother and make sure these kids didn't have any more pain than they already had.

"I know Bruce has a trailer," she said. "Do you think that you could go over and pick up all of Sydney and Justin's belongings and furniture from their rooms and get it down here to us?"

"Of course," I said.

Bruce and I hooked the trailer to the back of our truck and drove over to Nicole's house. I was so apprehensive about walking into her town house, which was once filled with her beauty, grace, and laughter and was now filled with death. I was freaked out, devastated, and, okay, scared. I had helped Nicole move into that town house. I had helped her unpack and put her clothes in the closets. I had helped her get everything organized. She was so happy to be there, to be on her own, and to have her independence. It was to be the home for her children, whom she loved so much, and she just wanted to make it amazing for them.

We pulled up to the back of the town house, and I retrieved the key and a garage remote where Judi had told me to get them. When we walked inside, I felt like I had been punched in the gut. This beautiful town house, with its beautiful white walls, was covered in gray-black soot, because the police had fingerprinted the entire house. I had never been to a crime scene before. I had never seen a house that had been fingerprinted, a home where police had searched for evidence. The town house was destroyed and with it, the life that Nicole had created there for her and her two children. She had made the place so special, so beautiful, so perfect in every way, and here was her pride and joy, ransacked and destroyed and blackened, fingerprint dust everywhere.

Poor Bruce didn't know what to do because I was crying, crying, crying. We walked upstairs and into those kids' rooms, and it just was devastating anguish to see the bedrooms and their little clothes that they had worn the night of the murder, which had occurred while they were asleep in these very bedrooms. Sydney's ballet recital costume was still lying on her bed, kind of hanging there, sort of half on the floor and half on the bed. These two little precious children's lives had changed forever in that instant, but their bedrooms were as if they had been frozen in time, even though it had been several days since the murder.

Sydney's and Justin's little toys were in their rooms, along with all of their personal treasures. Nicole had made sure they had everything that they ever wanted and needed. She just loved those kids so much and was so proud of them. Their rooms reflected that: their little school things and their artwork and their clothing were all beautiful and perfectly arranged.

Sydney's dance recital outfit on the bed was significant because so much of the talk by the D.A. over the last several days had been about what went on at that recital the night Nicole was killed. Remember, O.J. showed up at the recital but didn't sit with Nicole and wasn't invited to dinner afterward. This became a big focus of the investigation, and people around the world were talking about it. So to walk into the room and see that costume was profound.

Bruce and I had brought boxes and packing materials, and Ron Hardy came over to help us pack. Meanwhile, the television news crews were multiplying out front. They had of course gotten wind that we were there. I could hear the helicopters hovering over the house. We all started loading up the trailer while the reporters in the helicopters watched the house from above. We took apart the kids' beds and loaded their mattresses, belongings, artwork, and clothing—every single thing in those bedrooms—into the trailer.

As we were removing Sydney's bed and putting the pieces of it in the trailer, I looked at one of the bedposts and saw what I thought was blood. I panicked.

"Oh my God, Bruce, look at this!" I screamed.

"Oh my God, that is blood," Bruce said.

I immediately called Marcia Clark. Sydney's headboard was the last thing to go in the trailer, so the entire trailer was ready to go, and we were going to drive to Judi and Lou's house and immediately set up the kids' rooms.

"You cannot take that bed down to Lou and Judi's," Marcia Clark told me. "It has to go into evidence."

"Evidence?!" I asked.

"Absolutely," said Marcia. "Where is it?"

"It's in the trailer!" I said.

"Go park the trailer somewhere, and I'm going to send my forensic specialists to take a look at it," she said.

By then, the helicopters were all over us. We had to get out of there. We drove off, but instead of going down to Lou and Judi's house, we went to my house. We parked the trailer in the garage, detached it from the car, and locked it up and waited for Marcia's specialists to get there. When they arrived, they did some preliminary tests on this "bloodstain" and determined right there on the spot that it was red Jell-O.

That was the only thing that made us laugh.

Once the investigators determined that there was Jell-O, not blood, on Sydney's bedpost, we got back in the car and drove all the stuff down to Lou and Judi's house. We unloaded everything, and when we were done and back in our home, I kept thinking of Nicole and her town house on South Bundy. Being in that abandoned house was just so sad and so devastating. It had once been so full of life and joy and music and laughter and happiness. Now it just held silence and sadness, destruction and tragedy. I also noticed that there was sort of a smell coming out of the kitchen. It had been a couple of days since the murder, and somebody had opened up the refrigerator and didn't close it back all the way. It was creepy, and the kitchen was a mess because of the fingerprints. All I could think was that I wanted to get back over there and clean it up.

I asked Nicole's mom if I could go back the next day and clean out the refrigerator and pick up the mail for her. She said okay. So I did that, and it was a hard thing to do, but it gave me a way to take care of things for Nicole one last time.

The funeral was on June 16. It was held at St. Martin of Tours Catholic Church on Sunset Boulevard in Brentwood.

It was one of the saddest and strangest days ever. Every funeral is sad, but I've never been to one where someone died so suddenly and so tragically. Funerals are supposed to be an ending and have some sense of closure. This was anything but. This was only the beginning of a crazy ride that we were all embarking upon.

As part of the funeral procession, Bruce and I were driven up to the church in a limousine along with a few other friends. I remember arriving and thinking what a horrible reason to be at St. Martin of Tours, which was also the elementary school my son, Rob, and daughter Khloé had attended. I was used to bringing them to school and dropping them off. Now here I was pulling into the same parking lot to pay my last respects to a friend. The media weren't allowed inside but reporters and TV news crews were everywhere: on the street outside the gates of the church and flying above in helicopters. The *Los Angeles Times* described A. C. Cowlings as a "gatekeeper" who "waved through familiar cars, briefly questioned some arrivals, and greeted most guests with warm hugs." I just remember going through the motions and trying to hold it together.

I saw O.J. almost immediately, standing in front of the church with his older children as well as Sydney and Justin. Everyone was standing together but not speaking to each other at all. In the middle of the group was Kato Kaelin. All I could do was wonder what he really knew. I knew Kato because he was friends with Nicole before he became friends with O.J. I had met Kato through Nicole when she had a party to celebrate her move to the house she rented on Gretna Green Way.

According to his later testimony, when Kato first visited Nicole on Gretna Green Way—apparently at the same housewarming party I attended—he asked Nicole who lived out back. "Nobody," she said. "Could I?" he asked. "You have to clean it out," she said. "Great," he said, and that was how he began his journey as her tenant.

I thought he was nice, and Nicole apparently thought it was nice to have a guy living on the property, so I thought it was a good idea. She felt safer with him there, and she had two small children.

Later, he changed sides and started living with O.J. Nicole was upset about that. Kato knew Nicole and O.J. were having problems, and O.J. wanted to keep Kato close to him because he thought Kato could help him with Nicole somehow. So O.J. paid Kato a salary and had Kato live in his guesthouse. Kato had the best deal in the world.

We all quickly headed inside to escape the noise of the helicopters and commotion from the never-ending media gathering at the gate. There were about two hundred people in the church. During the service, Kato happened to be sitting right in front of me. But he never said a word, not to me or anyone else. Kato, in fact, barely said hello. I couldn't help but notice that no one on O.J.'s side was friendly or talking to anyone else at the funeral. It was the oddest, most uncomfortable, surreal, creepiest, most horrendous experience to be at a funeral with people who seemed to know more than they were saying.

I just had the overwhelming feeling, *I can't wait for this to be over.*

I looked over at Nicole's parents, Judi and Lou, and tried to imagine their devastation, which was impossible to do. Everyone was overwhelmed with grief. Again, I felt the urge to want the funeral to be over with so that we could find out what really happened to Nicole. But I tried my best to suppress that urge and remember that this was a day just for Nicole and nothing else, and she deserved that. She deserved to have everyone there whom she loved. She didn't deserve the mystery that surrounded her death to overshadow this commemoration of her life. So I just really tried to be there for Nicole and only Nicole, to pray for her and love her for that one last moment. I so wanted to be close to her and remember her as that laughing, loving, generous, gorgeous young woman, and not a murder victim whose blood had to be washed off the front steps of her home.

Once the funeral began, I was stunned at the poise and the courage of Nicole's mother and sisters who were actually able to stand before the crowd and speak calmly and eloquently about their beloved Nicole. I sat there thinking how heartbroken they must have been.

Other than that, I was in a fog and cannot remember some details. Please allow me to quote the *Los Angeles Times*:

> *Former football players, Olympic athlete Bruce Jenner and former baseball player Steve Garvey were among those attending the Mass, celebrated by the church's Msgr. Lawrence O'Leary. Simpson's lawyers also were in attendance. Reporters were kept out.*
>
> *"It was beautiful," said Garvey after the service in the church, a mixture of traditional and contemporary. "Msgr. O'Leary gave probably the most poignant and moving homily I've ever heard."*
>
> *Among the latecomers to the service—who were forced to wait outside the church—was comedian Byron Allen, who said he last saw O.J. and Nicole Simpson together five or six weeks ago at the House of Blues on Sunset Boulevard. "They were happy, hanging out, having a good time," Allen said. "They sat down at my table for about 10 minutes, had a bite of my salad . . . I figured they were working it out."*
>
> *Allen peered at the parked hearse. "It's devastating," he said. "It's really hard to believe."*
>
> *After the hour long service, family and friends paused outside the side entrance, surrounding O.J. Simpson, who was dressed in a black suit and wearing sunglasses. Guests embraced.*
>
> *Simpson's attorney, Robert L. Shapiro, said later that Nicole Simpson's mother had expressed a wish to him at the*

service. "Mrs. Brown told me: 'Please take good care of him (Simpson). The children need their father.' "

A mile-long funeral procession headed south to Orange County about 2 p.m. for burial services at Ascension Cemetery in Lake Forest. The site was not far from Dana Point, where Nicole Simpson graduated from high school in 1976 and where her parents still live.

Security was so tight at the service that even the Rev. Bruce Lavery, who would officiate, was made to show identification to sheriff's deputies who kept guard at the iron gate in front of the cemetery.

Simpson, holding the hand of his son and followed by about 50 relatives and friends, walked slowly after the pall-bearers onto a green baize carpet and under a light gray canopy that had been set up beside the grave site.

Lavery said Simpson looked "very solemn and hurt" during the service, where he was seated with Nicole Simpson's family.

"There was no estrangement at all," Lavery said.

At the gravesite, I wondered about the dynamic between O.J. and Nicole's family. Nobody wanted to come out and say anything about anything. You wondered: What is going on here? What's going to happen? It was like being in the middle of a mystery and nobody knew the outcome. We were all in the cramped little area beneath a burial tent and a gaping hole in the ground, all thinking the same thing: What happened and how did we get here? How did our lives end up at this place and what is going to happen next? That was the strongest question: what's going to happen next?

Later it would be reported in USA Today that O.J. leaned over Nicole's coffin during this incredibly dreadful day and kissed her on the lips.

"I'm so sorry, Nicki. I'm so sorry," he was quoted as saying. After that, Nicole's mother, Judi, supposedly asked O.J., "Did you have anything to do with this?"

"No, I loved your daughter," O.J. reportedly replied, according to a 1994 television interview with Judi Brown.

Nicole was buried next to her grandparents and that's where we left her. After the burial, I remember walking across the grass to the limousine and turning around and looking at the grave to say my last good-bye. Instinctively, I did what Nicole always did: I raised a hand in the air and flashed a peace sign. Finally, I thought, she was at peace.

After the funeral, everyone went back to Nicole's mom's house in Laguna. O.J., Robert, and A. C. Cowlings were all there, along with three of Nicole's sisters: Minnie, Tanya, and Denise. We were all in her mother's living room, which was an intimate kind of space. As always, we could hear the media helicopters overhead, closing in and taking over the house with their noise, a sound that was becoming the perpetual backbeat for these horrendous days.

Suddenly, I heard Robert say to O.J., "I think it's time."

I immediately walked over to him and said, "Time for what?"

"Never mind," Robert answered.

Then I watched in shock as O.J. and A. C. Cowlings went into a back room and traded clothes in an attempt to mask their identities. I thought that was so weird. I mean, they were both wearing suits. How different can your suit be at a funeral? But they took off in their exchanged apparel, and Robert and O.J. drove off. God only knows where they were going.

The next day, June 17, was the day of the infamous low-speed, two-hour Bronco chase, when O.J. fled Robert's house in Encino with A. C. Cowlings driving just before the police arrived to arrest him. Before news of the chase came on television, Bruce and I were sitting in our den in Beverly Hills. Before the chase began, two detectives, one of whom was Philip Vannatter, called the house. I picked up the phone, and Vannatter, the lead detective on the case, told me that O.J. had taken the Bronco and was missing.

"Do you know where he is?" he asked.

"Me?" I asked. "Why would *I* know where he is?"

"Well, Bruce has a plane," he said. "We thought maybe he was with Bruce."

"No, Bruce is sitting right here," I answered.

"Can we talk to Bruce?" he said. He wanted to make sure I was telling the truth. Once they confirmed Bruce was with me, Vannatter asked me, "O.J.'s not there, is he?"

"No, O.J.'s not here," I answered.

A short time later we were watching TV when the regularly scheduled programming was interrupted by a special report. The screen showed O.J.'s white Bronco speeding down the 405 Freeway.

The LAPD had ordered O.J. to turn himself in for the murders by eleven that morning. He kept delaying. When the police finally came to pick him up at Robert's house, he was gone, along with A.C. I was sitting at home that evening when I turned on the TV and, along with everyone else, I couldn't believe what I was watching: O.J. and A.C. in the white Bronco, helicopters overhead, filming their every move, in what everyone agreed looked like a getaway scene from a movie.

No one really knew what was going on or where O.J. was going—except maybe Robert, who reportedly kept in touch with him by phone during the chase. There was much speculation. Some reporters said he was going to visit his mother. *Right.* Most reports speculated that O.J. was going to commit suicide. Some radio and TV stations put people who knew O.J. on the air to try to talk him out of it. KCBS sportscaster and former NFL player Jim Hill, who knew O.J., was one of those begging O.J. on the air to surrender: "You do not want to be remembered as someone who ran from a bad situation," he said. On another station, USC coach John McKay asked O.J. to stop the Bronco and give himself up to the police.

As the chase continued, the Bronco never going more than sixty miles an hour, the police blocked freeway entrances so traffic wouldn't interfere with their operation. People gathered on overpasses, actually cheering on O.J. and A.C. in what *Newsweek* later described as "equal parts police chase, VIP motorcade and demented victory lap."

"More than a dozen news and police helicopters, flying in formation like some urbanized 'Apocalypse Now,' and a phalanx of patrol cars followed at a cautious distance," read the report. "Inside the truck, Simpson held a gun to his head and told authorities on his cellular phone that he'd kill himself unless he got to see his mother. Spectators jammed the overpasses and frontage roads. 'GO O.J.' signs popped up, a grotesque parody of his airport dashes for Hertz. Old football friends, horrified by what they were watching, called L.A. television and radio stations, beseeching him to give up. 'I love you, my mother loves you,' said a weeping Vince Evans, a former University of Southern California quarterback."

The chase would turn out to be one of the biggest television events in history, with an estimated 95 million people watching. Later, the court released a tape of LAPD detective Tom Lange speaking with O.J. on his cell phone during the chase, with O.J. telling the detective that he wanted to be with Nicole.

"I wasn't running . . . I was just trying to go to Nicole's grave and go to her," O.J. told the detective. "I just can't do it [commit suicide] here on the freeway. I couldn't do it in the field. I want to do it at her grave. I want to do it at my house."

O.J. also told Lange that he had tried unsuccessfully to visit the house where he had lived at the time of his first date with Nicole, saying, "That's where we were happy."

During the whole conversation, Lange pleaded with him to pull over and toss the gun out the window.

"Don't throw it all away," Lange told O.J., who replied, "I can't take this."

On the tape you can hear an emotional Lange repeatedly trying to convince a clearly distraught and emotional O.J. to go home. On that same day, June 17, 1994, as Detective Lange was talking to O.J. behind the scenes, I, like everyone else in America, was consumed with the case at home. Our TVs were on in every single room, every channel covering the case, 24/7, the entire nation transfixed, wondering what was going to happen next. At one point, I froze in absolute shock: there was my ex-husband, Robert Kardashian, in his light gray suit with a pink, black, and gray tie and an extremely serious expression, standing in front of a group of reporters, unfolding a piece of paper, which he was about to read.

What the hell? I thought I was going to fall to the floor.

Before I could process what was going on, Robert began speaking, reading what I could only interpret as a suicide letter from O.J. The letter, disjointed and long-winded, had supposedly been written by O.J. by hand right before he was supposed to turn himself in for the murder charges.

I'll quote the letter here in part:

To Whom It May Concern:

First, everyone understand I have nothing to do with Nicole's murder. I loved her. I always have and always will. If we had a problem it was because I loved her so much . . .
Nicole and I had a good life together. All this press talk

about a rocky relationship was no more than what every long-term relationship experiences. All her friends will confirm that I have been totally loving and understanding of what she's been going through.

At times, I have felt like a battered husband or boyfriend but I loved her, make that clear to everyone. And I would take whatever it took to make it work.

Don't feel sorry for me. I've had a great life, great friends. Please think of the real O.J. and not this lost person.

Thanks for making my life special. I hope I helped yours.

Peace and love, O.J.

Again, surreal. It would become a moment in television history, replayed continuously on televisions around the world. The TV would cut from the white Bronco to the cheering crowds on the freeway overpasses to Robert solemnly reading O.J.'s letter. Over and over and over again.

"Why are you doing this?" I practically screamed at Robert as he spoke on TV. "You can't possibly believe O.J.! And he's got you so on his team!"

The chase finally ended around nine that night, with O.J. back at home on Rockingham. After the chase was over, O.J. supposedly went inside, made a call to his mother, and drank a glass of orange juice. I was shocked that nothing more serious had happened. You would think that I would be relieved that the day had come to a peaceful end, but there was nothing peaceful about it.

Robert knew I was angry, and he was angry with me in return because he felt I was doubting his friend for no reason. I really believe in my heart of hearts that Robert truly thought at the time that O.J. was innocent and that he had nothing to do with Nicole's murder. I believe Robert was determined to help his friend in a time of need. I know it's hard to understand why Robert would stand behind O.J. so faithfully. But Robert was such a good person and had invested a lifetime of friendship and memories in O.J., whom he'd known since their days together at USC. They had been through marriages, divorces, babies, celebrations, and holidays. They were as close as brothers. As our friend Larry Schiller, who wrote *American Tragedy*, the book about O.J.'s defense strategies, would later tell the *New York Times*: "He [Robert] stood by O.J. irrespective of how he felt because he felt that nobody else was standing by O.J., not because of his innocence or guilt, but because there was a friendship there." Robert didn't know everything that I knew, everything that had happened between the time that he and I got divorced and I married Bruce, and Bruce and I became friends with O.J. and Nicole. As a girlfriend of Nicole's, I knew so much more about what was going on than Robert did, even though I didn't know everything.

So the cast of characters would soon be assembled: O.J.'s "Dream Team" of defense attorneys—eventually including Johnnie Cochran, Bob Shapiro, F. Lee Bailey, and Robert Kardashian. And on the other side, Marcia Clark, the lead prosecuting attorney assigned to the case by the D.A.'s office, along with her co-counsel Chris Darden.

During the trial, I spoke constantly with case coordinator Patty Jo Fairbanks, an amazing woman who worked for Marcia Clark in the D.A.'s office. Patty kept us all sane, communicating with us when Marcia Clark couldn't. She kept us all calm and gave us our updates. She would call witnesses and say, "You have to testify, and this is what time you have to be downtown."

CHAPTER NINE

O.J. All the Time

*T*estify.

That was the least I could do. Oh, wait, it's not like I had a choice. I was subpoenaed by the court to testify at O.J.'s trial.

We all felt like we were in uncharted territory, going through something that nobody could advise us on. I felt isolated, alone and scared. Everybody had an opinion. If you were Team O.J., you were really nasty to Team Nicole, and if you were Team Nicole, you were really nasty to Team O.J. What a lot of people didn't understand is that when we lost Nicole, at the same time, oddly, we also lost O.J. O.J. and Nicole were two of my best friends, so while I was mourning the death of Nicole, I was also mourning the emotional death of O.J. Simpson. He had been in my life since I was seventeen, and he had been someone I admired and looked up to. He was like my big brother. I felt he would've done anything for me, and I would have certainly done anything for him. I loved him.

Two people I adored, loved, and considered family were both

gone, along with the entire world as I had known it. Everything was just gone.

Our future memories were gone and our former memories were obliterated by this tragedy. Our Saturday tennis games were gone, our dinner parties were gone, our family vacations were gone. Everything was so messed up. These were the people with whom we spent Easter and Christmas Eve and Mother's Day. We celebrated the births of our children with them. When I gave birth to my kids, Nicole and O.J. were there, and when Nicole gave birth to their kids, I was there. My daily runs with Nicole, after we both dropped off our kids at school, were how I started my day. Our weekends were spent together too. Without her, my life, and so many other lives, would never be the same.

There wasn't anything that we didn't celebrate together. I thought about the football games that we went to in San Francisco when O.J. was a San Francisco Giant, and all the times that Robert went to support O.J. when he played for the Buffalo Bills. I never went, because I worked for the airline and was always flying, but Robert would always fly back to Buffalo when we were dating to support O.J. I thought about the happy times, the fun and the laughter—all gone. Nicole was no longer there to represent herself, and I was consumed with mourning her. Everybody has his or her own personal journey to go through when a loved one dies, but this was unique in that it was so tragic and public, a death that became international news every single day, all day long. It was as if I was watching intimate details of my life and the people in it unfold on the most public of stages. When it all began, I didn't know if I had the tools to be able to deal with that. I would have to tap into my inner strength and become a lot stronger than I ever knew possible. This would come to serve me well later in life, but for now it was overwhelming. I honestly didn't think I could get through it.

By the time the trial was getting ready to begin in January 1995, around six months after the murders, there had already been a lot of innuendo and leaked information from both sides of the case. It was chilly between Robert and me, for sure. It was a difficult time for us. It was hard to be neutral and civil to each other in front of the kids because the situation was so volatile, and there was so much going on, and there were issues cropping up daily.

Robert was doing media interviews. I did *Larry King Live* and *The Barbara Walters Special*, with Nicole's parents' blessing, and a handful of other interviews that the family wanted me to do. We taped my interview with Barbara Walters in a suite at the Peninsula Hotel in Beverly Hills. I was frankly scared to death; I had watched enough *Barbara Walters Special*s to know that her specialty was making every guest cry. She always asked the most interesting yet the most dramatic questions. And in those days, if you wanted your story told to the widest possible audience, you did an interview with Barbara Walters. I was such a fan and admirer of hers. But never in a million years did I dream that I would ever be interviewed by Barbara . . . and especially not in the context of a murder case.

They didn't give me questions in advance, and I was so nervous and anxious. But I kept reminding myself: this wasn't about me. I felt like I was there to be a voice for Nicole. Somebody had to speak about her, someone who knew her and loved her, and that somebody was me.

I came to the interview with my friend Ron Hardy, who had washed Nicole's blood off of her stairs. We sat down in the hotel suite, me sitting across from Barbara. The lights came on, and Barbara stared at me with her intense eyes and began asking questions. I can't remember specific answers, although I know I told Barbara what a good person Nicole was and how much we missed her, all while refraining from giving my opinion about the case and trying my best not to cry. The interview seemed to last two minutes.

Barbara was famous for taking her guests on a walk during her interviews. She did our walk after my interview was over. As I was walking through the Peninsula Beverly Hills hotel grounds with Barbara Walters, I felt, *This just keeps getting crazier.* It was surreal, but it was only the beginning.

When the trial started, Robert would come over to pick up the kids. We would meet in the driveway, because he actually thought that if he came into my house, someone might be taping him.

"Are you wired?" he would ask.

"No, are you wired?" I would say.

"Nope," he would say.

Robert and I would stand there in the driveway, a healthy distance from each other, because neither of us truly trusted what we'd told each other about not being wired. It was very weird. We'd pass off the kids, and they'd get in the car and wave good-bye.

Finally, after a few of these ridiculous driveway encounters, Robert called and said, "I want to come over and talk to you. Do you have a minute?"

It was the night before the trial was to begin.

"Sure," I said.

The enormity of the knowledge that the trial would begin the next morning was swirling around us. We were at the epicenter of this storm. At last, I felt, Robert wanted to talk about it. He came over, and this time he came into the house. We sat down in my living room and he pulled an envelope out of his suit jacket pocket.

"I can't stay long," he began. "I don't want you to ever have any bad feelings about me and I need to give this to you."

He handed me the envelope, which contained a handwritten letter from him.

"I just want to tell you that I know you'll probably never understand why I'm doing what I need to do, but hopefully this will be over soon," he said, and then he left.

I opened the envelope, and read.

January 22, 1995

Dear Kris, Kourtney, Kim, Khloé and Robert,

I feel I must explain my feelings about the O.J. case on this the eve of the trial. First of all, I want all of you to please understand that I did *not* want any of this to happen. God allowed this horrible tragedy to occur for whatever reason. I just happened to be in the "wrong place at the wrong time." I am not a public figure and really do not enjoy the horrible invasion of privacy of you, me and my family.

I think that the division in our family between guilty and innocence is very sad. I do not want our family torn apart by this case. Please understand that I am trapped in the position I am in and can't get out. I must see this case through. I truly believe in O.J.'s innocence and unless they find him guilty, I will continue to support him. I realize, Kris, that you also strongly believe in his guilt. You are entitled to your beliefs—just as I am. However, our individual beliefs should not interfere with our family. Neither of us should take pride in the outcome. The bottom line is that two innocent people were brutally murdered.

The past 7 months have taken such an emotional toll on my life—you have no idea. The other day, someone asked me a simple question about something that happened during the week of June 12 and for no reason, I started to cry.

My life will never be the same. I'm sorry for what has happened but I was only helping my friend—just as any of you would do. Please don't let whatever is going to happen in this case affect our family. Our lives are much more important than this one case.

The next few months will be difficult and time consuming and emotional. If I am abrupt or harsh or rude in any way, please don't take it personally. It will be a very stressful time.

Remember, I love you all and just want the best for our family. Please be understanding.

Love,
Robert

I burst into tears. He was finally acknowledging that we were in the middle of the Trial of the Century. I still felt like we were on different sides, but at least, on some level, we were on the same side as a family. We were going through the same things at the same time over the same friends, all of us experiencing similar emotions about two people we had known intimately. That he had brought the letter to me was monumental and was one of the things I will always remember about how good Robert was. He didn't have to do that. He didn't have to explain anything to me. We were divorced. Yet, he still felt he had to say, essentially, "I still care about you enough that I need you to know why I am doing this." That's how much Robert loved us as a family, and I will never forget that.

A few hours after Robert left, the phone rang.

"You have a call from a prisoner," came a voice from a recording from the Los Angeles County Men's Central Jail, asking if I would accept a collect call.

"Yes," I replied.

Then O.J.'s deep voice came on the line.

"Hi, Kris," he said.

"Hello," I said.

"I could never have done this," he said. "I don't know what's going on."

He began talking . . . and talking . . . about everything. What was so crazy was that he even started talking about the bloody glove that was found at the crime scene and that would loom large in the upcoming trial. He seemed more concerned about Nicole's relationship with our friend Faye Resnick and what had been going on between Nicole and Faye than anything else. Faye had written a book that was published four months after the murders: *Nicole Brown Simpson: The Private Diary of a Life Interrupted.* In the book, she talked about her relationship with Nicole and their friendship. O.J. was very upset about this, because the book had come out while O.J. was in jail. In the book, Faye claimed that she and Nicole had experienced a "night of girlish passion" around the time of the murders. O.J. was really angry about this, and he wanted to talk about it and talk about it.

Everyone who knows O.J. knows that he can be very long-winded. He can talk a lot. I told him I didn't know what he was talking about, because I truly didn't. I really had very little insight into Faye and Nicole's intimate friendship. I obviously knew they were great friends because I introduced them. But I didn't know what was going on between the two of them. But O.J. was convinced I did and that I wasn't telling him something. He was more concerned with that than the fact that he was sitting in a jail in Los Angeles for the murder of his ex-wife. He was obsessed.

I had to go run errands and get things done for my business

before the end of the day, and I just couldn't talk to him anymore.

"I'll call you back," I said, forgetting for a moment that he was in jail.

"No, you can't call me back," he said. "I'll call you later."

I left my house and went straight to Beverly Hills Stationers on Beverly Drive, where I had shopped for a decade, although I don't remember driving to the store. That's how distracted I was. I walked into the store and began ordering office supplies. I couldn't concentrate. All that kept going through my head was the phone call with O.J. When I got up to the cash register to pay, the telephone behind the counter rang. The sales clerk behind the register, who I had known for years, turned to pick up the phone. She answered it and shot me a strange look. "There's a collect call for you," she said. "From jail!"

I was shocked. "What?" I said. Then I thought, *How the hell did he find me here?* It was scary.

"Oh my God, it's O.J.," I said under my breath.

"Would you like to take the call in the back?" the clerk asked.

"Uh, yes," I said, practically running to the back room. I was so freaked out. A manager was back there. "Where's the phone?" I asked. He pointed and I grabbed the phone, punching the line that was lit up.

"Hello," I said.

"Hey," said O.J.

"How did you know I was here?" I asked. "How did you find me?"

"Your assistant told me," O.J. said.

Now I was stunned. "What?! What do you mean, my assistant told you? Why are you calling me at Beverly Stationers?"

"I just need to talk," he said.

"O.J., I told you to call me later at home."

But he wouldn't let me off the phone. I talked to him for about ten minutes, and then I said, "I will call you when I get home." I realized then that I couldn't do my errands because he was going to call me wherever I went. Somehow he knew where I was and where I was going. So I went home, and the minute I walked in the door, the phone rang: O.J. again. I went upstairs and I talked to him and talked to him and talked to him and talked to him. I would put the phone down and go do something in my bedroom and come back and he was still talking.

O.J. was desperate to talk, but I was used to that side of him. The needy O.J., the obsessive O.J. This was a guy that I had known my whole adult life, and I felt like he was trying to make me believe that he hadn't killed my friend, but not actually explaining how it couldn't be true. He just kept saying, "This is why this couldn't have been like this." Or: "The glove wasn't mine." Whatever. He tried to explain away all of the accusations, and he would keep going back to Nicole and her relationship with other people. He was still totally obsessed with whom she had been seeing and whom she had been sleeping with and whom she had been friends with. He was just sort of way out there, talking about stuff that didn't really matter. It was all really odd and very upsetting.

Finally, I said, "Okay, let's talk in a while. I'm exhausted."

That series of phone calls were the last time I ever spoke to O.J. Once the trial got under way, I never spoke to him again.

The trial began on January 23, 1995.

What struck me most was the whole entire thing was bigger than life. It wasn't just a trial; it was a spectacle. Bruce and I parked in back of the courthouse, where we were told we had a spot. Marcia Clark's case coordinator, Patty Fairbanks, met us there and took us under her wing. She told us all about Judge Lance Ito, who would preside over the trial. She told us what to expect. She gave us a tour of the entire facility: where to park, where to go through security, where to eat, what to say, what not to say.

"Never talk when there are others in an elevator," she said, "because you don't know who may be there."

The biggest surprise for me during this time was that I was finally pregnant. I pulled out the maternity clothes that Nicole had given me before she died, and I decided to wear those clothes to the trial every day. Every day on my way to the courthouse, I would think, *Please don't let me have a miscarriage.* I thought I was going to miscarry about five times because I was so upset all the time and I didn't sleep at night. I was terrified of testifying. It absolutely took over my life as I watched my friends and acquaintances being called to testify on the witness stand one by one. I knew I was next. It was a very scary time, and I was overly emotional anyway because of the baby.

Before the first day of the trial, Bruce and I had to go into Marcia Clark's office several times and talk about our relationship with Nicole and O.J. She wanted to know what we knew about them and their lives, and what could be possible reasons for O.J. to murder Nicole. At first it seemed like there was this whole domestic violence side of the trial that Marcia Clark was building her case around. It seemed like Marcia was planning for some of Nicole's girlfriends, including myself, to testify on Nicole's behalf on the subject of domestic abuse. I remember Marcia asking me if I wanted to see the crime scene photos, because I'm sure she didn't want me to see them in court for the first time, as it would be such a shock.

In her office one day, Marcia put the crime scene photos up on the wall for me to see. They were very big and very shocking. I could see Nicole lying at the bottom of the steps in front of her town house in a huge pool of blood. I looked at them and just wept for her, wept for her family, and wept for her children. They were horrible pictures of her.

The photographs were so shocking that I felt like I wasn't in the room with them but somewhere else, looking into the office and seeing those gruesome images. Maybe my mind was protecting me. The mind acts in very strange ways, and it can be very strong when you need it to be, and that is what happened to me that year. When you go through things of such enormity, you can wallow in your misery and you can feel sorry for yourself, you can become defeated and turn to drugs or alcohol, or you can become bitter and nasty. Or you can rise to the occasion and you can be strong and you can try to overcome your circumstances, and you don't let yourself fall down. It's really all about how you choose to overcome adversity.

I was trying to be there for all of my children and my friends who needed my support and who were also in pain, and to be there for Nicole's parents and family if they ever needed me. But I also had to support myself. I didn't want to lose myself in all of this because it was so tragic and it would've been so easy to be destroyed by all the pressures. Anger helped. I was really angry when I left Marcia Clark's office after seeing the photographs. I was subpoenaed to testify and Marcia was preparing me for it.

The proceedings began each day at nine a.m. and went on until five p.m., and each day everybody would check in with everyone else on Nicole's team—her parents, sisters, and friends—to see how everyone was doing and discuss what had happened on that particular day. Every day, as Bruce and I sat in the spectators' seats with Nicole's family and friends, I could see my ex-husband, Robert Kardashian, sitting at the defense table, always beside or near O.J. Sometimes my daughters Kourtney and Kimberly came to court with Robert and could see the division between us: Robert beside O.J., me sitting with Nicole's family, Kourtney and Kimberly somewhere in the middle, all of us intimately involved in this crazy murder trial.

We became entrenched in the daily proceedings. To carry on with our daily routine became difficult. Whether I was watching the trial on television or sitting in the courtroom, on some level I thought about Nicole all day long. Outside the courtroom, things were even more insane. It became an absolute circus. During the 133 days of testimony, the trial, which cost $15 million, was all anyone talked about—on the news, at cocktail parties, in the gym, in the supermarket, you name it.

Everyone was watching the trial, glued to their televisions all day, every day. Every major journalist, media outlet, and public leader in the country was discussing the story: Larry King, Geraldo Rivera, the Reverend Al Sharpton, Tom Brokaw, Ted Koppel, Barbara Walters, Dan Rather, Connie Chung, Jay Leno. CNN, ABC, NBC, CBS, and of course the *New York Times*—many of whom somehow got my home phone number and left countless messages asking for interviews.

It was surreal to walk into the kitchen and press PLAY on the answering machine, only to hear Barbara Walters and a dozen others say, "Hey, Kris, we'd love to get an interview."

As I continued to think of testifying before millions watching around the world, I felt awkward. I wanted to be there for Nicole and do the best I could for her. At the same time, well, there's no other way to say it: I was scared. Every commentator in the world would be analyzing, criticizing, and commenting on what I said. When my girlfriend Candace Garvey testified, all people had to say was something negative about her black headband. I could only imagine what they would say about me. What we wore was all so irrelevant; all we cared about was Nicole. Still, I knew I had to testify for Nicole if I was called.

In the end, I was never called to testify—and the reason why turned out to be the saddest thing of all. Marcia Clark decided that the jury wouldn't be receptive to the whole domestic violence component of the case, and she decided to pull it from her prosecution strategy. We were all shocked.

It's all still foggy, even today, but I believe Marcia's office called to tell me that I had been relieved from the witness list. However, they added, I was still under a gag order and couldn't speak to the press without permission.

On one level I felt relief that I didn't have to get up and testify. I wouldn't have to look Robert Kardashian and O.J. straight in the eye. How did things get so twisted? But on the other hand, I was confused. How could Marcia present the domestic violence side of our case if I wasn't able to tell my side of the story about what I knew had happened to Nicole?

"Why aren't I and Nicole's other friends going to testify?" I believe I asked. "We have such valuable information."

We all felt like if there was a reason Nicole was murdered, domestic violence was an important aspect of it, and why wouldn't Marcia have all of us tell the countless stories about everything that we had seen over the years? Marcia knew the whole story, but she had to prosecute this case the best way she saw fit. I was upset. I kept thinking: *I hope this woman knows what she's doing*, because this decision not to include domestic violence in a case that was all about domestic violence could be a make-or-break decision.

"We'll call you if we need you" was all Marcia's office told me.

Once I knew I wouldn't be testifying, I felt a lot of relief despite my feelings about eliminating what I thought was *the* only defense. I was still officially a witness, so I wasn't allowed to give interviews or to talk about the case. I couldn't even leave town without permission from Judge Ito, who issued his directives in writing.

I so admired Robert for bringing the letter explaining his situation at the start of the trial. But that didn't mean I agreed with the pro-O.J. stance he was taking. Once or twice as the trial dragged on, I talked to Robert about his role. I tried to be subtle, but that was tough. "Are you crazy?" I asked him more than once about his un-flagging belief in O.J. I guess that wasn't a very subtle thing for me to say. "Look, do you know what you're doing?" I asked him.

"I really feel like you're wrong," I would continue. "You weren't there with her when we were all there with her and you didn't see what was going on, because you weren't as close to them at the end. I mean, you were still close to O.J., but you weren't as close to O.J. and Nicole socially. You weren't going out with O.J. and Nicole like Bruce and I were. I was seeing Nicole every day, and you weren't, and you've got to listen to me."

"No, you're wrong," he would say, cutting me off.

One day, when he came to bring the kids back to me after a visitation, Robert and I talked in the driveway after the kids went inside.

"You're going to end up in a weird place here because I think you're going to lose this trial," I said.

"The only way we're going to have a problem is if they find Nicole's blood in the Bronco," he answered.

When investigators did find Nicole's blood in the Bronco, I told Robert, "Well, I guess you guys have a problem."

"Oh, no we don't," he said.

That's the way it was with everything with Robert. With every new piece of damning information, he would come back to me and explain it away. I think that's what he was doing to himself in his mind, and I think he really believed it.

Then strange things started happening in the trial.

First, the whole Mark Fuhrman situation. Johnnie Cochran very passionately accused Fuhrman, the lead detective on the case, of being a racist, tampering with evidence, and essentially setting O.J. up for the murders.

"Fuhrman wants to take all black people now and burn them ..." Cochran said in court. "That's genocidal racism. ... Maybe this is one of the reasons we're all gathered here this day. Maybe there's a reason for your purpose. Maybe this is why you were selected. There is something in your background, in your character, that helps you understand this is wrong! Maybe you're the right people at the right time at the right place to say 'No more!' "

Fuhrman was then caught on tape making racist comments multiple times in crude contexts after saying that he hadn't, under oath, which was a field day for Johnnie Cochran. Cochran was a really confident and well-spoken attorney known for representing Michael Jackson, Tupac Shakur, Snoop Dogg, Sean Combs, and many others throughout his career. And he often involved race and police corruption as part of his arguments.

Race was definitely a valid issue in the trial, but at some point, it seemed like it had outweighed the basic question of whether or not O.J. was guilty, and the fact that Nicole had been murdered.

Then came the moment when O.J. tried on the gloves.

I was at home that day watching it all unfold on TV. When I heard Chris Darden ask O.J. to try on the gloves found at the murder scene, I panicked.

"What are you doing, Chris?" I literally screamed at the TV. "Don't let him try it on!"

The gloves had been soaked in blood. I knew they weren't going to fit. Anybody who knows leather knows that if you get it wet on any level it's going to shrink and change the integrity of the material.

The famous courtroom scene of O.J. seeming to struggle to pull the gloves on, saying, "They're too tight," would lead to Cochran's famous and much-repeated quote: "If it doesn't fit, you must acquit."

Cochran would use this saying throughout the trial whenever he was trying to prove to the jury that a piece of the defense's evidence didn't make sense. In his closing arguments, Cochran would bring up the gloves again, and try on a similar pair of gloves himself in front of the jury to try to drive in his point: "You will always remember those gloves," he told the jury. "When Darden asked him to try them on and they didn't fit. . . . If it doesn't fit, you must acquit."

It was such a ruse. The fact that the gloves didn't fit and that the jurors bought that sideshow was shocking to me. Later, they even had O.J. try on a new pair of the gloves in the same size, and they fit. Wow. I couldn't believe it. What I flashed back on was when Nicole and I were in New York at Bloomingdale's and she bought those gloves as a treat for O.J.

According to the court testimony from Richard Rubin, the former vice president and general manager of the glove manufacturer, Aris Isotoner, the brown gloves were part of a limited batch of the Aris Isotoner Lights line, which were sold exclusively at Bloomingdale's. Between 200 and 240 of the gloves were sold in 1990.

Richard Rubin knew every fact, detail, and statistic about the gloves. "No other retailer in the United States had this model," Rubin testified. "And because of this particular type of sewing, which was unique to this model as well as the weight of the cashmere lining, the weight of the leather utilized and the way the vent is put into the palm, this could really not be any other style except 70263."

I know Nicole bought a pair of this type of glove at Bloomingdale's when we went to the store together during the first week of November 1989. She must have gone back for more gloves in December 1990. Had we only known what the future would bring.

There was a mountain of evidence piled up against O.J., but Johnnie Cochran and O.J.'s "Dream Team" of attorneys were really smart and clever. Independent of whether O.J. was guilty or innocent, race had become a *huge* component of the case, and many people believed that the police department had framed O.J. In a CNN-*USA Today* Gallup poll that came out in August, 67 percent of Americans thought that O.J. was guilty, and 30 percent thought that Fuhrman had planted the bloody glove.

The February before the verdict was announced, Dominick Dunne wrote in *Vanity Fair* about the country's obsession with the trial: "The Simpson case is like a great trash novel come to life, a mammoth fireworks display of interracial marriage, love, lust, lies, hate, fame, wealth, beauty, obsession, spousal abuse, stalking, brokenhearted children, the bloodiest of bloody knife-slashing homicides, and all the justice that money can buy."

I was sitting at home and got a call from Patty Fairbanks in Marcia Clark's office.

"Come down to the courthouse immediately, and come to Marcia's office," she said. "The jury has reached a verdict."

I couldn't believe the trial was finally coming to an end. After almost a year of this spectacle, the jury was ready to announce a verdict on October 3, 1995, nine months after the trial had begun. It only took them around four hours of deliberation. Because the deliberation was so short, we thought for sure that meant a guilty verdict. One reason why: they had asked to once again hear the timeline for when the limo driver, Allan Park, picked O.J. up for his flight to Chicago. The driver was supposed to pick up O.J. on Rockingham at 10:45 p.m. on the night of the murders and take him to the airport for his flight to Chicago, but O.J. was late. All the lights of his house were off, like no one was home, so Allan Park called his boss, who told him to go around the back of the house, because O.J. sometimes watched TV in the room that was back there. The driver ran into Kato Kaelin in the side yard of O.J.'s house, carrying a flashlight, and later also saw a man Marcia Clark described in court as a "six-foot, 200-pound African American person in all dark clothing" walking into the front of the house at "a good pace." A minute or so later, someone finally answered the intercom, and it was O.J. The timing of this weird sequence of events made it seem so obvious that O.J. was the man in dark clothing who had entered the house. Allan Park also testified that on the ride to the airport O.J. kept complaining about the heat and asking him to turn on the air-conditioning.

We thought for sure that the jury asking about the timing of all of these things involving the limo driver meant they thought O.J. was guilty.

When it was announced that the jury was going to give their verdict on October 3 at 10:00 a.m., Bruce and I drove to the courthouse. I was eight months pregnant, and Marcia Clark and Chris Darden didn't want me to go into the courtroom because they weren't sure what was going to happen. I was to watch the verdict on a television upstairs in Marcia Clark's office with two of Nicole's sisters. We drove up to the courthouse. As always, it was a circus and the media swarmed around our car. Marcia Clark had security officers waiting for us to take us into the building. They met us at the car and walked us inside to the elevators to Marcia's office. As I walked through this sea of media, everybody was calling my name and yelling out, "Good luck, Kris!" Or "We love Nicole!" Or "O.J.'s innocent!"

Everyone on both sides thought they were going to win, I believe. I don't know for certain about O.J.'s side, but I knew we had a strong case and I knew Marcia Clark believed we would win.

Nobody really said it out loud, but I think everybody was pretty confident because of the jury only taking four hours.

While I was watching the television in Marcia's office, Peter Jennings was broadcasting live from the courthouse and did some commentary about our arrival, which had occurred moments before. "And here comes Kris and Bruce Jenner," I roughly recall Jennings saying over footage of Bruce and me walking into the courthouse. "Now, you know Kris is the ex-wife of defense attorney Robert Kardashian and . . ." He explained my whole history and why I was relevant to this trial. It was one of the most surreal things I've ever been through in my life. I was in such an emotional place, I don't think I even remember walking into the building, and here I was, watching it played back on television. The rest of the country was watching too.

"Essentially the whole country stopped," Jeffrey Toobin of the *New Yorker* said of America's absolute fascination with the trial. "Long distance phone calls dropped during that period. Trading on the stock exchange dropped. Everything simply stopped for the announcement of the verdict because that's how much the country was interested."

I'll never forget what happened next. Judge Ito invited the deputy to bring the jurors into the courtroom. Judge Ito said, "Good morning again, ladies and gentlemen," and then asked Mrs. Deirdre Robertson, the law clerk, to hand the sealed envelope containing the verdict to the deputy, who returned it to the jury foreperson to make sure the verdict was correct.

"Madame Foreperson, would you please open the envelope and check the condition of the verdict forms?" Judge Ito said. Those few minutes leading up to the actual announcement felt like the longest moments of my life. I was sitting up in Marcia's office and it was so still. The office was full: Bruce, Nicole's sisters and friends. The closed-circuit TVs were on as well as regular TV. But no one spoke. No one even seemed to breathe. It was like we were all frozen. In that moment, I said a silent prayer for Nicole.

Dear Lord, just give her justice and bring her peace, I prayed, and then repeated it over and over in my mind while waiting for the woman to speak.

As all this was happening, O.J. looked like he was trying to stay calm, but I could see that he was on edge, looking back and forth between the jury and the judge and the deputy and fidgeting in his seat. It was hard to wrap my head around the fact that the man on television was the same man I had known all my life. The foreperson agreed that the verdict forms were accurate and then the judge asked everyone to "carefully listen" to the verdicts as they were read by the clerk and to "remain calm." He warned that the bailiffs would remove anyone causing "any disruption."

Then everyone stood up and Judge Ito asked O.J. and his lawyers to stand and face the jury while she read the verdict. O.J., looking almost bewildered, was the last to stand. At one point Johnnie Cochran, wearing his bright blue suit, pressed his palms together beneath his chin as if he were praying. The law clerk, Deirdre Robertson, began reading:

"In the matter of the people of the state of California versus Orenthal James Simpson, case number BA097211. We the jury in the above entitled action find the defendant, Orenthal James Simpson, not guilty of the crime of murder in violation of penal code section 187A, a felony, upon Nicole Brown Simpson, a human being, as charged in Count 1 of the information."

Not guilty.

The words burned in my brain.

Robert had the most serious expression on his face the entire time that both of the verdicts were being read. It almost seemed like disbelief. He didn't smile or hug O.J. He just looked right at him and then turned back to face the jury.

I looked over at O.J. at the moment he broke into that soon-to-be-infamous little grin the moment the words "not guilty" rang through the air. He shot a little wave to the jury and mouthed the words "Thank you." I watched so many intense feelings of relief, disbelief, and then joy go across O.J.'s face in those few seconds. Johnnie Cochran immediately gave O.J. this little victory hug from behind right after the verdict was read. Then right away the sounds of sobbing from the Team Nicole side of the courtroom. Fred Goldman held his daughter, Kim, as she immediately collapsed and began weeping in his arms. O.J.'s smile got bigger and bigger as the court reporter kept reading:

" 'The Superior Court of the State of California, County of Los Angeles, in the matter of the people of the state of California versus Orenthal James Simpson. We the jury in the above entitled action find the defendant, Orenthal James Simpson, not guilty of the crime of murder in violation of penal code section 187A, a felony, upon Ronald Lyle Goldman, a human being, as charged in count 2 of the information. We the jury in the above entitled action further find the special circumstances that the defendant . . .' "

The courtroom was in shock. Women were holding their heads in their hands, or running their fingers through their hair, or collapsing with their heads in their laps and their hands covering their faces. That image of Fred Goldman holding Kim, shaking his head, will always remain with me.

Marcia Clark's and the other prosecutors' faces were just stone cold—expressions of either complete exhaustion and pure defeat or shock and bewilderment. As the court reporter asked the jurors to confirm the verdict one by one, O.J. and his lawyers bowed their heads in a huddle. Then O.J. leaned toward Robert for a hug and

Robert held the back of O.J.'s head. Robert took his glasses off and rubbed his eyes almost like he was wiping away tears or stress—or maybe tears *of* stress. This entire time, sobs were just racking the courtroom. O.J.'s side of the courtroom was crying and holding their hands in prayer, too, but out of happiness. And then it was over.

We couldn't believe it. *Not guilty!* I was sitting in a chair in the office, and I just bowed my head, said a prayer for Nicole, and cried my eyes out. *Wow, there is no justice for her,* I thought. *There is no peace for her.*

"He's going to kill me and he's going to get away with it."

I couldn't get those words out of my mind. Not then. Not now. Those were Nicole's words, and I could just hear her voice saying, *See, I told you.*

Nicole's sisters were sitting with me, but we couldn't even talk. I mean, what do you say? We just kept saying, "I'm so sorry, I'm so sorry," to one another. We were all so devastated.

Another thing I couldn't get out of my head: O.J. thanking the jury. He was relieved, I think, that he could get out of there and go home. The thing is, not only was Nicole's life over, O.J.'s own life, as he had known it, also was over. To have been and to continue to be shunned by his community and his peers and the people who had always adored him would be as devastating as a prison sentence to O.J. Simpson. If you know anything about O.J. Simpson, you know that that fact itself would be torturous for him. So I knew that, on some level, he would suffer for what I felt he did. I took some solace in that.

Robert rode with O.J. back to his house on Rockingham, where there was a celebration. I was not there, obviously, but I heard all about it. There was champagne and laughter and tears. Everybody was so happy. O.J. was innocent, of course, and blah, blah, blah. Everybody on Nicole's side just went back to his or her own home.

At some point during the early evening, Robert came over to my house. He knocked on the front door and said, "Can I come in? I need to talk to you."

He had been to O.J.'s celebration party and he looked good. But he wasn't gloating. Anything but. He had a calmness to him, and I sensed that he was hopeful that I would welcome him into the house. I felt that he had something important to say.

"Sure," I said, wondering what could come next after this already insane and exhausting day.

Bruce was there. Robert asked me to go out to the patio with him. So we went outside and sat down.

"What's up?" I asked.

"I know you must be upset because we won," he said.

I know he wasn't gloating, but just to hear him say "we won" really upset me.

"What do you want?" I asked.

"I just think that you and I need to put this behind us," he said. "We can't let this be a part of our lives anymore. It's almost ruined mine. We really need to be great parents for our kids, and that's all that should ever matter. I really want to go back to just being a great dad and a good friend, and I don't want this to get in the way of our friendship, because it could really destroy our family, and we're still a family."

I couldn't argue with that. I told Robert that I didn't agree with what had just happened, but I certainly never wanted to let our family be pulled apart as a result. Eventually, Robert and I were both crying, and Bruce, poor Bruce, was standing there probably feeling very uncomfortable, thinking: *What am I watching here?* Robert and I both told each other that we loved each other as people, and then I told him I was really happy he was the father of my children. We agreed to carry on as parents and friends, and from that day forward we really started working on our friendship and our relationship as parents, vowing to always put our kids first.

We weren't going to let O.J. Simpson eat away at us anymore. We decided that day that after being on two opposite sides of something so big—something so much bigger than we were—we had to take control of our feelings and move forward for the sake of our kids. The case could either destroy us or it could make us stronger. We decided to let it make us stronger.

As for O.J., I never saw him again after the trial. Often, I've thought about what would happen if I did see him. What would I do? What would I say? I still don't know. As for Nicole, there isn't a day that passes when I don't think of her.

The day after the verdict was announced, Robert Kardashian sent a letter to the *Los Angeles Times* in an attempt to explain why he had decided to stand by O.J.:

"O.J. Simpson never lied to me," he wrote. "He has told me that he did not commit these horrible crimes and I have no reason not to believe him. It is from that perspective that I came to stand by his side during his trial. For me, the question was: What would you do for a friend? Would you give up your business, put your personal life on hold and devote a year and a half of your life to a friend? I did, without realizing what an awful journey I was about to take."

A year later, in an interview on *20/20*, Barbara Walters asked Robert what he thought when he heard that O.J. had failed a lie detector test a few days after the murders. "I was devastated," Robert replied. "I didn't know what to believe."

"What's your relationship now with O.J. Simpson?" Barbara asked later in the interview.

"The relationship is not the same as it once was nor will it ever be," Robert said.

"Why not?" Barbara asked.

"Because I have doubts," Robert said.

To this day and quite often, considering it has been sixteen years since the trial, I will be watching TV and for one reason or another the powerful image of Robert and O.J. together at the defense table will come flashing across the screen. It will literally stop me in my tracks. It's always the same image: the moment the not-guilty verdict is read, and I can see the serious expression on Robert's face. It never fails to jolt me and take me back to that exact moment in time at the end of the trial, while simultaneously sparking the same exact emotions I had that day. Now, sixteen years later, with Robert gone, the televised image of my former husband with O.J. Simpson still brings me to tears. Watching it, I often crumble and pray for both Robert and Nicole with everything inside of me, hoping that somehow, through some miracle, we could bring them both back.

CHAPTER TEN

The Haven

After the verdict, it was time for a new beginning. Robert and I decided to move on from the conflict the O.J. trial had created between us for the sake of our kids. I had to end the sadness and pain of those years. It wasn't fair to Bruce, whom I had dragged into all of it, to live my life in the past anymore. I had to move on, and I had to move swiftly. My focus reverted back to my lifelong dream: to be a wife and the mother of six kids, which meant I had two more children to go.

By then, I was eight months pregnant. It wasn't that hard to juggle full-time work and motherhood because I had my amazing assistant, Lisa Frias, who helped me with Bruce's business. We had developed a pretty impressive speaking business for Bruce. He was traveling all over the country, giving motivational speeches for Fortune 500 companies like Coca-Cola while attending Olympic events around the world.

Just before our baby was due, Bruce and I went back east to

stay with Kathie Lee Gifford, one of my best friends. I had known Kathie Lee since the 1980s when she was still Kathie Lee Johnson. Back then, she came to a baby shower I had given for a girlfriend, Shanon Christian. As you know by now, I love giving parties and showers, and that shower was an example of my style and taste for over-the-top celebrations. Kathie Lee fell in love with the Tower Lane house. She and I were on the exact same page: we both loved architecture and decorating and design. We hit it off instantly.

Kathie Lee and I had drifted apart during my divorce from Robert. But when I started dating and then married Bruce, who had known Kathie Lee and her husband, Frank Gifford, for decades, the four of us became the best of friends. So during that time I was pregnant, Bruce and I spent some time at Kathie Lee's house in Connecticut. From there, we flew down to Atlantic City, where Kathie Lee and Regis Philbin were hosting the Miss America Pageant. Bruce was a judge in the pageant along with fashion and bridal designer Vera Wang. Little did I know that, fifteen years later, Vera would be designing wedding gowns for my daughters.

In Atlantic City, recovering from the trial and trying to unwind before giving birth to our first child together, Bruce and I asked Kathie Lee and Frank Gifford to be the godparents of our new baby. We hadn't chosen a name yet. We were only considering *K* and *J* (*J* for "Jenner," of course). I told Kathie Lee and Frank about how all my girls were *K*s, so this baby should be a *K* too. All my daughters were still living under my roof, and if I had named this baby girl a *J* name—I loved the name "Jade," for example—I was afraid she wouldn't feel like she was a part of the rest of the family. I wanted her to feel just as loved and wanted and adored as the rest of my girls. So I knew that as long as Bruce was okay with it, I needed to commit to another *K* name. I thought it was fitting, too, because I was a *K*, and Kathie Lee, her godmother, was a *K*. We decided it would be the K Club.

I started throwing names out to Kathie Lee—"Kameron" ... "Kendall"—and she stopped me at "Kendall."

Luckily, Bruce loved the name "Kendall" too.

On November 3, 1995, I gave birth to Kendall Nicole Jenner. I decided to make her middle name "Nicole" in memory of my dear friend Nicole Brown Simpson. Giving birth to Kendall, as well as all of my children, has been my greatest blessing. I know that some women dread pregnancy, and not everyone looks forward to the birth experience. But it's been my biggest joy. I cherished those few weeks at home, bonding with my baby girl and feeling so blessed and happy to have my beautiful, ever-expanding family around me. I was surrounded by five children now, and I couldn't have been happier.

One of the toughest things I have ever done in my life was to introduce Kendall to Robert Kardashian. He had called shortly after she was born to offer his congratulations, both on the new baby and for my birthday, which came around the same time. He still called me often, even if we were battling over something, and he always called me on my birthday. *Always*. He had this goofy birthday song that he had put on a cassette, and he would just play the song on the phone. It was so silly and so cute and so Robert. We had this bond after having four children together. Now I had number five, but it wasn't with Robert.

I burst into tears when he called me on my birthday that year and offered congratulations on Kendall's birth. "Come meet the baby," I said.

He came over a few days later, when Kendall was just a week or so old; I can still see him walking through the front door. I went to greet him, saying, "Hi, Robert!" first, before introducing him to Kendall. I could tell that he was a little nervous as I led him into the other room where Kendall was sleeping in her straw Moses basket on the floor. I stepped aside as Robert moved in front of me, leaned over, and stared into the basket. When he saw her, he started to cry a little.

"Oh, Kris, she's so beautiful, it makes me cry," Robert told me.

He picked her up, and I could tell it broke his heart. My life had gone on, and it was a very hard moment for both of us to acknowledge that it had gone on without him. He knew the joy and the memories we had with each of our babies together, and I am not sure he ever expected I would have more. I don't think he dwelled on it, but it was a tough moment in time.

Although I was so happy and felt so content, there was still one important part of me that wasn't complete. I still felt unsettled, and I knew it was time for Bruce and me to finally commit to buying a home of our own. When Bruce and I got married, I had just moved out of Tower Lane and into our Malibu rental. Now we were still leasing a house in Beverly Hills with no gate or security, and I really felt like we needed a larger house. Our family was constantly growing and shifting and evolving. So I started looking for houses again. As always, I didn't have much time. We were planning to take the entire family and all five children to Atlanta for a month for the 1996 Olympic Games, and we would be gone for at least six weeks total. Bruce had worked for the 1992 games in Barcelona, and the two of us were able to live in a hotel for six weeks because Robert took care of the kids for me. But this time we had four kids and an infant in tow. We were also working for Coca-Cola, so it was going to be a ton of work and a huge month for us. I felt we needed to buy a real home in Los Angeles before we left to ground us when we came home. We needed a home to come home to.

There was, of course, more to it than that. I'm such a nester, and I've always needed a home to build memories. Of course, I had no idea in 1996 that I was searching for a house that would literally become a stage for my family on television, although it would still take several more moves before we landed in the first of the houses featured on our show. Nesting just comes naturally to me. Many of the important women in my life, like my daughters, are the same way.

I have to have everything in my life completely organized and perfect—otherwise, I am a complete mess. I can't think straight if my home isn't just right. That was the way I was brought up; my environment just feeds my energy. I love creating a home, and I thrive in the order of what I create. So living in a rented house—somebody else's house, with somebody else's refrigerator and somebody else's washer and dryer, somebody else's walls and tile and decorations—is not how I thrive. I *had* to get us out of that rented house and into a place of our own. I became fixated on it. It became a goal, a quest.

Once I put that vibe out there, amazing things began to happen.

One day, one of my best friends, Lisa Miles, called.

"Hi, Kris, I would love to have you over to my house," she said. "You've never seen it. Come for lunch. I want to show you the house."

Lisa, who I had known since I first met and married Robert, had moved from Beverly Hills out to someplace called Hidden Hills.

"Where in the hell is Hidden Hills?" I asked.

It was in Calabasas, fourteen miles from L.A. She gave me directions, and I felt like I had to drive on the 101 freeway forever to get there. It felt like I was driving to San Francisco! But when I finally reached the community of Hidden Hills and drove through its magnificent gates, I did an audible exhale. It was like driving into another world. I saw these huge parcels of property with white fences, winding trails, beautiful homes, and trees every-

- 197 -

where. I drove a bit farther into the neighborhood, and I saw horses, llamas and cows, and people walking their dogs and riding their horses. I saw a dog walker with about fifteen dogs on leashes. When I rolled my window down, I could hear birds chirping and singing. It was heaven. *Where am I?* I thought. *Who even knew this existed?!*

When I finally pulled up to Lisa's house, I could hardly even speak.

I was so happy for Lisa. She was living an amazing lifestyle in a gorgeous home on a beautiful piece of property. She was so excited to show me her house. She had a tennis court, a basketball court, a stable, a barn, two horses, three goats, about ten chickens, and a bunch of bunnies and cats. She was happy and calm and thriving.

Doesn't every fairy tale end with a happily-ever-after? I was already deliriously happy with a new baby, an amazing marriage, and a great life. Kourtney, Kimberly, Khloé, and Rob were all in school, and Kendall was, of course, still an infant. I was determined to take care of my kids and make the most beautiful home possible for them and for Bruce.

Hidden Hills looked like the perfect place.

"How did you find this place?" I asked Lisa at lunch that day.

She told me the story of how she had discovered her home, and when I drove back to Los Angeles that night, I just *knew*. I had found our home. Hidden Hills fit the bill and it was where I wanted to live. I didn't even know how to get there, but I knew I was *going* to get there.

I practically gushed about it to Bruce that night: Hidden Hills, Hidden Hills, Hidden Hills. All I could talk about was Hidden Hills.

"I am not living all the way out in Hidden Hills," he said of this elusive place just fourteen miles from L.A. but over the hill and a few freeways from Beverly Hills. "That's just not something I want to do."

"But you used to live in Malibu!" I said. Malibu was even farther.

"Well, Malibu is different," he said. "It's the beach."

He was definitely not on the bandwagon. But the more I talked about Lisa's beautiful house and the more I raved and raved about it, Bruce eventually did what he usually does: he came around.

"Well, if you love it that much, why don't you go look at houses out there with somebody and just see what you find?" he suggested.

I called a friend who lived in Encino. I loved her house too; it was large and spacious compared to what you could find in Beverly Hills. You really get a lot for your money when you're willing to drive out of town. Plus, it wasn't like we had bazillions to spend on a house. We had a tight budget and needed a lot of space for what was now totaling *nine* kids: my four, Bruce's four, and the baby we had just had together. We needed at least five bedrooms for Kourtney, Kimberly, Khloé, Robert, and Kendall, plus a bedroom for Bruce and me. That meant we needed a six-bedroom house, and a house in Beverly Hills with six bedrooms would have cost us $10 million. I knew I had to get creative to find the perfect house.

My friend recommended a broker named Lisa, and as we drove around the incredible neighborhood, I just kept thinking, *I've never seen anything like this*. The houses were so far apart from each other and each one was absolutely beautiful. Then the real estate agent pulled up to a house that didn't seem to fit in. It was a sprawling house that wasn't at all like my friend's house, the house that had made me fall in love with the area in the first place. In fact, it was borderline ugly. It looked like it might be a bit of a spec house with a sparse garden, not nearly as lush as the surrounding homes. It definitely looked like it could use a little TLC. *But who knows?* I thought. I still wanted to take a look inside.

But when I walked through the doors, I immediately called the house "the monstrosity," because it was sort of a bad shade of gray with purple carpet and black marble floors. It was so big—more than 9,000 square feet—and it had six bedrooms, nine bathrooms, a huge backyard, and a pool with horrible brick trim, but not a single tree. All I remembered when I left that day was the purple carpet. It wasn't the castle I pictured in my fairy tale, so I moved on. I had envisioned something really special. I didn't know exactly what it was, but I knew I'd know it when I saw it. We looked and looked and looked at all kinds of houses, and I fell in love with one right down the street from that first purple and black monstrosity. I really loved this one. It was Spanish in style, it was in Hidden Hills, it had a tennis court and everything else I wanted. It was divine. It had extensive damage from the '94 earthquake and was in need of repair, but regardless, I loved it.

The house was in foreclosure and we tried to buy it. We made an offer, and the sellers accepted. A few days before we left for the Olympic Games in Atlanta, thinking that when we returned home we'd move into our new, big, beautiful, Spanish-style, Mediterranean villa in Hidden Hills, our real estate agent, Lisa, called.

"You didn't get the house," she told me. "Somebody else heard that it was going really cheap, and they bought it out from under you."

I was crushed. I mean, I actually cried myself to sleep that night. *Now what are we going to do?* I had exhaustively searched every single house in both Hidden Hills and Calabasas. I just knew that that's where our life would be. I just didn't know what I was going to do to get there. There wasn't time to think about it now. We were off to Atlanta for six weeks. Bruce, Kendall, our nanny, Jackie, and I went first, while the rest of the kids finished up school at Robert's house. While I was in Atlanta, I got a phone call from Lisa. "You know that house that you saw with the purple carpet and the black marble that you thought was so ugly?" she said. "Well, they've lowered the price one more time, and if you want it, I think I can get it for you. You've got to act quickly, though, because there's somebody else interested."

Bruce and I talked it over in Atlanta and decided that there was nothing about the house that we couldn't fix. It was the first house we saw in Hidden Hills, and we thought, *Why not?* We could take it on as a big project and redo the house, room by room. We would transform it; we would single-handedly turn it into our dream house. Both of us were ready for the challenge.

So we bought the purple monstrosity in Hidden Hills. Escrow closed in thirty days. Being out of town that month was a blessing, because it distracted me and kept me from obsessing about all the things that I'd have to do to turn that purple house into a home. This was a big deal for Bruce and me, because it was the first house we bought together. *Is it going to close? Is someone going to buy it out from under me?* I was stressed, but we were so busy in Atlanta that I couldn't let it get to me.

The arrival of our kids in Atlanta would have made a great scene in *Keeping Up with the Kardashians*, only it wasn't so funny—at least, not in the beginning.

I knew that Kourtney, Kimberly, and Khloé were going to be something special even then, when they were still in their early teens. They were raised in a family full of big personalities, after all, and we were always doing something really exciting, whether we were filming an infomercial or going on a fabulous trip. Everything was larger-than-life because that's just the way our family did things, and this trip to Atlanta was not going to be any different.

My son, Robert, and Khloé came to Atlanta separately from the other girls. They flew in with my mom and dad. Kourtney and

Kimberly were to come a few days later. Before their arrival, a bomb exploded during a rock concert in Centennial Olympic Park, killing two people and injuring more than a hundred. Kourtney and Kimberly had not only been really spooked by the bomb explosion, they were scared to death. They didn't want to come to Atlanta because they thought that they were going to be bombed. It took me hours on the phone to convince Kourtney and Kimberly to even get on an airplane.

On the day they were to fly to Atlanta, Kourtney and Kimberly went through security, which was, of course, much lighter than we have today. Still, an escort had to take them onto the plane because they were unaccompanied minors. They were flying coach and sitting on the plane. But before the plane left the ground, the girls, still spooked about the bomb that had gone off in Atlanta, were distracted by a particular fellow passenger: they were sure he was a terrorist. The girls started watching this guy's every movement. They got each other so worked up that they started hysterically crying to the flight attendants and eventually screaming, "That guy has a bomb! We want to get off this plane!"

By then, the plane was taxiing onto the tarmac, and Kourtney had a full-blown panic attack. She started screaming that she just *had* to get off the plane, that a bomb was about to go off. You can imagine the effect that yelling about a bomb would have on an airplane, even back then. Complete chaos. Kourtney and Kimberly rattled the flight attendants so much that they told the pilots and the pilots turned the plane around and took Kourtney and Kimberly off, even though their luggage had already been checked.

Bruce and I were at an event for Coca-Cola when Bruce's cell phone rang. It was the agent at the gate in Los Angeles. "Mr. Jenner?" he said. "This is the supervisor . . . I have your daughters here, and they have created a nightmare."

The supervisor explained the situation to Bruce, then added, "We're going to let this go this time. We're not going to suspend the girls from flying. But I do not want them on one of our flights until tomorrow at the earliest."

He insisted that the girls go home and think about what they had done and the panic they had created. "Right now, everyone's really upset," said the supervisor. "Your kids have to go home."

So the girls went home and the next day, they boarded another flight to Atlanta. The second time, they made it without incident. In hindsight I guess it should have been foreshadowing to me about the kind of shenanigans Kourtney and Kimberly would get into later. At the time, I was so mad at them, but never happier to see them when they finally landed in Georgia.

We stayed in three adjoining hotel rooms: all four of our kids in one room with twin beds; Bruce, me, and the baby in another; our nanny in the third room. It was crazy, like a big dormitory, and a great adventure. The kids had a ball. I took them to Olympic events, but the biggest event was celebrating the twentieth anniversary of Bruce's gold medal. I had spent months planning a surprise party for him with all his Olympic buddies, our families, and our dearest friends, including Steve and Candace Garvey, who had set us up years before. We had the party at Planet Hollywood, and *Access Hollywood*, Pat O'Brien, and NBC Sports covered it.

A couple hundred people came to the party. I had hired a producer in Atlanta and spent months making a video of Bruce's entire life. It included every commercial he ever shot and all the footage from the Olympic Games. I had a crew go around and interview all these people from Bruce's life about Bruce. We even interviewed President Gerald Ford, because after he sent Bruce a congratulatory telegram when he won the gold at the Olympics, Bruce and

President Ford became friends. I interviewed Kathie Lee and Frank Gifford. We set the whole video to inspiring music and there were cheers (and tears) when we played it at the party.

We had custom-made chocolate gold medals and a gorgeous cake—complete with an image of Bruce crossing the finish line—flown in from Hansen's Cakes in Los Angeles for dessert. I had to buy that cake its own seat on an airplane, and my girlfriend Stephanie Schiller flew to Atlanta in the adjoining seat. The party was a roaring success. It made Bruce feel so special, which was all I wanted. Bruce had a new baby, a new house, and a new wife, and we wanted to celebrate his life.

I had asked Bruce to meet me for a "business dinner" at Planet Hollywood, where I had a crowd waiting. My heart was racing when someone alerted me by walkie-talkie: "Bruce is here, and he's in the elevator! He'll be there in a second." I was so excited. When those elevator doors opened, he was going to see all of his family and the friends he had gathered throughout his lifetime. Even my parents were there, and Bruce's dad had flown all the way from Lake Tahoe. When Bruce stepped off the elevator, everybody screamed, "Surprise!" He had accomplished so much in his career and in his life, and I was so happy to see the look of joy on his face. I'll never forget that moment. He was touched, excited, and over-whelmed. It was perfect.

While we were in Atlanta, I kept thinking about the house.

Before we left, we got the news that the escrow on our new house in Hidden Hills had closed, and it was such an exciting day. We had this big new house, which, while not so beautiful at the moment, we were determined to *make* beautiful. Our family had so much anticipation, so much joy, and so many blessings.

In our large and crazy family, our houses have always been our anchors, the places where we can all find one another no matter how many different directions our individual lives go. That's why, to this day, our weekly Sunday family dinners are really important to all of us. When we bought that first big house in Hidden Hills, it would quickly come to symbolize to all of us that life was good again. We were really looking forward to going home and packing up our rented house and moving to Hidden Hills.

As soon as we landed in Los Angeles, we immediately went to work. Thank you, Lord, for making Bruce Jenner a handyman! The house was so big, we didn't even know where to start. We rolled up our sleeves and started with the weather-beaten front doors, which sorely needed a fresh coat of paint. Bruce began sanding the front doors and then painted them. Then we worked our way from front to back. I remember thinking: *This is going to be hard work, but a lot of fun.* Bruce and I changed all the black marble floors. We pulled up all the purple carpet. We painted the house yellow. We put a picket fence out back and a pool fence around our pool. We started transforming that house into a haven.

We moved in on August 16, 1996, making a million trips from Beverly Hills to Hidden Hills and unpacking rack after rack after rack of clothes. It was 116 degrees in Hidden Hills on the day we moved in. I swear, I don't think I have ever seen it as hot since! Still, Hidden Hills was fabulous. Every year the community has a parade, and everyone dresses up a vehicle—golf carts, bicycles, even horses—and marches in the parade. Then there is a bake sale and a carnival and a horse show. There is also a riding ring for the horses and also pancake breakfasts every so often. It was like living in the 1950s, so peaceful and quiet. There weren't even streetlights at night. It was an oasis. It felt like I was dreaming, but I had this beautiful big house in a wonderful community, and we were making it amazing.

Bruce started painting rooms by himself, one by one. Before

we moved in, he painted Kendall's room this gorgeous lemon yellow. Then he painted Robert's room navy blue; Kourtney's cream; Khloé's shabby-chic green; and Kim's pale pink. The rooms all took on their own personalities, and they were each so beautiful.

All the rooms in the new house were huge, and each bedroom had its own patio. We were redoing all the floors downstairs with big Mexican paving stones, because they fit the style out there. The construction crew gave me extra tiles. I had them mix up cement for me, and I ended up tiling Kendall's patio all by myself, plastering, spreading, and leveling each tile by hand.

Bruce and I were having the times of our lives painting and tiling. Then one day I saw a magazine cover with a picture of a picket fence and white iceberg roses all over it. I woke up the next morning and told Bruce, "We have to have white iceberg roses!" We went to a nearby nursery and bought three hundred white iceberg rosebushes. Poor Bruce not only built and painted the picket fence with a fence digger by himself—he had a whole workshop set up in the garage by now, with a table saw and a virtual paint store with brushes and gardening tools—he also planted all three hundred white iceberg rosebushes.

While we were renovating our new house, we were also raising five kids. Bruce was flying in and out of town on personal appearances, and the house was slowly being transformed into a magical place. We finally redid the pool and put a putting green in the backyard for Bruce. One day my friend Mary Frann, who played Bob Newhart's wife on *Newhart*, came to stay overnight in our new house. We were walking back from the community bake sale when she noticed that my house didn't have a sign with the name of the house in the yard like the other Hidden Hills homes all did. Every house in Hidden Hills has a name, and we hadn't named ours yet. "You should name it 'The Haven,' " Mary Frann told me. The next day, we ordered a sign for our house: "The Haven." That has been the name of our house ever since, even as we moved from one house to another, and that's sort of how we've thought of all the houses we've lived in together as a family.

We were obsessed with our new house; it signified the end of a long journey for Bruce and me as a couple. We were *so* proud to be in this place in our lives. Once again I began entertaining with as much passion as before, hosting birthday parties, Easter egg hunts, Thanksgivings, and ginormous Christmas Eves and Christmas Days with Santas and elves.

The house brought us luck and good fortune. On our first Christmas in Hidden Hills, Bruce and I discovered we were pregnant again. On August 10, 1997, our second daughter together—and my sixth child, the realization of my lifelong dream of having six kids—was born. Of course, we had to name her with a *K*, and we found the perfect name, "Kylie."

CHAPTER ELEVEN

Healing and Forgiveness

The next several years were peaceful, wonderful, busy years. Kourtney and Kimberly each took turns living with their dad at the end of their high school experiences. I think both of them felt there was just always so much going on in my household—a whirlwind of activity every single day, with babies and people (business and personal) in and out—and the girls found peace and more attention at their dad's house. It was good for them. Robert had gone to law school, obviously, and was really into study skills and the importance of excelling in school, which was not really my cup of tea. Robert was also single at the time, and he could devote himself to dinners with them one-on-one and good, quality bonding time.

Kourtney went off to college at Southern Methodist University in Dallas, Texas. Having Kourtney leave for college was a significant moment. As you know by now, I have always dreamed of having the perfect family, complete with a wonderful husband and six beautiful kids. But I never got to the part in my dream when one of them would leave for college. I certainly wasn't ready to let Kourtney go. I was so preoccupied with changing diapers and keeping Bruce's business going, I didn't give much thought to the fact that Kourtney was actually and truly going to leave for college. When the day came, I was an absolute mess.

Her dad and I decided that it would be a good idea for the entire family—Robert, me, and the four kids we'd had together—to fly to Dallas to get Kourtney settled at SMU. We arrived and spent a couple of great days in Texas together. Then it came time to say good-bye, and a pit began growing in my stomach, probably the biggest pit I've ever had. I just didn't know how to say good-bye. I had never been away from my firstborn, *ever*. Now here she was, moving to another city in a distant state. I had once told her she should go to college in a different state so she could have all of these new and fresh experiences. Now I realized that she would be so far away, and it totally turned my world upside down. What was I thinking? I started to uncontrollably sob and become a complete wreck; this exact same emotion would continue before and after every single visit with Kourtney in college until the day she graduated from the University of Arizona, to which she would eventually transfer from SMU.

I knew then that being separated from my children would never be something I could handle. I knew I had to figure a way to keep my babies close in the future. The answer would come soon enough, and, as with everything, it would come in a big and dramatic way.

During those years in Hidden Hills, Khloé, my youngest daughter with Robert, grew up a lot. She was very mature for her age. She was too young to be in Kourtney's peer group and she wasn't quite in Kimberly's tight circle of friends, and she didn't really have a developed circle of her own. Those kinds of friendships are developed when children are young, and they often have something to do with the parents nurturing those relationships. By the time Khloé came around, I was entrenched in my own friendships and I never really made a group of friends centered on her. I believe all of these factors played into who my girls would eventually become.

For me, Khloé was a godsend. She had decided to get her education via homeschooling—and she was an incredible student—which enabled her to become a built-in babysitter and my right arm. Khloé was so loving and nurturing, and she loved playing with our two babies and helping me feed them and watch them. I would have had to give up so much if I had not had Khloé there to help. Without Khloé, I don't know how I would have gone on with my life. After all, I was forty by then, and I was starting over with a new husband, two new babies, a new house, and a new business—all of which added up to a lot of new responsibilities. Because of Khloé, I was able to attend business meetings, work out, get my hair cut, even have lunch with a friend. Because of Khloé, I was able to get back to being myself again, and I will never forget the sense of freedom this gave me.

Khloé gave me the world's biggest gift and she probably doesn't even get how important she was to me. To this day, Kendall and Kylie feel that Khloé is their second mom, which she is. The love that I felt for Khloé for so selflessly helping me in those early years would bond Khloé and me together forever. I will always be grateful to her.

So while Khloé was happy to be part of my life with Kendall and Kylie and to be the ultimate big sister, Kourtney and Kimberly were more eager to leave the nest and test their independence. After Kourtney spent her last year and a half of high school with Robert and left for college, Kimberly moved in with her dad in Kourtney's place.

I had no idea that my family, my home, would someday become an entertainment empire. Like everything else in my life, it would just flow from my love of home and family. However, our daily life and the environment in which my children were raised were always dramatic and exciting. There was never a dull moment, good or bad. I think part of what shaped my girls is the constantly evolving family dynamic and unconditional love. During this time, my kids developed independence, responsibility, character, integrity, and a work ethic. They were on their way.

Kourtney and Kimberly both got new cars as soon as they got their driver's licenses, and soon it was Khloé's turn. Initially, Robert just gave Khloé one of his cars, and definitely not a Rolls. It was an old jalopy. Khloé felt like the odd sister out: her sisters had both received brand-new cars, but Khloé got Robert's hand-me-downs. I finally talked Robert into giving Khloé a new car for Christmas that year. It was so cute. On Christmas morning, Robert came over to our house and snuck in the back door before the girls woke up. We all gave her the keys to her brand-new Mercedes together. She was thrilled.

As each child took turns living with Robert, I would buy each of them all new bedding and redo the bedroom in Robert's house so that they felt at home in her or his own space. When Kourtney moved in with Robert, we decorated her new bedroom at his house in all new Ralph Lauren sheets and décor. When she moved out to go to college, I redecorated the same room to fit Kim's tastes and style. Khloé didn't go that route and stayed with me, but Rob decided to move in with his dad when he was fifteen. He was going through some tough years in school, along with puberty, and he needed his dad. So each of them had that time there with him.

My oldest girls, Kourtney and Kimberly, grew up fast and began to date very seriously very early. Back in 1992, when Kim was around thirteen, she began dating TJ Jackson, Tito Jackson's son and Michael Jackson's nephew. At that time we were still living in our Beverly Hills rental. I knew all the Jackson boys—Michael's nephews—because Kourtney and Kimberly had started going to the Buckley School with them in preschool. The girls made most of their lifelong friends at the Buckley School, and they had known the Jacksons forever. So when Kim started dating TJ, I was thrilled, because he was so great and our families really liked each other. TJ became one of my own and I adored him.

Tragically, right after we lost Nicole is the summer of 1994, TJ's mom, Delores "Dee Dee" Jackson, was also brutally murdered. Dee Dee was an amazing person and such a good mother. The Jackson kids all loved their mother so much. After the murder, TJ moved in with us briefly and healed a bit at our house. He and I really bonded. We all just kind of held each other close, as all of us were healing from various things. We became like one big family.

For Kim's fourteenth birthday, Michael Jackson invited all of us up to the Neverland Ranch for her birthday party. Kim invited all her friends, and I rented a Mercedes bus. Bruce and I came with all the kids, as well as TJ, Taryll, and Taj Jackson, and we all spent the night at Neverland. We had the time of our lives. I can only imagine how much fun Kim had and what a memory it was for her, because it was one of the most magical places I had ever been— and I was an adult!

When you walked into Neverland, you felt like you were in a very magical place. The house, amusement park, carnival rides, flowers, and the petting zoo . . . all were too astonishing to believe.

We never saw Michael. I was told he was there that night, but he never came out to say hello. However, we couldn't miss seeing his generosity and the love and the passion that he put into his home. The people who worked there were so accommodating and sweet, and the whole ranch had such good energy. We watched movies, we ate candy, we rode go-karts, we had a water balloon fight in the fort, we went horseback riding, and we played with the monkeys.

Kim and TJ dated for several years, and TJ would come along on family ski vacations with us. We all became extremely close and felt like TJ was part of our family. Eventually, though, Kim and TJ's relationship ended. We were devastated when they told us. I felt like *I* broke up with him. I was in my bathroom when the two of them told me, and I just became inconsolable. I felt so bad for TJ, because he had to try to make *me* feel better about their breakup as I was bawling in my bathroom.

"It's going to be okay. It's going to be okay," TJ kept repeating.

I think that, somehow, everything that I had been through in the previous couple of years just kind of manifested in the breakup of Kim and TJ. He was her first true love. They went to the prom together and had so many memories. We love TJ. To this day, I feel like he's one of my kids.

Several years after they broke up, he called me out of the blue. "Hi, Kris, where are you?" he asked me.

"Running an errand," I said.

"Can you come home? I have a surprise for you."

"You do?!"

"Yeah, but you have to come home right now."

So I rushed home to the house in Hidden Hills.

"Where's TJ?" I asked Bruce.

"He's in Khloé's room," he answered. I walked into Khloé's room, and TJ was standing there, hiding something behind him.

"What's going on?" I asked.

He stepped to the side, and this tiny toddler was sitting on the floor.

"Who's that?" I asked.

"This is my baby," he said. "I just wanted you to meet him."

He explained that he had a new girlfriend, to whom he would soon be married. I cried like a baby myself when he showed me his child. It was the sweetest thing. TJ and his wife have a couple of kids now. He's living his dream of being a dad and a husband, and I still feel like he is one of my own children.

Unfortunately, all of Kim's boyfriends wouldn't be so dear to my heart.

In 1999, when we were in our new house in Hidden Hills, Kim, nineteen at that point, started going through a phase. At first, I wasn't sure what was going on. She was acting a little funny, but she had been living with her dad, and I didn't know if she was just getting ready to spread her wings or what. At that time she was working at a high-end clothing store in Encino called Body, and she was very independent. Kim has always had an amazing love of fashion, and when she figured out I wasn't going to buy her everything she wanted at the drop of a hat, she took it upon herself to make it happen on her own. So she got the job at Body, where she shopped herself, and she started building a client list of people she would buy for and style. She was really good at it, and she started to earn commission on top of her salary. Everyone fell in love with Kim, and she began making a good living.

About this same time, Kim started dating an older man. She started acting really funny, and one day I said to Kourtney, "Your sister is acting really suspicious and odd."

Shortly after that, Kim told me she wanted to get her own apartment.

"You mean you don't want to live with Daddy anymore?" I asked her.

"No, I need my own place now," she said.

I took her to Bed Bath & Beyond and bought her all new things, and then I found out where she was living: Northridge. That was a really odd choice for her, way north of the city and even north of Hidden Hills.

"Why would you want to live in Northridge?" I asked her. "You're not going to school there. There's no reason for you to live there."

"Oh, I just like it over there," Kim answered, but I didn't buy it. It got even odder. Another day, she pulled up to my house out of the blue in a brand-new Jaguar. How did she buy herself a brand-new car, and a Jaguar no less, without my help?

I called Robert.

"Did you buy Kim a new car?" I asked.

"No, I didn't buy her a car," he said. "How did she get a car?"

Kim suddenly had all these new things and she was acting really weird about them, never explaining where she was getting all the stuff. Kourtney and I became very suspicious. She started doing some research, fishing around on the Internet. We did know that her apparent boyfriend was friends with Justin Timberlake. Justin Timberlake had just celebrated his birthday in Las Vegas, and Kim had gone to the celebration.

So Kourtney went onto an Internet search engine and typed in "Kim Kardashian," and lo and behold, and to the utter shock of all of us, up pops a marriage certificate for Kim and the older man.

Kim had gotten *married*!!

For three months, she had been fooling all of us.

We were all devastated. I immediately called Kim.

"Kim, first of all, you better get your husband to give me a call," I said. "Second, you have twenty-four hours to tell your dad before I do."

"You married my teenager," I said when I finally spoke to Kim's new husband. "You married my *teenager*!"

In the end, there wasn't anything I could do about the situation. Kim was nineteen and legally an adult. She could marry whomever she wanted. What was I going to do? I didn't like it, but I realized I would have to learn to live with it.

I made Kim tell her dad herself. Robert didn't speak to her for two or three days afterward, but I knew I needed to take a different tack. I had come to the conclusion that if I wanted to remain close to my daughter and keep our family together, I had to be the one to set the tone. Everyone was going to take my lead. It was up to me to be a mature, calm, loving parent and wrap my arms around her, let her know how much I loved her and that she would always have my unconditional love. That is what being a mom means: *unconditional*, all of the time.

I asked Kim to come over. One thing I know about Kim: she always wants me to be okay with her decisions. So she walked through the door, looking happy and hopeful. She wanted me to be on Team Kim, no matter what, and, of course, I always am. Kim is no quitter. What was done was done, and I knew she wasn't one to admit defeat quickly.

She explained that this was what she wanted for her life, but she wasn't very convincing. She was very, very young. I thought to myself, *Well, I was really young when I got married the first time, and maybe she does know what she wants, but she just doesn't know how to articulate it.* But the words coming out of her mouth just didn't sound passionate enough to me to be believable. Still, I had to see it through with her, because I'm her mother. I had always told her that my job was to be there for her, through thick and thin. I knew she depended on me for that.

What I didn't realize at the time was that this was a real turning point in my relationship with Kim. She knew, from then on out, that we were family and it was the real deal. Our bond could never be broken.

I was happy when Kim moved into a house close by. I helped her stock her kitchen and do all the shopping. Kim didn't need much help; she was already divine when it came to design. I was so impressed by her innate domesticity. She was a nester, just like me. She loved making her house into a home, from the décor to the way she had everything organized. The closets were perfection, and I was so proud of Kim, because homemaking is not an easy thing to do.

During this time, Kim also started working hard building a business on eBay, buying and selling clothing. She started to design clothes herself and worked as a stylist too. She eventually became a closet organizer, and she would go to people's houses and completely restyle their closets and organize everything to make it beautiful.

One Mother's Day, Kim restyled my entire closet. That was something I will never forget. She knew by now that I needed my environment to be just so, because I am so much more productive when things are organized and perfect. Kim understands this perfectly because she's exactly the same way. She came over and worked on my closet, and it made her happy to help me. It was so nice to see her happy, because I could tell that she was pretty miserable in her marriage. I really didn't know where it was going to go, but I sensed the relationship wasn't going to last much longer.

Tensions came early. On the first Easter after Kim got married, I remember sitting in Bel Air Presbyterian Church. Our family took up the entire pew, with Robert Kardashian and Bruce sitting at one end of the pew and Kim and her husband at the other. I was smack dab in the middle. I looked down and waved at Robert and Bruce, then looked down and waved at Kim and her husband, and they seemed strangely distant and so far away from the rest of us. I wondered: *How in the world are we going to get through this day?* Still, I was there to support my daughter. Her decision to marry wasn't popular, but I had to do my best to keep the peace.

We all went back to the house and had a big Easter dinner and an Easter egg hunt. That was our family's way of wrapping our arms around Kim and saying, "No matter what, we love you, and we'll accept whatever you decide to do."

Meanwhile, Kourtney had come home from college newly single, and she started dating Taryll Jackson, TJ's brother. Taryll is just as amazing and special as TJ. They are just really good kids. Kourtney and Taryll adored each other and made a really cute couple. I had known the Jacksons forever, and everybody felt safe with everyone else in that situation. We both had high-profile families. Kourtney and Taryll moved in together, and they became like a little family. They lived in Taryll's house, and his brother, Taj, lived with them. Khloé wasn't dating anyone at the time, and Rob lived with his dad.

Life settled down a little for us during the last years of the 1990s. Bruce was still traveling around the world, giving motivational speeches, and our life still had a lot of moving parts. But it was an amazing life. Those years were spent making huge pasta dinners at the Hidden Hills house and watching the boys play basketball outside nonstop. Bruce enjoyed his putting green. Life was idyllic.

Until, as always, things began to change.

It started with something I did. For Bruce's fiftieth birthday on October 28, 1999, I wanted to make one of his lifelong dreams come true. A half hour north of our house in Hidden Hills was the most amazing, beautiful, exclusive golf course and tennis club called the Sherwood Country Club. Located outside of the community of Thousand Oaks, Sherwood also has an exclusive residential community where we had many friends living and loving the Sherwood lifestyle. Bruce often talked about golfing with friends there, which gave me an idea for a surprise: a membership to the Sherwood Country Club. "There's no better country club than Sherwood," Bruce kept telling me.

When you want to become a member at Sherwood, you are supposed to attend a board meeting. Obviously, since it was a surprise, Bruce couldn't go. Instead, I had to figure out a way to represent him at the meeting. So I came up with a great idea: I delivered a Wheaties box with Bruce on the front along with the little Bruce Jenner dolls that Hasbro had produced and little Bruce Jenner race cars from Ford. I wrote a letter to each board member as if it was from Bruce, saying, "Dear Board Member, I can't be at the meeting today, but enjoy these Wheaties. I'll be a fantastic member and I would appreciate your vote."

The next day, I got the call: "He's accepted!"

Mission accomplished.

"Happy birthday, baby!" I exclaimed when we woke up on Bruce's birthday.

I told him that I was going to take him to a very special dinner that night and to be ready to leave at 5:00 p.m. sharp. After getting ready for dinner, we went to get into the car and Bruce hopped into the driver's seat.

"You're not driving," I said, and I whipped out a blindfold.

"What are you doing?" he asked.

"This is your birthday surprise," I said.

Bruce got out of the driver's seat. I put the blindfold on him and led him into the passenger's seat. After driving around for ten or fifteen minutes to get him really disoriented, I was on my way to Sherwood Country Club. I had told the guard at the gate ahead of time not to ask any questions when I pulled up, because if Bruce heard the guard, he would surely know where we were. We drove through the gates and I pulled into the parking lot at the golf course. I took Bruce onto the green, where a group of about twenty of our closest friends was waiting in silence.

When I got Bruce into position, I said, "Okay, honey, you can take your blindfold off now!"

Bruce whipped off his blindfold and looked around in a state of shock. Then a huge grin spread across his face. He was so happy to be standing on that putting green. I just screamed, "You're a member! You're a member!" and started jumping up and down. I think I was as excited as he was. We immediately had cocktails on the veranda to celebrate Bruce's birthday and his new membership at Sherwood before walking down the stairs to the club's wine cellar for a gourmet birthday dinner.

By this point, Kourtney was living with Taryll, Kim was married, Khloé wanted to move out right after her high school graduation, and Rob was living with his dad in Beverly Hills. Bruce and I started to feel like maybe The Haven was too much house for us. We had enjoyed the past eight years there, but now we had a nine-thousand-square-foot house and two babies, and we were wondering why we needed so much space. Bruce was dying to move near his precious Sherwood Country Club in Thousand Oaks, about twenty-nine miles from L.A.

Sometimes you need to take a breath and evaluate a situation. But back then, I was all reflex and little analysis. We had just finished decorating our whole Hidden Hills house: new fireplaces, new bathrooms, and new floors. We had redecorated every single room with the help of our dear friend and talented designer, Nancy Whaley. We had finally gotten it perfect, down to the china, when Bruce and I started talking about moving out. It all made sense on some level. We had all these rooms we didn't use. Even though family and friends were still coming over every night and I was still having big pasta dinners with salads and wine and huge board game parties with Monopoly and Scattergories, the truth was that we were only using half the house.

So one day Bruce and I looked at each other and said, "You know what, maybe we'll start thinking about moving on to something a little smaller." We decided maybe it wasn't that we needed something smaller but that we just wanted to be in a different place. We got antsy when we saw our friends moving to Sherwood Country Club and buying these big lots and building new homes. We thought: *That's exactly what we're going to do. We're going to buy a lot and we're going to build in Sherwood.*

We went to Sherwood and started looking around. A friend of ours told us, "If you're going to build a house at Sherwood, then you also need a townhome."

"We do?" I asked.

"Yes, in case you have guests, so they can stay near the golf course, inside the gates."

A friend of ours called and told us about a townhome for sale at a great price, so we bought a townhome. We moved to Sherwood to live in the townhome while building our new house.

I'll never forget the feeling I had driving out the gates of Hidden Hills and on to a new chapter in my life that day we moved to Sherwood. It was such an exhilarating feeling. I was so proud that I had the nerve to start another chapter. I'll never forget what I asked myself that day: *At what point during your life do you stop evolving?* Driving out the back gate of Hidden Hills toward our new home in Sherwood, I had my answer: *Never.*

I'll never stop evolving, never stop dreaming, never stop wanting and never stop following dreams. Even though sometimes my dreams haven't always worked out exactly as I'd planned, I've always been determined to try something new. I've always believed that there's a reason for everything, and it's the journey that has gotten me to exactly where I am today. I'm exactly where I'm supposed to be because I know God has a plan for my life.

But what was the dream? In this case, I was following my husband's dream of moving to Sherwood. I thought, *He's done so much for me, and now it's my turn to do things for him and to try it his way. That's grown-up, right!?* Not only was I trying it his way, but also I was moving to one of the most beautiful paradises on the planet.

To drive through the gates of Sherwood is like entering heaven. It's decadent; it's gorgeous. When I drove through those gates, I could feel the sense of extravagance and power envelop me. When we moved in, Tiger Woods was hosting his annual golf tournament there, and anybody who was anybody in that neck of the woods was living in Sherwood Country Club.

So we left our nine-thousand-square-foot dream house in Hidden Hills for a four-thousand-square-foot town house in Sherwood, which meant that half our stuff ended up in storage. I thought that was a good place to park it until we built our dream house. I had no idea when that would happen, but I was pretty confident that it would happen soon. We put only our favorite things in this beautiful townhome.

The first two weeks we lived there, everyone came to see the new digs. All my friends came by. The kids were obviously there. Everyone said they loved Sherwood as they helped me unpack. Then, a few days after we moved in, it was Halloween—and things got a little scary, at least for me.

As I've said repeatedly in this book, I love holidays, and the big holiday season begins every year at Halloween. In Hidden Hills, Halloween is the most fabulous event. There are kids running around trick-or-treating on foot or on their golf carts and everyone has parties. Every Halloween, I hosted a complete extravaganza. We all dressed up in costumes with a family theme. One year we were all baseball players; another year we were all the characters from *101 Dalmatians*. I was Cruella De Vil in an actual Cruella costume lent to me by a friend who worked at Disney, and I dressed up all my kids as white fluffy Dalmatians. If you pressed their hands, the costume would bark. One year we dressed as characters from *The Wizard of Oz*. I was Dorothy, Bruce was the Scarecrow, my dad was the Cowardly Lion, my mom was the Wicked Witch, and Kendall and Kylie were both Dorothy, too, just like me. We've done the same thing for our holiday cards year after year. Everyone in matching and coordinating outfits. We do a full-on photo shoot and have the best time making yet another memory out of it.

Halloween in Sherwood on the year we moved in was . . . *dismal*. Nothing happened! Absolutely no one was even on the streets! Our older kids scattered and did their own thing in L.A., and Bruce took the little girls out trick-or-treating. Sherwood had its annual fabulous Halloween party the week before, and Kendall and Kylie had a ball at the party. But on Halloween night, it just wasn't the same.

After we had lived there about a week, Robert Kardashian drove up to see our new house. He parked in front of the townhome and came inside.

"You live on a cul-de-sac" was the first thing he said, matter-of-factly.

"Yeah, I know, isn't it great?" I said.

"Not really," he said. "There's no parking."

He was right. We lived in a place where there was no parking on the street. There were actually signs that stated NO PARKING. If you didn't have your car in your driveway or in your garage, you were shit out of luck. Well, we had a lot of kids with cars at that point. It was not the best configuration for visitors. Or for guests at a party. Or for friends to drop by.

"This is really pretty," he said, looking around. "Really, really nice . . . and a little small for you guys."

"Hey, don't rub it in!" I said. "We're building a house!"

He listened to my grand plans, skeptically, while I was wondering, *What have you gotten yourself into now?* But Robert knew me well enough to know that I was very stubborn and determined to make it work. He teased me, but he didn't push.

Two weeks later, I was getting really lonely. Sherwood was farther north than Hidden Hills, and nobody wanted to visit me way out there. My friends wouldn't come to visit. They all had excuses. Nobody had the time to drive out to Sherwood. To show you how bad it was: Soon after we moved in, I had bunion surgery on my toe. I was flat on my back and unable to even go downstairs for two weeks, and not one person even came to see me. I knew then: I was officially living in the boondocks.

In the meantime, Bruce had been asked to star in a new prime-time reality TV special for ABC called *I'm a Celebrity . . . Get Me Out of Here!* It had been a huge hit in Europe and they now were bringing the TV show to the United States. Bruce and several other celebrities traveled to Australia to live in a jungle with absolutely no communication with the outside world. So off Bruce flew for three and a half weeks, leaving me all alone in Sherwood. *Yippee!*

While Bruce was gone, my mom and my dad, Harry Shannon, came up to stay with me the first week because they knew I was new (and not very happy) in this new neighborhood, and they didn't want to leave me alone for almost a month. Plus, I had never been away from Bruce for that long before. The first week was great, because I had my independence and I had some room to myself, living in the smaller quarters. After that, though, I got lonely, and I really missed him. I missed my kids, my friends, and my wonderful life in Hidden Hills. To make matters worse, Kendall and Kylie, who had zero friends in Sherwood, kept asking me a single question: "Mommy, when are we going home?"

Pretty soon, I felt I was marooned in my own reality show: *I'm a mother, friend, neighbor,* I kept thinking, *all alone in a town house in Sherwood. Get Me Out of Here!*

I found myself working out of my town house with nothing really going on, and I would go to lunch at the clubhouse just for something to do, thinking maybe I'd run into . . . *somebody*. I found myself having extensive conversations with the personable waiters. I had no one else to talk to. Within two weeks, I was crying myself to sleep.

"What's wrong with you?" Bruce said when he returned from the jungle.

"I've got to get out of here," I said. "I think we've made a big mistake."

It wasn't like when I was unhappy in my marriage with Robert Kardashian years before. This time my marriage was wonderful. I had just landed in the wrong place. I never knew my environment could have such a powerful impact on my happiness until that moment. I came to realize that I had disrupted my mojo with that move. All of the people I loved were at least thirty minutes away. I didn't have the same cleaners or the same drugstore. I had a new market. It was a whole different environment. I thought that, living in such a glorious place, none of that would matter. But it did. I liked being stuck in my old routine and my old ways. I suddenly realized how important that was to my life.

My older kids were telling me, "Mom, what happened? You moved to Sherwood, and it's just weird." We were all really unhappy, and Kim was struggling in her marriage, and I felt like I needed to be closer to her. Hidden Hills, Hidden Hills, Hidden Hills. All I could think about was getting back to my old wonderful life in Hidden Hills. I had made a huge mistake and I needed to admit I was wrong. I had made a mess of our environment. My kids had left all of their friends behind, and we were driving an hour each day just to get to and from school. I felt so guilty and horrible that I had done this to my kids. Now it was up to me to fix it. I was determined to make everything right again.

No big deal, right? Just move back? Not so easy. I went looking for houses again in Hidden Hills, but by then the home prices had skyrocketed. There was nothing for sale under $15 million that was big enough for the large family I now knew I still needed in my everyday life. I needed my kids to be there every day, or at least have the space for it to be an option.

In the end, I put our Sherwood Country Club townhome on the market and sold it as fast as possible. I was probably the only person in the history of real estate to lose money that year, because it was a really good year for real estate. I scrambled out of Sherwood with my tail between my legs and a lesson burned in my brain: Don't ever discount your environment. Where you live, work, and play has a powerful effect on your happiness and productivity.

Since we couldn't find anything remotely affordable in Hidden Hills, I expanded my range to Calabasas. There was absolutely nothing. Then one day I suddenly got a call from my real estate broker, Marc Shevin. "Kris, there's a house up off of Parkway Calabasas," he said. "It's in one of the new communities, and it's beautiful. Somebody just fell out of escrow today. Do you want to look at it?"

"I'm on my way."

I drove straight to the address, walked in the house, looked around, and as I walked out the front door, the broker said, "Well, what do you think?"

I had seen enough crap by that point to know that this was the perfect house at the perfect time. I said, "I'll take it."

Bruce was on the road and was coming home that night. By the time he got home, I had made an offer, gone back and forth with the seller, agreed on a price, and signed a contract. All I could think now was: *Bruce is going to shit when he gets home,* because I just bought a house. Without telling him! He didn't even know what it looked like. *What have I just done?* I thought.

If you've watched our show, you know Bruce is so easygoing, just a really chill guy. He's so laid-back, he's practically horizontal. But even the chillest guy in the world might not take this so well. He came home that night, and I waited until the next morning to tell him.

"Well, you want to go see our new house?" I asked him.

"What?" he asked.

"I bought a house."

"What?!!" he said. Nothing shocks Bruce Jenner. I was a little worried. Then he shifted and said, "Okay," with a raised eyebrow, surely thinking, *What is she going to do next?*

Maybe he thought I was kidding. Then I showed him the house with the broker. I waited for his response. The house was empty, because the sellers had left already and moved to Seattle. It was beautiful and clean, and it didn't need one thing done to it. Bruce had brought a video camera with him. I was watching him as we toured the house, trying to read his mood. Was he upset? Or just exhausted from being on the road? When we were done, Bruce turned the video camera on me.

I said into the lens, "Well, what do you think?"

He turned the camera back onto himself.

"I love it!!" he said. He started jumping up and down and acting all silly and happy. It made me cry. I stood there and cried because he was so happy and I was so happy. That is when I knew I had married the absolute greatest guy in the world. I mean, who else would put up with all of my nonsense and move here—no, move there, do this, repack, move that table, plant those rosebushes? The guy would have done anything for me. He just wants everyone to be happy, and he knew moving from Sherwood into this new house would make me happy.

Things got worse, however, before they got better.

Around this time, my dad Harry's health went into a rapid decline. The first signs had come when he and my mom came to stay with me in Sherwood while Bruce was away on *I'm a Celebrity . . . Get Me Out of Here!* My mom and I had gone shopping for Shannon & Co., the children's store she owned in La Jolla. On our way home, we called Dad to tell him we would meet him at the Sherwood clubhouse for dinner, but he didn't answer the house phone or his cell phone. We didn't know where he was.

I called one of the guys at the country club and asked him to go to my house and check on my dad. He called me from outside my house and said, "I'm ringing the doorbell and nobody is answering, but your dad's car is in the driveway."

I started to panic. "Pound on the door," I told him. "Walk around the back and look through the windows!"

He could see Dad napping on the couch inside, and the poor guy had to pound on the door for a long time before he finally woke him up. Dad was totally disoriented when he came to the phone. "I was just napping," he insisted, but it was unlike him to take naps in the afternoon, and I thought it was weird that it was so hard to wake him up. Red flags.

As he had grown older, Harry had started having health issues, specifically with diabetes. He started to get more tired, and we had to start reminding him to eat so his blood sugar would not drop. One day that April, after my parents left my house, I don't know what happened, but I got up and had the biggest urge to go see my dad. He had been calling me regularly, saying how much he missed me, which was very powerful for me to hear. I just felt like I needed to go visit him.

I remember thinking back, many, many, many years ago, to when my biological dad passed away in his terrible car accident. Right before he died, he had wanted to get together with me, and I had told him I was too busy. I always felt guilty about that because I never saw him again. I also remembered visiting my mom when she was undergoing chemotherapy for cancer and sitting in the parking lot with Ryan. I had so much guilt for not being there for my mom. This was my chance to make amends for that. My instincts were trying to tell me something: if you feel like you need to go visit your loved one, then go! My instincts would prove to be right.

One day when Dad called, I decided to visit him immediately. I called Kourtney. "I'm going to drive to San Diego today just for the day to go see Papa. He's not feeling great. Why don't you go with me?"

She said, "Great."

So Kourtney and I got in the car and we went down to La Jolla. We stopped by my mom's store to visit her, and then we drove over to their house in Clairemont and saw my dad. We spent some time with him and we had a great visit with him, then drove back to Los Angeles.

Not forty-eight hours after we left, my mom called me—I remember I was working at my house—and she said, "I don't want you to be worried, but your dad was in an accident today."

My heart stopped.

"He went to go see your sister and he must not have eaten lunch," Mom continued. "He got off the freeway and was coming up to a red light and he kind of had a little blackout and bumped the car in front of him lightly. His air bags went off."

He was in his brand-new Mercedes, a very safe and heavy car.

Still, the air bags inflated, so he was taken to the hospital for an examination. "We're here at the hospital and he's fine, and everything's good. I'm going to take him home in about an hour," my mom explained.

I offered to drive down the next day, but she wouldn't hear of it. "No, we're fine," she said. "He's going to be great."

About an hour later, she called me to say, "We're still at the hospital." Apparently, when they tried to put my dad in the car, he was in excruciating chest pain. X-rays showed he had suffered a broken sternum in the accident.

Eventually Harry went into the intensive care unit. Mom traveled back and forth from her home to the hospital in Palomar, and then later Scripps Hospital in La Jolla. After a few days and the next time I saw my dad, he was in bad shape. We all realized that he wasn't going to get out of there anytime soon. Now he was having a hard time breathing and they were putting him in an oxygen tent. The news got worse: he was suffering from a staph infection that would literally eat him alive. We always thought he would come home from the hospital. He had been in a minor car accident; it wasn't a big deal. It was the staph infection that was killing him, not the accident.

While my dad was in the ICU, my mother was at his bedside twenty-four hours a day. She was faced with the decision to shut down her beloved children's clothing store, Shannon & Co., which she had run for thirty-five years and which was a La Jolla institution, so she could devote all of her time to Dad.

"I'm going to close the store for a while," she said.

I wouldn't hear of that. It was her livelihood. She didn't have any employees; it was just her. I said, "You can't close your store. You just bought all your stuff for spring and Easter." This was April, which was the beginning of their biggest season in La Jolla. I said, "I'll tell you what: I'll come down and run the store for you while

Dad's in the hospital, and you can go to the hospital every day. That's that."

"I'll take care of the kids," said Bruce, ever supportive. "You take care of your mom."

So, for sixteen weeks, I drove down to La Jolla every week to run my mom's store. I would spend four or five days in a row there, then come back home for a few hours, then return to La Jolla. I just kept going back and forth from my kids and my husband to my dad and my mom. Sometimes I would come home for five hours and then go back for five days; sometimes I would come home for a day and return to my mom's for ten days. I just kept going back and forth while my dad and my mom were in this horrible limbo. My dad wasn't getting any better.

I knew I was losing my dad, and almost more difficult was knowing that my mom, the love of my life, was losing the love of *her* life. Our family was so close, and I was heartbroken for my mother. Mom and Harry had been married for four decades, and she was losing him. She was devastated and didn't know what to do. I was grief-stricken, too, but I knew I had to rally to help my mom and dad.

Every day for those sixteen weeks, I got up and I made Mom breakfast. We went to the hospital together, and I would say good morning to Dad, who was using an oxygen tent to help him breathe. Watching that staph infection take his life one day at a time was one of the hardest things I've ever had to do. After leaving my mom at the hospital, I headed straight to the store, keeping any problems I had at the store to myself. I could tell that my mom was really grieving, so I never, ever wanted to complain or tell her I wanted to go home. I just wanted to be there for her and help get her through this.

Dad was not the only person I worried about during that time period. Earlier that year, I had gone to see my son, Rob, play in a basketball game at the Buckley School. Robert Kardashian was there, too, and in the middle of the game Robert asked me, "Can I talk to you outside? It's really important." Bruce, my kids, and I all exchanged glances that showed we wondered what was up, but I followed him out of the gym and around the side of the building.

Once we were outside, Robert started to cry. "I don't know how to tell you this," he said, "but I have cancer."

"What?!" I said. *"What?!"*

"Yeah," he said, "I have cancer. I'm sure it is going to be okay, but I am really scared."

I don't remember him telling me what kind of cancer. All I knew was that he had said the *C* word, and I felt the whole world spin. We cried and cried, then pulled ourselves together and walked back inside. He said he was going to get a second opinion.

The next week Robert called with the greatest news: "Guess what? I don't have cancer! It's a miracle. I am okay. It turned out to be a bad test."

A few months later, though, Robert called again. I was working in my mother's store in La Jolla.

"Are you sitting down?"

I sat down. I felt a bombshell coming. Just in case, I got up, put up the CLOSED sign, and locked the door.

"I do have cancer," he said.

He had just returned from a trip to Italy, and he literally couldn't swallow. His throat had been bothering him for a while. He had seen a doctor again, and he was diagnosed with stage IV esophageal cancer. I stood up and started pacing around the store, which wasn't easy, because it was a tiny place. I was walking around in tight circles, talking to him and trying to listen to what he was saying, but I really didn't hear anything. The room was spinning and my ears were ringing. It was a very difficult conversation to have with someone I loved so much. Still, Robert really didn't think cancer was going to beat him.

"I'll get treatment," he said. He told me about a healer in China whom he was going to fly into L.A. He was so confident he could beat it. That night I told my mother about Robert's cancer. The next day I got up in the morning and I said, "Mom, I have to go home and do something. I'll be back tonight, but I just need to go home for the day."

I drove all the way back to Los Angeles, and I locked myself in my bedroom, and I wrote a letter to Robert. I told him everything I felt about him. I don't know what possessed me to do that, but I felt like I needed to just talk to him in a way that was tangible, and that he could read in his own time. I needed to tell him how much he meant to me and how sorry I would always be for hurting him.

July 19, 2003

Dearest Robert,

I know you are going to think I am crazy, but for the longest time, probably for years, I have wanted to write you a letter expressing some of the feelings I have for you and for the family we have together. I always put off such a letter because for one it's painful to think about, and very emotional. Secondly, it just never seemed like the right time, but something I told myself I must do before anything ever happens to me, and then it's left unsaid. Well, when my dad got sick, I promised myself that when it was finally "over," I would sit down and write the letter I have been wanting to write . . . And now, with the news last week of your illness, I just don't want any more time to go by.

Where do I possibly begin? I find myself in awe of how quickly so much time has gone by since we first met. Sometimes, when I think back, it seems like only yesterday that you were picking me up at the airport from one of my trips on American Airlines. And it seems like only yesterday my dad was walking me down the aisle at the Westwood United Methodist Church and I was so scared with all of those people watching . . . It seems like only yesterday that we were on Tower Lane with our babies. I owe you an awful lot for the wonderful and amazing life that you gave me. You allowed me to grow up with incredible privilege, in a beautiful home, in beautiful surroundings, with amazing friends, a loving husband and precious children. I remember being pregnant . . . and being pregnant . . . and being pregnant . . . and being pregnant. I have so many wonderful memories, and I am grateful to you for being such an incredible man. For loving me the way you have since I was seventeen years old.

I very foolishly threw all of that away, and for that I will always be sorry. I was a very stupid and foolish girl. If I could turn back the hands of time, I would change it all. But I can't. The only thing I will ever be able to do is apologize for the pain and misery I put you through. I am so sorry to have ever hurt you in any way. I hope you will one day understand it really had NOTHING to do with you, but obviously something inside went terribly wrong with me. I can't explain my emotions or actions back then. I can't explain how tortured I was inside. I just know it was wrong of me and I am truly sorry.

I spent several pages thanking him for everything, reliving the memories we shared, thanking him for the incredible gift of the four children we had together, and thanking him for being the greatest father and friend, ending with my sorrow over his illness.

I am very sad about the recent news that you have cancer. I know you must feel scared and anxious and mad and confused, all at the same time. My heart aches for you. I just wish there was something I could do for you. I really believe that you are so strong. Your faith is strong and your body is strong and your mind is strong. I just wish you didn't have to face this challenge. You don't deserve it. I just want you to know that I am always here for you no matter what. It must feel really good to know that you have been blessed with wonderful children who love you uncon- ditionally and would do anything for you. They are a gift from God and I know they will comfort you.

You have been a huge and tremendous blessing in my life. You are one of the greatest loves of my life. And fi- nally, you are and always will be one of my most treasured friends. I love you and am thankful God put you in my life. Not knowing the path it would take me along or where it would end up . . . I am eternally grateful and will cherish each and every memory for as long as I live.

With all my love,
Kris

After I wrote the letter I drove over to my daughter Kim's house and said, "I have to go back to San Diego, but please give this to Daddy." By this time Robert had told the kids about his cancer. They were devastated and needed me, too, and I was feeling badly because I couldn't be there for them. I had to go back to San Diego.

The next day, Robert called me at Mom's store, sobbing.

"That was the most beautiful letter I've ever read," he said. "It was an amazing letter, and I'll never forget your writing it to me."

After I closed the store in La Jolla each day, I went to the hospital, saw my dad, and then my mom and I would have dinner. Mom and I would go back to her house after dinner and watch *American Idol*. We especially loved to watch the auditions. It was watching those silly auditions and laughing at all those bad voices that helped get us through that joyless time. That laughter helped get us through all of it as Dad continued his rapid decline in the hospital.

We knew he didn't have much time left.

One day toward the end, I remembered something someone told me: people need to tell their loved ones good-bye and hear that it's okay for them to go, because once they hear that, they can pass on in peace. My mom, my sister, Karen, and I took turns at my dad's bedside, and we filled his room with love. One day, I walked in and leaned down close to his face.

"Dad, I love you so much," I said, and I spent the next half hour thanking him for everything he had done for me and telling him how much he meant to me. I told him how everything that he had done in my life added up to make me the person that I had become. I thanked him for embracing my sister and me as if we were his own daughters. I thanked him for driving hours to be with me at every holiday, for attending the births of each of my children, and for watching them grow up. I thanked him for getting on the floor and playing Barbies with the girls and for endless games of catch with Rob, for helping me move from house to house, and for attending every single grandparents' day at each of my kids' schools.

I promised him I would take care of my mom and that we were all going to take care of one another. I knew that was important to him. I told him everything that was on my mind and in my heart and, most of all, I told him how much I loved him. I don't know if he heard me or not, but I believe he did. I left the room and changed places with my mom, and he passed away as she stepped out of the room for a second.

Dad died sixteen weeks after he first went into the hospital. He was seventy-eight.

I watched my mom die a little inside at the same time. She had been married to this good, kind, and decent man for thirty-five years. Her whole world was wrapped around him. To this day, I think about him for one reason or another at least six times a day. He gave me a little birdhouse when we lived in Sherwood because he thought it would make me feel at home, like I was back in Hidden Hills. I've hung it in the tree outside my window in my backyard, and I look at it every day and think of him.

Both Bruce and Robert Kardashian came to the funeral, along with all my kids, of course, and many of my friends. We had the gathering after the funeral at the La Valencia Hotel because Dad loved La Valencia. He and my mom had spent a lot of happy times there for birthday dinners and celebrations. La Valencia has a beautiful room overlooking the sea. At the gathering, Robert came up to me. "I love you, but I have to go," he said. He told me our son, Rob, was going to drive back up with him so he didn't have to be alone. "This has been a lot for me," he told me. "I'm feeling really tired and really weak."

Oh, God, I thought. Not good. Robert was only fifty-nine. He shouldn't be feeling weak. He wasn't really getting aggressive treatment for his cancer, and I could see the disease taking its toll on him.

A couple of days after we buried Dad, I went home to my family. Robert was going downhill fast. Soon, he was bedridden. Kimberly and Kourtney spent practically every waking moment being there for him, taking care of him and feeding him. It was a huge life lesson for them for sure. It's terrible to watch the person who brought you into this world waste away. I felt so bad for my kids, and I knew exactly what they were going through at that exact moment because I had just suffered through the death of my dad. It still broke my heart.

The girls were there for him, just as I had been for my dad. Kourtney read to Robert, and Kim would make him Cream of Wheat, oatmeal, or a cup of tea. They called me regularly to give updates and reports. Khloé, however, emotionally shut down. She just couldn't handle the sadness. She had already lost her beloved grandfather, and now she was losing her father. She couldn't eat, sleep, or talk about it. She began losing weight, then gaining weight. She started going out and partying, which just wasn't her. Khloé just couldn't handle seeing someone she loved so much sick and dying.

At one point Robert's sister, Barbara, called me. "Why don't you come over? I'm going to be over there. Why don't you come see Robert?" So I went over to see Robert, and he and I sat outside talking for a while. He was really frail, but he was still coherent.

Soon after that, we all knew: it was time to say good-bye. Priscilla Presley had been a big part of Robert's life, and I called her and told her he didn't have much time left and asked her to call him. We facilitated a call between the two of them, and Priscilla was able to say good-bye.

Four weeks before Robert died, a woman he had only been dating a short time married him. She made it very difficult for us to get in to see him, and she made my children feel like they could not have easy access to their dad. I know that O.J. called the house to talk to Robert, and she wouldn't let him talk to him. No matter what you think about O.J., if Robert wanted to speak to him, he should have had the right to do so. When Robert's two best friends,

Larry Kraines and Randy Kolker, tried to visit him, she denied them access.

Finally, Larry just said, "I'm coming over." A second time, the woman denied Larry access to Robert. As he was driving away with his wife, Joyce, Larry turned around and decided nobody was going to keep him away from his friend. He finally got in to see Robert and say good-bye. It was weird and certainly uncomfortable, but at least they got to see him. I will always admire and respect Larry for his perseverance. It showed me he had great love for his friend.

The only moment of levity in the days before Robert died came when I told Kimberly, "We will probably never have the chance to go in his house again. Is there anything we can do to maybe get the things that I loaned to Daddy or any of the things that you want?"

There were things that held memories for both of us at Robert's house. But knowing that we had such limited access, Kim and I were afraid that we would lose those memories forever. Robert and I had lent each other things ever since I could remember, and when I moved from the big Hidden Hills house to the town house in Sherwood, Robert stored a lot of my stuff for me. After all, these were my belongings, and I just wanted them back.

"Pull up your car, and when she's not looking, I will run things out to your car!" Kim told me.

I pulled my Range Rover up to the front yard and driveway of Robert's house in Encino and left it running. We were like Bonnie and Clyde: Kim would come running out to my car with something, and I would wrap it up in a blanket and stash it in the back. Then she'd run back in and come out with something new, over and over again. We recovered the statues that Robert and I had bought from Angelo Donghia back in the 1970s, and we also retrieved my gorgeous Lalique vase that Robert and I bought when we were on a vacation in Paris the year we went to the Louvre. Sadly, we never found the many pieces of art I had lent Robert when I moved from Hidden Hills or the big, beautiful Dutch antique cabinet that Robert had given me for our tenth wedding anniversary. I'm sure that ended up in his Palm Springs house.

These things didn't hold a great deal of monetary value, but they were part of my memories with Robert. They also meant something to my kids. Later, Khloé was able to finally get Robert's childhood monkey, "Jocko." All Khloé wanted was that monkey. My kids just wanted the sentimental things that had belonged to their father, and let's just say they became increasingly hard to come by.

The day Robert passed away, September 30, I went into his room. It looked exactly the same as it always had. On this visit, my heart sank. He wasn't in his big, beautiful bed; he was just lying on this little gurney the nurse had set up for him. He couldn't have weighed more than eighty pounds, and it was horrible to see him suffering. He wasn't conscious, but I felt like he knew I was there. As I had done when I said my good-byes to my dad, I just talked to Robert, feeling that he heard me through the haze. I told him that our kids would be okay, that we were all going to be okay, and that he needed to know that before he left this earth. I told him how much I loved him and how much his kids adored him and I thanked him for being such a huge part of my life. I was able to tell him how much he meant to me. A moment or two passed after I finished speaking, I felt like he just wasn't there anymore. I could see his chest moving up and down and I could see that he was breathing, but I felt that he was already gone.

We had all had more than our shares of horror and grief for one month. On the day Robert died, just eight weeks after his diagnosis, part of me died with him. All of the kids were devastated. Poor

Khloé, though, had the worst time of all. She couldn't bring herself to see her father before he died, and now she couldn't go back and change that. She was so grief-stricken that she lost all her hair. It fell out in big clumps until she had no hair at all. She started wearing hats. She just couldn't get over the fact that her dad was gone, and her body was reacting to her tremendous stress and grief. She didn't know how to process it herself, so her body processed it for her. It took a lot of TLC to bring Khloé back to life.

On the day of Robert's funeral, Bruce and I drove up to Inglewood Park Cemetery, where Robert's entire family is buried, to find a capacity crowd. Hundreds of mourners packed the church. It was literally standing room only. People were pouring out the front door and onto the streets. I just looked up at the heavens and smiled, because I knew Robert would have appreciated a packed house. Robert's friends just loved him so much.

The whole Kardashian family was there, of course, and my kids were sitting with Robert's family in the front row. Bruce and I sat down next to our dear friends Shelli and Irving Azoff. Shelli is my best friend, and Irving had an amazing loyalty to Robert and he was one of Robert's best friends.

When I sat down next to Irving and Shelli, Irving turned to me. "What are you doing sitting here?" he asked. "You need to be sitting in the front with your children."

"Oh, no, no," I said. "That's not my place."

"No, actually, it is," Irving replied.

He rose from his seat and took a chair from the end of an aisle, and he put it beside the front row next to my kids. He directed me to sit in it. It was a powerful moment. I was, by then, Kris Jenner, but in some ways I would also always be a Kardashian, thankful for everything that Robert Kardashian had done for me through his incredible generosity and his love. He will forever be the father of the four wonderful children we had together; he will forever be in my heart. Irving somehow knew I would always love Robert. I will never forget that gesture on that day and it will always mean the world to me.

After the funeral, there was a gathering at the Bel-Air Country Club. Robert's family, along with A. C. Cowlings and every other familiar face from my past with Robert, was there—everyone but O.J.

Standing in the middle of that room with all of the friends and family that Robert and I had shared together, I realized that this was the same room where Robert and I had had our wedding reception. Almost all of the same people who were here now for Robert's funeral had been at the reception so many years before. *Life is so short*, I thought as I stood there, realizing that we really do have to make the best of every single second that we are given. I knew then that I had to be even stronger now for my kids.

Because now it was just me.

It's a profound moment when your children lose a parent and you are the only parent left. It was up to me then to help them make something of their lives. I had realized my lifelong dream of having six kids, and now I was done with the birthing and ready for the work. It was time to stop screwing around. It was time to get off my ass and get to work.

Shortly after my dad and Robert died, I realized that I really missed going to work at my mother's children's clothing store. The routine of the store centered me, and the hard work was an outlet for what I was going through. I had spent those months making sales, changing out display windows, selling T-shirts, and reordering stock, and I had a ball doing it. It freed my mother to take care of Dad and it took my mind off what they were going through.

Coming home after Dad's funeral and then coming home again

after Robert's funeral was a tough transition for me and my family. We couldn't "go back to normal" just like that. I was worried about my mom and my kids. Back in my house, with no job to go to, I felt useless. I couldn't figure out what to do with myself. But I knew I had to do something. I couldn't let grief get the best of me. I had to get moving, and I needed a new direction—fast. I realized that I was the only one who was responsible for ME. I couldn't change everything, but I could change ME. Life was going to pass me by if I didn't snap out of this funk.

Finally, I decided that I needed to open a store of my own. I had always wanted to do that, and I missed working in my mom's store. So, what better time was there? I have always tried to see the glass as half full. I had to find a way to bring my family together again for something joyful instead of something heartbreaking. Something fun, instead of funerals. Nothing could erase what we had been through, but creating a new direction for our family with something like a store could help us get back to the good in our lives.

"Just go out there, Kris, and do it," Mom told me when I mentioned my store idea to her.

I got out of bed the next morning and started scouting store locations. I didn't have a business plan. I didn't even know how I was going to pay the rent. I did have a vision of what the store would be. I've always loved fashion, and I obviously love kids, so the perfect match for me was to open a children's clothing store.

I was going to take out of storage Kendall and Kylie's gorgeous baby furniture that I had used when I decorated our house in Hidden Hills. Now they had big-girl rooms and didn't use it anymore. I was going to decorate the store with their baby furniture, just like a store I had always admired in Beverly Hills called Auntie Barbara's Kids, and make it look adorable and cute and sassy. I found the perfect location for the store, in Plaza Calabasas, the very first day.

I had grown up in a family business, so I instinctively turned to my family for help. First call: my eldest daughter, Kourtney. "I'm going to open a children's store," I told her. "Do you want to be my partner?"

Kourtney had just graduated from the University of Arizona, where she had studied fashion. She is great at design and has an eye for fashion, and I knew that she could open a store of her own someday. That was her dream. After all, she had gone to college for this very reason. She had always wanted to be a clothing designer, and she was already designing a line of her own T-shirts and selling them to different stores around town. I knew that she had fashion in her blood, but I don't think she had ever thought about designing or opening a store for children.

I convinced her that we were going to have the time of our lives. I knew I could sell ice to an Eskimo, so I knew I could talk Kourtney into joining me. She could be my partner, and it might help take both of our minds off my dad and Robert.

Everyone needs direction and motivation, and I felt that if I could motivate my kids, one by one, to find their dreams, I would be doing my job as their suddenly sole parent. The kids were coming to that point in their lives where it was time to say, "You're an adult. You're at the starting line. It's time to pull the trigger and go out there and do something with your skills."

I figured the store could be a starting point.

Kourtney said, "YES!"

As I had with my mother's store, Shannon & Co., I would use the new store as an outlet for my emotions. When I was feeling really sad, I started to imagine just how my beautiful children's store could look. I thought about all that fabulous furniture I had in storage and how perfect it would be in the store. I thought about how Bruce could help paint and build cabinets and do all of the things we loved doing together. Most businesses are all about the money, but this one was all about passion and dreams, recovery and renewal, and, most of all, bringing our family together in something good. I knew if we did all of that, the money would eventually come.

Four months after Robert died, we opened our children's store, Smooch. My best friend, Shelli Azoff, came up with the name. We all immediately loved the sound of it. It just sounded happy.

CHAPTER TWELVE

Keeping Up with the Kardashians

We opened Smooch to great success in 2004.

The store did well. For me, it was an enormous validation: Never give up on your dreams just because life gets in the way. I was almost fifty when I opened Smooch, and here I was, finally achieving something I'd spent a lifetime dreaming of doing. Working at my grandmother's store and my mom's store since I was thirteen, I knew I would end up someday with a store of my own. This was a really big deal. No matter how long you've had a dream, it can still come true if you persevere.

We worked there every day for three years. We didn't have any help or any employees. It was just Kourtney and me. I think that is what gave it a personal touch, and it really taught Kourtney

the business in shorthand, because she had to just jump in and
do it.

Within a couple of years, Kim and Khloé saw how much fun
we were having with Smooch, and they decided they would love to
open a store too. One store was enough for me, but I told them, "If
you two want to open a store with Kourtney, just the three of you,
I think you should."

Soon a space became available next to Smooch, and the girls
grabbed it. They thought long and hard about a name for the store
and finally ended up calling it DASH—first, because it's part of
their name, KarDASHian, and second, because Robert's friend
Chris Christian used to call him "Dash" as a nickname. So the
name DASH is a nod to both their name and their father. Just as
with Smooch, DASH found great success, and the girls developed
an amazing business.

At the same time we opened Smooch, we moved from the Sherwood Country Club back to Calabasas into our new house on a
street called Cordova Drive. Pretty soon everybody who knew our
family kept telling us the same thing: Your family is so crazy, you
should have a reality TV show.

I wasn't crazy about the idea, at least not at first. I knew what
Bruce had endured in *I'm a Celebrity . . . Get Me Out of Here!*
He had to fight for survival in the Outback of Australia with other
celebrities, including Robin Leach, Melissa Rivers, and Downtown
Julie Brown. That's pretty much what I knew about reality television. However, I also knew the power of success on television from
what it did for Bruce and me when we filmed our fitness infomercials in the nineties. So, whatever the basis of the show, I felt this
would be a piece of cake. That's just how I felt: *I can do this.*

I always thought our family was certainly entertaining enough—or maybe just crazy enough—to make a good reality show. So when someone told us we should film a pilot, we found the idea very interesting.

We shot a pilot in our house in Calabasas, and it was a lot of fun and didn't take very long. The producer was a woman who said she just wanted to capture the spirit of our family. When I saw the result, it didn't blow my socks off, but it was a start and I thought it was fun and interesting. The pilot included the three girls and myself and basically just followed us as we worked at our stores and hung out at home, doing our thing.

By then, my girls were getting some attention. Especially Kim, who by now was divorced, and began to go out, really for the first time in her life, frequently with her longtime friend Paris Hilton. Paris's mother, Kathy, and I had known each other since the 1980s, back when we were both having babies, and Kourtney, Kim, Khloé, and the Hilton daughters, Paris and Nicky, had all grown up together. As the girls grew older, they all stayed in contact, traveling to places like Vegas or the Hamptons together, and we always saw Kathy and Rick at all of their beautiful parties and around town. Kathy and Rick even gave me my baby shower when I had Kendall. I adore Kathy and Rick and will always consider them dear friends.

Eventually, Paris took off in the public eye and became very, very famous. Paris started asking Kim to go everywhere with her. The girls traveled the world—Australia, Europe, all over. Kim was Paris's sidekick, and they had a ball together. The media started noticing Kim because she was always with Paris. They really started paying attention when Kim, the hopeless romantic among my girls, was introduced to Nick Lachey shortly after he split from his first wife Jessica Simpson. I heard Nick and Kim were going out on a date to the movies, and I thought, *Well, that will be fun.*

I didn't hear much more about it, but the next morning I woke up to find Nick and Kim plastered all over the Internet. Every single media outlet was reporting it: TMZ, *Entertainment Tonight*, *Access Hollywood*, and more. When the weekly magazines came out that week, it was the same thing: they were the hot new couple in every magazine. I thought, *But it was just one date!* It was so funny to me that things could get blown out of proportion that quickly. I mean, I knew the media, but that was an introduction to pop culture I had not had before.

Even more important than any of this was the fact that I still had to get my son into college. Rob was finishing up high school, leading me to my greatest mission: to get him accepted at the University of Southern California.

That had been Robert Kardashian's dream: for his only son to attend his alma mater, USC. From the day Rob was born until the day Robert passed away, he talked about it, dreamed about it, planned it. There was no other college in Robert's eyes. He wore USC caps, USC T-shirts, USC everything. Having one of his children get into USC was his life's dream. It was the only choice.

College was a very big deal for Robert Kardashian. He was the one who studied with the kids and emphasized academics. He talked about college endlessly with all of them, and he helped Kourtney when she was applying to SMU. He helped the kids fill out the paperwork; he helped them study for tests; and he helped them finish their homework. I was so grateful that he took over the educational component for my older kids, because when they were preparing for college, I had two babies to care for. College became Robert's department.

Now Robert was gone. College was my responsibility. Rob was finishing high school at the Buckley School. We had sent our kids to Buckley since 1980, and the school knew our kids like family. They knew what Rob had gone through when his father was sick and passed away. They really got behind me and wanted to help me get Rob to USC. Without the faculty and staff of Buckley and their guidance, I would have been lost. I started going to meetings there regularly to talk about the college application process.

Then it came time to get recommendation letters for Rob's application, and I went on a full-fledged promotional campaign for my son. I called my dear friend, USC alumnus Frank Gifford, and he wrote the most wonderful recommendation letter for Rob. My dear friend L.A. attorney Howard Weitzman had known Rob since he was born and was able to write about Robert Kardashian's passionate wish for Rob to go to USC. I talked to everyone I could think of; it was like waging a political campaign.

I will never forget the sense of relief I had after Rob's application was submitted and completed and in the mail. Of course, my relief was coupled with a terror that he would not be accepted.

The day of Rob's interview on campus, I dressed like I was going to meet the queen of England, from my high heels to my business suit. Walking onto that campus that day was very emotional. I knew that someday I might be there for something like this, but I never thought I would be doing it alone. I never thought I would be doing it without Robert Kardashian. Actually, I wasn't alone: I had Bruce Jenner by my side. And that proved to be extremely important. Bruce Jenner, in fact, has always been by my side since I met him, picking up the pieces and propping me up. Bruce was amazing. Bruce *is* amazing. He is always there to love and support me. I will always be grateful for this man, who loves my children and me unconditionally, even the children who are not biologically his.

That day, parking the car at USC, Bruce was as excited as Rob and I were. He got himself completely wrapped up in this excitement—the Getting Rob into USC Campaign. Bruce had promised Robert Kardashian when he was dying that he would be there to take care of his children, and I think Bruce saw this as an extension of that promise. When we stepped into that meeting with the dean of admissions that day, Bruce knew how important it was to all of us and he was just as devoted to the cause.

There was an audible buzz in the department when we arrived.

Not about me.

It was all about Bruce.

Bruce Jenner is here.

With Rob Kardashian.

After the meeting, I felt good about Rob's chances. Still, after his application was complete, it was a waiting game. I rushed to the mailbox every single day. Some days I would just sit on the steps outside my front porch, waiting for the mailman to arrive. Soon we became really friendly. I felt the mailman was part of my family. After all, he was about to deliver one of the most important letters of my life. When the mail was delivered, I would rifle through it, sifting through the junk and the catalogs, searching for the envelope with the USC seal. I knew that this would be a really big deal in Rob's life. Oddly—and irresponsibly—I didn't have a Plan B. You know how kids apply to different schools? Rob applied to exactly one: USC. There was no other school; there was no other option. I just focused all my attention and my energy on that one school, and I wasn't about to take no for an answer. "If someone says no, you're talking to the wrong person." That's been my lifelong motto.

One day I rushed to the mailbox, and there it was: the letter I felt I had been waiting for my entire life. I saw the USC seal. I started to shake, I got so nervous. I ran inside and sat in my living room, holding this letter in my lap, thinking, *It's addressed to my son, but I really need to open this.* I wanted it to be a big surprise.

But if I opened it and it was a rejection, what was I going to do? How would I tell my son that his dad's dream of him going to USC had gone up in smoke? I remember sitting there so scared. The uncertainty was driving me crazy. I just had to know. Finally, I slid a fingernail under the back of the letter and pried it open. Just a little. So it wouldn't be obvious that it had been tampered with. I opened it just enough and very slowly, carefully . . .

I peeked inside. I could only see the first word . . . and it said, "Congratulations."

I screamed. I burst into tears. I was alone, but felt like Robert Kardashian was there with me. I started jumping up and down in the living room, yelling, "We did it! We did it! Robert, we did it! We did it!"

Of course, I knew all along that Robert Kardashian was probably running the show from up there in heaven, and I really felt his presence that day.

What to do now? Celebrate! I ran out to Chick's, a sporting goods store where I knew they sold USC merchandise. I bought everything with a USC logo on it: USC caps, USC T-shirts, everything USC. Back home, I took the acceptance letter and all of the USC stuff and put it in a box, which I gift wrapped. I called Bruce and told him to come home immediately. I called all of my kids and told them to rush right over. Soon the whole family was gathered in our house in Calabasas. Finally, Rob came home from school.

"What's up?" he said.

"I just bought you a present," I said, and gave him the big box.

He opened the box and saw all of the USC paraphernalia, and we all started crying and screaming and congratulating him. Wow. I knew Robert was smiling, just as we all were on that amazing day.

Rob went to USC, to the business school, and he became a straight-A student. I know that part of his motivation was that he knew he needed to do his best for his dad. He wanted to make his dad proud, because they had talked about USC so many times. That was the mission; that was the goal. Mission accomplished. I am so proud of my son.

After living on Cordova Drive in Calabasas for about eighteen months, I was still on a never-ending search for the perfect house for my family, bugging my real estate agent, Marc Shevin, on a daily basis. Even though we had a beautiful house on Cordova Drive, I was bound and determined to get back into Hidden Hills. Every day I called Marc. "Is anything for sale? Is anything for sale?" I would ask him. But there was nothing on the market.

Then, right after we shot the pilot for the reality show, Marc called me. "Kris, there's a house that might be coming on the market," he said. "I want to drive you by it."

I jumped in the car and met him in front of Hidden Hills, where I hopped in his car and we drove through the gate. He started driving me down one particular street, and my heart started racing. "Oh my God . . ." I said to Marc. "Could we possibly be going to my favorite house?"

As we drove closer and closer, I could barely breathe.

"I don't know," said Marc. "Which one is your favorite house?"

There was one particular house that I used to drive by all the time in Hidden Hills. If you were going to write a fairy tale about a cottage in the woods, this house would be that cottage. It was set back from the street, a Cape Cod–style home with a long driveway over a stream with a big wraparound porch with rocking chairs and a porch swing. It had beautiful pink roses all over the place.

Sure enough, we pulled into the driveway of my fairy-tale house. I knew instantly: this was *the* house I had been searching for for so long. This was the perfect house for our crazy Hollywood family, a modern-day Brady Bunch, in an adorable, Cape Cod, all-American dream. We had found that house for a reason, and I would discover that reason soon enough.

"Oh my God, oh my God!" I screamed "This is the house I have been walking and driving by. I love this house!"

"Well, the owner wants to sell it," Marc said.

"I'll take it!" I said.

"You haven't even seen the inside yet."

"I know, but I love this house. I *have* to have this house."

I had Marc make an offer immediately. I didn't even go inside of the house until after we'd made the offer. When I saw the interior, I loved the house even more. By that evening we had a signed contract. It was the craziest thing, but it was also the perfect thing. Once again, I had to tell Bruce. This time he was excited! He actually sat up with me all night with the negotiations back and forth. By midnight we were moving, this time back into my beloved Hidden Hills.

Yet again I had the feeling: *This is exactly where I'm supposed to be.* Finding my dream house after such a long and winding search was almost surreal. I realized it had all been part of a long journey on which I had to take every single step. Every move and everything we had gone through had led us to this incredible house, and even one step not taken—no matter how painful— might not have brought me here. I knew it was God who had taken me on a path and I had to put one step in front of the other—to live in house after house after house—for a very important reason.

This house was more than a house. This house was a stage. This was the house that everybody would fall in love with. This was a house *dying* for an audience. I never could have dreamed of how large that audience would become.

———

Life was so good. Kim was thriving in her styling and closet organization business, styling and organizing the closets of friends like Bernadette and Sugar Ray Leonard, and Nicole Richie. Kourtney and Khloé were completely absorbed in their stores. Bruce's business was booming. And I had finally found what I felt at last was my dream house. Things began to fall into place in an incredible way. Thirty days after we unpacked and we were settling in, our dear friends Jerry and Deena Katz came over for dinner. Deena was the casting director for Bruce's reality show, *I'm a Celebrity . . . Get Me Out of Here!* and she had been a good friend ever since. When she visited us in our new house in Hidden Hills, she had become the casting director for *Dancing with the Stars*.

Deena was sitting in my kitchen of my Cape Cod dream house, watching the chaos of our life swirl around her.

Kim rushed in and announced, "I'm spending the night." Kourtney came over, changed into her bathing suit, and said, "Can I use your pool?" Our two little girls, Kendall and Kylie, were running around the house—all while I tried to make us dinner with the phone ringing off the wall. We were laughing and talking and I was booking speeches for Bruce even while all this was going on. Someone called for Kylie, and I pushed the intercom button and said, "Kylie, line one!"

Then: "Kim, line two!"

And: "Khloé, line three!"

When Kylie didn't answer, I hit the intercom again. "Kylie, line one!" I said.

Then I went back to cooking dinner.

Afterward Deena stared at me in bewilderment. "Did you just intercom your ten-year-old?" she asked.

"Yeah," I said nonchalantly. There was nothing unusual about that to me. This was my life.

"You are hysterical," said Deena. "This is the craziest house I have ever been in! You really need a reality show!"

"Oh, that's funny," I said. "Why are you the thirtieth person to say that to me this week?"

"Because it's true," she said. "Just being around your life and the people you hang out with and the way you guys all are together. Don't you see how unique that is? You, your daughters and your son, and your husband, and the little girls . . ."

She stopped in mid-sentence.

"You know, I really think you should talk to Ryan Seacrest's people," Deena said. "He is over at E! producing shows, and this is right up his alley. He would love this."

"I'm all ears," I replied. "Get me a meeting."

The next morning Deena called me and said, "Can you get over to Ryan's office?"

"When?" I asked.

"Now!" she said.

I jumped in my car and drove right over.

Ryan Seacrest had an office over at E! in this ginormous, gorgeous, sort of modern brick building on Wilshire Boulevard. I drove down Wilshire and couldn't believe I was going to talk to Ryan Seacrest about doing a reality show about our family. I pulled up and gave my car to the valet, then went up in the elevator to the lobby and this enormous area where you wait until someone comes down to get you. I sat in that room for five minutes or so, looking around at pictures of the iconic people who had done shows on E!, including Paris Hilton and Nicole Richie.

An assistant came down and took me to Eliot Goldberg's office. Eliot was Ryan's producing partner and the president of Ryan's company. He asked me to tell him what our show might be like. I winged it the best I could, saying that it would be a blow-by-blow look at our crazy, loving, fun, and incredibly close family. By the time Ryan walked in, it felt like I actually might be onto something.

I told them that it would be a show about Kourtney, Kimberly, Khloé, Kendall, Kylie, Bruce, Rob, and me. I was hoping to get some extended family members, too—including my mom and hopefully some of our friends.

"The family dynamic is what would make this a special show, and it is what we need to focus on," I told Ryan and Eliot. There was so much media coverage swirling around Kim then, both positive and negative, that we knew that we had to act fast and take advantage of the moment. "Timing is everything in entertainment and pop culture," I remember saying. "The Osbournes were so successful in their show," I added, "and we think we could have the same kind of success. The girls would be the stars of the show, but all of us around the girls will be the ones that people can relate to. We will be able to broaden our demographic and our audience because, together, we span all kinds of age groups. We could cover ten to one hundred."

They were nodding agreement, which I took as a good sign.

"This sounds like a project that could be really, really fun," Ryan and Eliot told me.

Just goes to show: passion can be as powerful as preparation. Other than the informal pilot that I shot, I had never done anything remotely like a reality TV show before. But I knew that if we could come up with a format, we would have ourselves a TV show. And it would be a hit. I thought about the show in terms much bigger than just the girls. I thought this could definitely be a family show, because anytime you do a show with that many personalities, you are bound to have both the funny and the dramatic elements that can appeal to more people.

Ryan is one of those guys who get very excited and animated—he has great energy—and I could tell he "got" it. He had a vision.

When you are pitching a show to someone, you want them to get on your bandwagon and see the same thing you are seeing in your head. It's organic. And Ryan and Eliot GOT it. They just did. It was one of those magical moments where everything clicked.

I was feeling so positive about the meeting, I pressed my luck a bit.

"I'd like to be an executive producer," I said. "I need to have my hands in this. I need to have some control."

"Let's do it," Ryan and Eliot said.

The next day, Ryan took the show idea to E!, since that was where his company had a production deal.

A few hours later I got the call from Ryan and Eliot.

"Congratulations!" they said. "We have a show."

That night, I invited the entire family for dinner in Hidden Hills. When everyone was at the dinner table, I stood up. "Family, you're not going to believe this," I said, "but we got our own reality show, and it's going to be on E!."

Kim and Khloé jumped up from their chairs, they were so happy.

Kourtney was a little quiet, because she was somewhat hesitant. She had just met her new boyfriend, Scott Disick, at that point. But she's a team player, and she eventually said, "Okay, Mom, I'll do it."

"You don't have to do it," I reassured her. "Nobody *has* to do it, but this is what I really, really want to do." Every single one of them said yes, they would do it.

Bruce was still sitting in his chair, dumbstruck.

"What?" he said. "We're going to do *what*?!" He shook his head. "I am a motivational speaker. I am an Olympic athlete! I am going to do a reality show about my family?"

"You won't regret it, honey, I promise you. You won't regret it."

Bruce is such a chill guy. He just shook his head.

"Oh, God," he said, preparing for another roller-coaster ride. "You guys are crazy. Okay, why not? I'll try it."

The morning after we sold the show, I woke up with butterflies in my stomach. *Buckle up, it's going to be a bumpy ride!* I thought to myself. I didn't know what to expect. I also knew I was going back to work on a whole different level than I had been at the store. I knew I was going to be running everyone's careers.

I was about to meld my roles as Mom and Manager: I was about to become a Momager.

Up until that point, Kim had been doing club appearances on her own, and she was very popular in that scene. The clubs were clamoring for her. She was also getting offers for deals with clothing manufacturers. The positive attention was thrilling for all of us. But I knew that once all the girls were on a television show, these opportunities were going to multiply exponentially, and quickly. That meant I needed to gear up for handling something very big, because I knew this was going to take 150 percent of my energy, effort, and creativity. Whatever it took, I wanted this venture to be a huge success.

First step? Meet our new producers at Bunim/Murray productions. Bunim/Murray was the production company partnering with Ryan and Eliot and E! to actually film and make our show.

The first person from Bunim/Murray who came walking into my house was Farnaz Farjam, our new show runner and producer, whose résumé included *The Simple Life*. She brought her entire crew, along with Jeff Jenkins and Jon Murray. Jon Murray is one of the owners and founders of Bunim/Murray, and Jeff Jenkins helps run the company.

I was so nervous meeting all of them that night. I made drinks and my famous guacamole and chips and we put out a little spread for all of them. I loved Farnaz the minute she walked into my house, but I was a little taken aback: she was so young, beautiful, and sweet.

This is the girl who is going to run our show? I thought. She would come to be one of my closest friends.

I didn't really understand how important that first meeting was, but because of our chemistry and the connection we all felt that first night, it turned out to be a great thing. We had a great night: we talked about our lives, where we lived, our Hidden Hills dream house. They asked us our thoughts on what the show could be. It was a really special night. We felt like a team already.

Next, we went to the Bunim/Murray team's offices—and their drawing boards—and started putting together the necessary camera crews and sound teams and pulling together the actual people who would make our show possible. They started talking to us about how the daily work would go: hair, makeup, microphones on every morning. They asked for one promise from us: no matter what happened, the cameras would continue rolling.

The first day of filming came a month later. Thirty days after we signed on with Ryan Seacrest and E!, a camera crew was at my house. On Day 1, we shot our show titles. Show titles are the iconic images that open every episode of a show. We stood in front of our house and there were cameras, booms, jibs, microphones, and 150 or so production people milling about—and all of us in full hair and makeup and dressed to the nines. We still have the same show title—the scenes that play before our theme song, a whimsical, whistled tune—the perfect reflection of the usually chaotic energy around us.

Here's how the show title goes: the camera bounces between close-ups of our faces and individual shots of us while we attempt to arrange ourselves as a family in front of a backdrop of Hollywood. There's a lot of shuffling and elbowing and nudging involved as we fight for the best angle and shot of each of us. Bruce and I are in matching plum colors (my dress, his shirt). Kendall and Kylie are dressed in glittery miniskirts and animal prints. Khloé towers above the rest of us in glamorous, sparkly gold sequins. Kourtney is in a little pewter dress. Rob says, "I need someone to make me laugh."

"Where's Kim?" I ask.

"Kim is always late," says one of the girls off camera.

Finally, Kim rushes up and inserts herself in the shot, hands on hips and filling out a ruby red Herve Leger dress, looking fabulous as always. When we are finally assembled, little Kylie pulls on a rope and the backdrop of Los Angeles falls to reveal a shot of the front of our Cape Cod dream house.

"That's it, we're done," says a crew member off camera.

"Money," says another.

Everything and everyone was in place, but we were having trouble coming up with a name for the show. All of us were trying to think of the perfect name: our family, Ryan and Eliot's company, everyone at Bunim/Murray. In the meantime, our show runner, Farnaz, was running in a hundred different directions trying to catch us all on film. Kim was in Vegas, I was running down to San Diego to visit my mom, Kourtney was in Malibu, and Khloé was running around Beverly Hills . . . crises, comedy, and cameras following us everywhere we went. We would go to meetings, and then Kim would need to rush right out for a different meeting—at the Playboy Mansion, for example. Bruce was driving carpool for Kendall and Kylie while juggling his own career and his regular golf game. We each had our own crazy schedule. The crew was like, "Oh my God, these people are driving us crazy! There's so many of them and they all go in different directions!"

One day Farnaz was late to a meeting. She came rushing in and said, breathlessly, "I'm sorry I am late. I'm just having a really hard time keeping up with the Kardashians."

Everyone stopped talking. There was total silence. Everyone turned and stared at her, and she said, "What?!" Then she got it. "Oh my God, that's it: *Keeping Up with the Kardashians*!" Farnaz said.

I wasn't in the meeting. When they told me the name, I loved it, but I said, "But what about Bruce Jenner?"

"Oh, it's going to be fine," they said, and of course, Bruce being Bruce, it was.

We wanted the show to be mostly about the girls. That their family just happens to include a stepdad who has his own name and celebrity, well, the producers thought that was just an added bonus. *Keeping Up with the Kardashians and the Jenners* just didn't have the same ring to it. So we went with *Kardashians* alone. Everyone, including Bruce, knew it was the perfect name. Bruce is such a good sport, and he would never let ego get in the way of something like that.

The producers were counting on our lives being interesting enough to be entertaining. We knew that for our reality show, we needed to show our life in full. In order to set that up, the producers needed to know all about our life. They were asking us questions: "What's going on? What are you guys doing? What do we need to film?" They needed to know all our comings and goings so they could get production clearance for any restaurants, clubs, hospitals, hotels, office buildings, and more. If we had a doctor appointment they thought might be interesting, they needed to make sure they could shoot it.

One day I called a family meeting.

When we were all together at Hidden Hills, I said, "Look, guys. We have to make a decision right now if we are going to go on this journey together and let everything hang out. I think the only way to make this show successful is to really be real about it, and if stuff happens—and I don't have a crystal ball, so I don't even know what that could mean—we have to be able to roll with it and let them tape it and show it, no matter what. Okay?"

I looked around the room. They all stared at me at first, surely thinking, *What has she gotten us into now?* But then everyone said yes; they all agreed to let the cameras keep rolling, no matter what. What did we have to fear? Nothing. We have no skeletons; everything about us is out in the open anyway. We all thought, *Why not?* We were now off to the races, ready to face the cameras, waiting for something wild, crazy, funny, dramatic, and exciting to happen. We didn't have to wait long.

Our show premiered on October 4, 2007. The first episode began with Bruce and my sixteenth wedding anniversary. But the show opened with me talking about Kim's ass. The opening shot showed Kim from behind, looking in my fridge, and me commenting on the "junk in her trunk" to the other family members in my family room. Khloé immediately called me out. "Mom, she's always had an ass," she said. "Where did this come from?" Kourtney called me "catty." "I hate you all!" Kim declared.

Then we cut to voice-overs and a montage of scenes about the main characters: our family.

"Welcome to my family. I'm Kim Kardashian. My sisters say I'm a bitch. But I always have their best interests at heart," Kim said.

"I'm Kourtney. I'm the oldest and the most mature."

"I'm Kris Jenner. I'm the mom and Kim's manager. Say what you want, but I know what's best for my kids . . . and my husband."

"I'm Bruce Jenner, and I am a pushover for my family . . . up to a point."

Me again: "And then Bruce and I together have Kendall and Kylie Jenner."

"So it's six kids and two crazy parents," said Kim. "We're the modern-day Brady Bunch with a kick. There's a lot of baggage that comes with us. But it's like Louis Vuitton baggage . . . You always want it."

The first season went by in a blur, beginning with our sixteenth anniversary party. One guest was our dear friend Robin Antin, creator and the choreographer of the Pussycat Dolls, whom Kim took into my bedroom to show her the anniversary gift she had given us as a gag: a stripper pole. If you remember, stripper poles were all the rage back then; even Oprah had Teri Hatcher on her show to demonstrate the newest exercise craze: pole dancing. It wasn't meant to be strip-club sexy; it was just meant to be an exercise tool to go along with the newest exercise craze. Robin started demonstrating a new routine on the pole, when Kylie, then ten, walked in and began imitating Robin's routine. It turned out to be a little more salacious than intended, and clearly Kylie was just being a kid. But when Bruce found her in there, he hauled her out quickly.

The cameras kept rolling. When the episode aired, people were absolutely outraged that I had my ten-year-old daughter on my stripper pole. If it had happened without cameras there, nobody would have flinched. Everyone was just talking in my bedroom, and Kylie was only trying to be included. It just looked scandalous when taken out of context.

During that first season, Kim made her first live television talk show appearance on *The Tyra Banks Show*. Not long after that, we got a call from *Playboy*: they wanted Kim to model for a spread. My instinct was to say yes. *Playboy* is iconic and historic. Marilyn Monroe was on the very first cover. Farrah Fawcett, Janet Jackson, Cindy Crawford, Ursula Andress, Jayne Mansfield, and Linda

Evans all did *Playboy*. It was an honor for Kim to be among the list of spectacular, beautiful women who have posed for *Playboy*. Kim was hesitant at first, but I assured her that she would not have to take all her clothes off. After the pictures came back, Hef was very pleased with them, but he wanted more photos of Kim—this time wearing less. Hef invited us to the Playboy Mansion and, camera still rolling, convinced Kim to do a second shoot, this time wearing nothing but a dozen long strands of strategically placed pearls. Determined to show me how it felt to be naked in front of the camera, Kim as a joke arranged for me to have my own photo shoot wrapped in American flags, wearing nothing but Bruce's gold medal.

Here my daughter had posed for *Playboy*, which was a controversial move. But for her to follow that by playing this joke on me spoke volumes and set the tone of the show. Kim came back at me with humor, because we love each other, and that photo shoot was yet another milestone for me. It showed me that no matter what we went through and no matter how much pain it caused, we could always overcome any kind of adversity through humor, laughter, and our love for each other. It also showed me that our show didn't need to be a train wreck. It could be funny! It could be about our family and how we get through things with laughter and love. It could show audiences that we're a real family, with real problems and real happy endings. This incident—Kim posing for *Playboy*, followed by me posing with the gold medal—taught us not to be afraid to make fun of ourselves. We were having a great time; why not show it? I knew right then that everything was all going to be okay.

Working with and for my children was a huge step in this experience. I realized that if I was going to tackle this whole situation and be there and manage my family, I had to commit emotionally, physically, and intellectually 150 percent. There was no way to do this half-assed. I knew I could not do this as a hobby, or part-time, or for just a couple of hours a day. This job required that I live, breathe, eat, sleep it 24/7, and once I decided to do that and make that emotional commitment to myself and to my family, there was no turning back. I was not only a mother, daughter, and wife but also a producer, a manager, negotiator, a publicist, a business manager, a stylist, and at times a caterer and a set decorator. Suddenly, I had to keep track of everyone's schedules and even tell the girls when to work out.

I was developing a brand, managing all these people who were practically living under the same roof, and what I didn't realize was that when things went wrong, which was inevitable, the natives would get restless. We knew how to deal with each other on the mother-daughter level, but adding the business element had its challenges. I had to learn how to deal with each child and his or her needs individually. They each have different goals, expectations, and personalities. It was a dance, and I had to dance differently with each one. Of my daughters, Kourtney is a tango, spicy and difficult at times. Khloé is a salsa, sassy and all over the place, perpetually changing directions. Kim is a waltz, easy, smooth, and beautiful.

Then, in our first season, Kim thought about firing me as her manager and finding someone else. I was devastated. Kim and I are like twin souls. So for me not to feel what she was feeling at that moment was unusual for us. It was a deeply raw moment. The cameras were rolling. I got upset and headed straight to the spa, leaving a message on my phone with Kim's cell number and instructing callers to call Kim directly. (She received hundreds of calls in an afternoon.) That was one of the several times when I did feel the urge to turn off the cameras—times when we went through deeply raw and personal issues—but I chose not to, and I am glad.

In the end, she and I got back on the same page. It was a reminder to me that although these are my daughters, they are also clients, and they need respect and consideration. And I think Kim saw how very deeply I cared not only about her but also about this job, and she had new respect for me too.

We taped a segment mourning the anniversary of Robert Kardashian's passing and did our best to come to peace with his loss while still desperately always missing him. In the aftermath of the anniversary of her father's passing, Khloé made a huge mistake and got a DUI. She had to face the consequences, which included a night in jail. At another point in the season, the girls and I were flown down to *Girls Gone Wild* creator Joe Francis's house in Cabo in Joe's private jet for a swimsuit photo shoot—without telling Bruce the truth about where we were going or why. (When he found out, he showed up furious in Cabo to confront us even as we posed on the beach in bikinis.)

We kept rolling through everything—the good, the bad, the crazy, and the scandalous—and *Keeping Up with the Kardashians* struck a nerve. People began talking about our family around the water cooler at work. We exceeded the hopes of our producers and the network in the ratings.

The bottom line was that our first season was ratings gold, and we knew we had a hit on our hands. We didn't have time to even celebrate because the network signed us up for Season Two. We immediately began filming our *E! True Hollywood Story* and Season Two of *Keeping Up with the Kardashians* without even taking a break.

CHAPTER THIRTEEN

Building the Brand: *Check!*

One of the challenges as I get up and go to work every day is that I know I will live longer if I can try on some level to keep stress to a minimum (LOL). My dear friend and Robert's cousin Cici and I have an amazing, long, and beautiful relationship. I don't know what I would have done without her in my life. We met when I met Robert and I was just a teenager, and we just bonded like sisters. We have a long-standing routine that whenever something iconic or BIG happens, or if we mark something off of our "bucket list," we just e-mail each other with "This just happened to me," or "I just did this, I'm so excited!" And we end the e-mail with the word "Check!" As in "Check that off the list!"

Sometimes I will email her some good news and she will simply write back "Check!" and I always laugh. I laugh because she is the most supportive and upbeat person I know and yet she fights for her life every day. She has taught me about what a positive attitude can do as she struggles daily with her battle with cancer. Cici will squeal with delight when she knows I have accomplished a goal of mine, or accomplished the impossible for the day. I have learned more from her than she will ever know. But the biggest thing I have learned from her is how to have laughter in the midst of adversity, and love in the midst of uncertainty. Her belief in God and her positive attitude get her through, and her selflessness and unflappable strength are something I admire and I strive to achieve. She helped to make me the woman I am today and has encouraged me to set goals and aspirations and given me the freedom to be my true self. She has never judged me, and she is the best friend I have ever had.

My list of things to achieve had a lot of boxes to check off . . . and I started working hard to check them off one by one.

First, the show, which was the vehicle for everything that would follow. We never took a break after filming the first season; we just continued filming the second season immediately. And then a third. And a fourth.

I knew we were onto something big. And I loved the business side of all of this. That's what drove me, that's what excited me: the possibility to make this into something so much more than a TV show. Every time we renewed for another season, I would think to myself: *How can I take these fifteen minutes of fame and turn them into thirty? How can I get paid to do what I love?* I felt like I had a responsibility to not only turn out a really good show season after season but to use the show for a springboard for something permanent, something lasting for the kids. I was, after all, now the manager of my kids. I was responsible for their futures. I took my job very seriously. So while I was producing that television series, I also had to find some time to think about what would come next.

Throughout my personal life, I've had to be the mom, the wife, and the daughter. Now I had to be the manager, the businesswoman, the television host, and the leader of the pack. I was the one that my family was looking to, asking, "Okay, Mom, what's next?" I had to be so on top of it all, because I didn't want to let anybody down. I had spent my entire life taking care of my family, and the last thing I wanted to do was waste this amazing opportunity.

I felt that if the girls were going to work this hard and show me that they could be this responsible and this devoted to something, then why not let them try their hands at whole new levels in the business world? Every six months, Kim and I would sit down and ask each other, "Okay, what are our goals?"

I felt like this was what I was born to do. I loved this process. First of all, I felt like the luckiest girl in the world, because I got to wake up every morning and work with my family. But even more, I loved being able to figure out what business opportunities suited which person, which person could handle what. It had to be a good fit. It couldn't just be "Oh, we're going to endorse this, do that, and make this appearance"; everybody has a different personality, so each person was going to have a different path, from which passions to pursue to which products to endorse. When you are doing a television show, you not only have eighteen-hour days of filming; you also have all the press and travel that go along with promoting the show . . . Before you know it, the show leads to other things . . .

The first thing that happened was our show went international. One after another, countries around the world started watching *Keeping Up with the Kardashians*. When audiences in the United States were watching Season Three, audiences in Brazil, Argentina, and Australia were watching Season Two. Soon audiences around the world were having the Kardashian experience. Little by little, the rest of the world was falling in love with the family. It was crazy. We were like, *What?!*

I remember going to Mexico and turning on the TV, and there

I was on the screen. I thought, *Wow, this is crazy. I'm in another country and I'm watching myself on TV.*

I think that foreign audiences fell in love with the same things people fell in love with in the States: our spontaneity and our willingness to let *everything* hang out for the cameras. It was definitely a universal acceptance, which was a very heady feeling.

I was able to check another goal off my wish list. International television show? *Check!*

The next goal was a lifelong one: to have a talk show or to be a television host. As I mentioned earlier, one of my best friends is Kathie Lee Gifford. For thirty years I watched her work as a TV host and was always so proud of her. I loved that she had this amazing career, and I really admired her and the fact that she always did so much, both professionally and personally. I always dreamed of having a great full-time TV job like hers someday. But who goes after dreams like that at the age of fifty? Who would think that anyone over thirty-five could re-create herself on television?

In 2008, Kim was asked to do *Dancing with the Stars* for ABC. I encouraged her to do the show because I thought it was an amazing opportunity to attract people who don't watch E! *Dancing with the Stars* could tap into a whole new audience. If Kim could gain some favor and win some hearts on *Dancing with the Stars*, maybe viewers of that show would wander over to our network.

Kim was a little nervous. She's not a dancer. She doesn't have any moves on the dance floor. She was never the kid who went to tap or ballet lessons. That wasn't Kim. But it was *my* thing—I loved to dance—and I persuaded her to do it. I would have loved to have done *Dancing with the Stars*, and here, as with things before, I was able to live vicariously through Kim.

Kim will listen to what I have to say, really think about it, and she will often take my advice. She commits herself 150 percent to whatever it is I ask her to do. It is amazing to have a kid who, as an adult, really sees the same vision and has the same goals that I do. Kim really gets it; and she's a trouper.

Well, after Kim accepted the job with *Dancing with the Stars*, the producer Linda Bell Blue, the producer from *Entertainment Tonight* and *The Insider*, called me and asked me for a meeting. At the meeting, Linda said, "Will you be a correspondent on our show for *Dancing with the Stars* while your daughter is in the competition?" Life was just getting better and better by the day. Now, not only was my daughter going to be on *Dancing with the Stars*, but they were asking *me* to be a cohost on *The Insider*. I was over the moon. I literally couldn't believe that a dream that I'd had for my entire life was coming true.

I worked alongside Lara Spencer, lifestyle editor of *Good Morning America*, who later became a dear friend. At first I had no idea how I could make it work. I was already shooting my own television show eighteen hours a day, seven days a week. I also had to attend every rehearsal and every performance for *Dancing with the Stars* because I was Kim's manager. How could I take on another show?

Luckily, *Entertainment Tonight* and *The Insider* taped at 5:00 a.m. A car picked me up at around 3:15 in the morning and drove me, in the dark, to Paramount's Radcliffe studios in the San Fernando Valley. By the time I arrived at the studio, it was about 3:45 a.m. and I would go into hair and makeup and be on set by 5:00. When I drove home after taping it was only 8:00 a.m. I was already in hair and makeup and I was able to walk right onto the set of *Keeping Up with the Kardashians*, which of course was being filmed in my house. I did that for nine months. It was a real test of my energy, my dedication, my passion, and my work ethic. And I pulled it off.

Next goal on my wish list, to cohost a major network television show: Check!

Kim did three episodes of *Dancing with the Stars* before the judges ended her run. Dancing is just not her thing and she is confident enough to admit it. But she challenged herself to do something outside her comfort zone and worked her ass off while making some lifelong friends in the process. I remember her first dance with Mark Ballas (who now, years later, is giving her dancing lessons for her wedding). It was a fox-trot, and Kim was so gorgeous with a flapper hairstyle and a long beaded gown. She looked elegant and confident, and took the judges' critiques very professionally.

Kim learned a lot from this experience, and I did too. It taught me a lot about my ability to work hard, get up early, and expand my horizons. It also taught me that you never know when or how one experience will lead to the next opportunity. After *Dancing with the Stars* ended, *The Insider* sent me to cover the Super Bowl in January 2009. As it turned out, it would be an extremely fateful Super Bowl for me businesswise.

Leaving my hotel for the game, I rushed into the elevator. I had to get to the stadium before a certain time or they wouldn't let me onto the field. Bruce Springsteen was performing, and I didn't want to be late. There was one other person in the elevator on that day. He was a big guy with white tube socks and a beach chair in his hand and binoculars around his neck, wearing a Super Bowl T-shirt and some crazy shorts that didn't match and were too short. I noticed that he had white legs and a sunburned face. A true fan ready to go to the Super Bowl.

"Hey, you're Kris Jenner!" he shouted as the elevator doors closed and we headed down to the lobby. He started telling me how much he loved the show, and, well, since I was in a hurry,

I sort of brushed the guy off. Suddenly the elevator made a funny sound . . . and then stopped.

I started pushing buttons like crazy. Nothing. We were stuck between floors, and I was really upset. I wasn't in the best of moods anyway, because I was under a ton of stress and a deadline, and I couldn't get the elevator to take me down to the ground floor.

The stranger in the bermuda shorts started pushing the elevator buttons, too, and talking a mile a minute.

Soon I was practically yelling at him: "Stop! Don't push the button again! Stop it!"

I was giving him orders. Finally, the elevator lurched to a start and opened on the seventh floor, where I got off. I was trying to get to the lobby and didn't want to get stuck on that damned elevator again. He got off there too. I got back on another elevator, and he followed me back onto that one.

"Don't touch the buttons," I warned him, and he did exactly as I said, like a little boy. When we finally got down to the lobby, I was already fifteen minutes late, and I needed to make up the time. I started running toward the BMW limousine waiting for me outside.

The guy from the elevator ran after me, calling out, "Hey, Kris, I just wanted to give you my card before we part."

I turned back to him impatiently, as if he was the last person I'd ever want to call.

Big mistake.

He handed me his card and said, "My name is Tom Dowd. I'm the senior vice president of GNC."

Instantly, my face switched into the biggest smile I could muster. I went straight from bitch to businesswoman.

"Oh my God, Tom, why didn't you say so?" I purred.

Ever since Bruce and I had launched our infomercial television career in exercise equipment back in the '90s, I had wanted to get into the nutrition and diet business. It was yet another dream, and GNC is the leader when it comes to vitamins and supplements. I wanted to jump back into the stalled elevator with Tom Dowd. I took another two or three minutes to talk to him and I said upon leaving, "I would love to talk to you more."

"We would love to have somebody like you on our team," he said.

Long story short, within ten days I was back at my house in California and Tom Dowd was sitting in my office. No shorts or white tube socks this time; he was in a suit and tie. I was ready to do battle with the supplement business. And as our relationship grew, Tom brought in a colleague of his, Keith Frankel. To this day, Keith Frankel is my business partner in our vitamin and weight-loss business, called Quick Trim. I was able to turn a near miss into what is now a very lucrative business. All of my children are involved in it—even Scott Disick got a job working for Keith—and Keith Frankel is now my business partner and collaborator in all things diet and nutrition.

This is something to remember: you never know what opportunity is going to present itself—or where. It's a lesson Robert Kardashian used to tell me on a regular basis. Business 101: *Be nice to everybody.* Never take anyone at face value. These are life lessons I needed to remember. I could've blown off Tom Dowd—and almost did!—but being stuck in that elevator with him was just meant to be.

Nutritional supplement business: Check!

As we added all these titles to my résumé and to my kids' plates, I realized that there were a lot of categories out there yet to conquer. The television show became my day job, and everything else became a passion, one move at a time. I had always had the energy and motivation and passion to pursue all these dreams, but it took a show like *Keeping Up with the Kardashians* to be the vehicle that could channel all my energies and turn them into viable opportunities. I started to look at our careers like pieces on a chess board. Every day, I woke up and walked into my office and asked myself, "What move do you need to make today?" It was very calculated. My business decisions and strategies were very intentional, definite, and—other than chance encounters in elevators—planned to the nth degree.

Every day, I had to answer a laundry list of questions: Where does this child need to be and how is she (or he) going to get there? It was work: filming the show and then traveling to events and appearances, all of which required intense coordination and scheduling.

On the day I am writing this, for example, Kim is doing *Project Runway* in New York. When she walks on set, I'll be on the phone with her. "Did you sign your contract?" I'll ask. "How's everything going? Did your hair and makeup go well? Don't forget, your car's picking you up at such and such a time to take you over to the television station to do another talk show."

On and on it goes. The coordination of the girls' schedules is like the engine that keeps everything running. It soon became insurmountable by myself. I had to begin building a team, starting with our agents, who began to diligently build the girls' calendars and run their master schedule with me. That, in and of itself, soon became a full-time job.

In 2009, I had an idea to tape the girls by themselves and give them a spin-off show instead of just featuring them in *Keeping Up with the Kardashians*.

It began one day when they said, "Mom, we want to open a store in Miami."

"You do? That's a great idea!" I replied.

Kourtney loves Miami. When she was younger, she and Kim

and Khloé would go to Miami to celebrate New Year's Eve. If we were opening a store there, why not add a television component? The show would be about the girls moving to Miami for the summer, where they would design and stock the store, hire the employees—or "Dash Dolls," as they called them—and get ready for the store's launch, which Kim flew in to attend.

We took it to Ryan Seacrest and the E! execs, and they said, "Let's do it."

Kourtney & Khloé Take Miami was born.

It ran two seasons. Kourtney revealed her pregnancy on the show, and the second season finale had 3.6 million viewers.

Spin-off show: Check!

Kim wasn't involved in the spin-off show. She was so busy with everything else that was going on. As I mentioned earlier, Kim and I would regularly sit down and talk about our goals. A recurring one for her as well as for me: her own fragrance line.

"Wouldn't that just be the dream come true?" we asked each other. "Wouldn't that be amazing if we could turn this into something that would be forever and real—a product and a business?"

The fragrance, Kim Kardashian, was an instant hit. The scent is a mix of jasmine, gardenia, and sandalwood, and we marketed the perfume as classic, glamorous, sexy, and feminine—just like Kim. The marketing tagline is "Kim Kardashian: The voluptuous new fragrance." The launch party at Sephora in Las Vegas was in February of 2010 and it was packed; one guy even got down on one knee and proposed to his girlfriend in front of Kim! After the launch at Sephora, there was an after party at Tao nightclub at the Venetian, and they rolled out a huge cake that was an exact replica of Kim's perfume bottle. Before Kim Kardashian went on the shelves, Kim was already gearing up to do her second fragrance, Gold.

Kim's (first) fragrance, Kim Kardashian: Check!

This was such an amazing experience for all of us that I would later develop a deal for Khloé and her husband, Lamar, for a unisex fragrance of their own called Unbreakable.

The next project I wanted to tackle was skin care. Everyone compliments our family on our skin, so it just seemed like a natural next step. We knew skin care was something they would all be proud of and love. I was able to find a partner with a lab that could enable the girls to develop their own skin care line. I would love for all the girls, at some point in their careers, to have makeup endorsements, like a L'Oréal contract or something similar, and each have her own skin care line. That's a dream we haven't realized yet, but I felt like one skin care line could be a precursor, and I really felt all my experience with infomercials and back-end marketing would help. We were able to develop a skin care line called PerfectSkin, and we shot an infomercial for it. It was a success.

The girls all have slightly different skin types, and PerfectSkin is a three-step line geared toward busy women with different skin types: oily, dry, sensitive, etc.

PerfectSkin skin care line: Check!

Another thing I had dreamed of doing with my daughters was a clothing line. The girls had their DASH clothing stores in L.A. and Miami by now, and they each had a gift for fashion. It was all about timing at this point. Once the fragrance was off the ground, then the next dream to tackle was the clothing line. It took three years to get this together. I believe in doing my due diligence and I researched the history of the different companies, the levels of marketing, retail, and what might be the best fit for us. Was it going to be mass-market? Mid-tier? I wanted to go to the professionals with already successful clothing lines and get their advice, because I really believe in talking to people and experiencing the whole gamut of trying to put something like this together. For three years I researched the entire retail market.

By then we were about to start out the sixth season of *Keeping Up with the Kardashians*. We finally identified our retail partner: Sears.

I have fond memories of Sears when I was a little girl shopping with my grandmother for holidays and special occasions. I've been going to Sears since I could walk. It's yet another surreal thing to me that my girls are going to have a clothing line, the Kardashian Kollection, in an iconic store. The girls will have their very own line, and it's going to be a store-in-store setup so that the customer can go into a Sears store and have a Kardashian *experience*. They're actually building Kardashian stores inside every Sears location. That's one of the things I'm proudest of, because we spent a long time putting a lot of care and thought into developing a line that reflects the girls. One hint: they're going to have shoes named after different metropolitan cities to reflect their fans and all the places they travel.

Clothing line: Check!

Still, as we checked off goals on our mutual wish lists, there was one thing missing for my daughter Khloé.

As I've written in previous chapters, Khloé struggled most visibly with her father's death. Just before Robert died, Khloé was so distraught over his illness that she couldn't even visit him. When he passed away, she lost all of her hair. I felt hopeless and helpless; I couldn't make Khloé snap out of her intense grief. When we started filming *Keeping Up with the Kardashians*, it was a godsend for Khloé. Her father's death still felt fresh to her at the time, and the show was a big distraction. She could focus on something productive and she felt like she might be able to move on instead of being stuck in a helpless place.

Still, that first season of the show proves that Khloé was still struggling, including the episode in which she got her DUI. We were all so shocked over her DUI, because that really wasn't who my kids were. My kids aren't alcoholics or drug addicts. They love to have a good time, for sure. We all do. But Khloé and her sisters have always been extremely responsible. They've made mistakes, they may not always make the right decisions, but they are definitely good girls. So to see Khloé fall apart like that was really hard on the rest of us, because we just really wanted the best for Khloé. Part of this was wanting her to find someone she really cared about.

Khloé was the girl who never fell in love.

She never brought any boys home.

She never even hinted that she might be in love with somebody.

Kim was the hopeless romantic, always dating various guys and falling for someone. Kourtney found her boyfriend, Scott, at a young age. Khloé was still growing up, still trying to figure out life, still trying to figure out who she was. Yet, nobody was more loving, giving, or adorable than Khloé. Nobody was more generous, kind, funny, funny, funny, funny, while also being very strong. She obviously learned to grow some thick skin and she was very vocal about how she felt about things. She was never one to shy away from giving her opinion.

Still, I never expected Khloé to fall head over heels in love, but I always knew that whoever she ended up with would be getting the most amazing wife, mother, companion, and friend that anyone could ever want. Because that is just who Khloé is.

I knew that eventually Khloé was going to be okay, but I obviously always worried about her finding someone, as I did for each of my girls. In my generation, everybody got married when they were in their early twenties and then had kids. But my kids were well into their twenties, and nobody was getting married.

After three seasons of *Keeping Up with the Kardashians*, we moved to our third house in Hidden Hills, the house where our show is filmed now, a sprawling cream-colored Mediterranean-style house with a huge green front lawn—yet another dream house come true. Ever since we had moved from our first house in Hidden Hills, Kendall and Kylie begged me to get their old house back. They wanted to live back on that street. They loved everything about that street: the location, the acreage, the houses. I felt like I was failing them because they weren't living where they wanted to live. I just wanted to make my kids happy. So I started looking for a bigger house back on that street. Lo and behold, I found an amazing house on our same street, and it was bigger and better than I could've ever imagined. I was so happy that I had found this place and was able to make a deal and buy the house. Nobody knew I had bought this house except Bruce and me.

On Christmas morning, 2008, we were at our old house opening gifts. When all the gifts were opened, Bruce and I said, "Well, Kendall and Kylie, we have one last present for you." We jammed everybody into Bruce's Escalade and we all drove over to the new house. We pulled up out front, and I think at first my little kids thought that we were going to see a horse, because we live in horse country, and they thought they were getting a pony or something. I whipped out the keys and opened the front door, and Bruce screamed, "Merry Christmas, family! Welcome to your new home!" Everybody went running through the house, screaming and yelling. I will never forget that morning.

One of the best things about moving into that new house was that it gave my older kids, one by one, the opportunity to live in our old house for a while while we were trying to sell it. First, Rob lived there for a few months. Then Kim needed to live there for six months while she scoured Los Angeles, looking for her own dream house to buy. A year later, it was Khloé's turn to move into that house. Finally, Kourtney and Scott moved in while they were looking for a new home of their own.

Life was going as usual, and everyone was working very hard.

One day in August 2009, while we were gearing up to start shooting Season Four, Khloé came over.

"Mom, I left a name at the gate," she said. "I have a friend coming over. When he gets here, let me know."

Khloé was doing a magazine interview in my family room, so when the doorbell rang, I opened the door. I looked out the door, and then I had to look up higher . . . and higher . . . until I was looking up about three feet, because there was a six-foot-ten guy standing on my doorstep. I was looking at Lamar Odom. Of course, I knew that Lamar Odom was the star forward for the Los Angeles Lakers basketball team. But Khloé hadn't told me that the "friend" coming to the house was Lamar Odom. She had told me her friend "Lamar" was coming over to say hi.

"Hey, Lamar," I said as he came walking into the house.

My girlfriend Lisa Miles was there that day. Lisa was always taking me to Lakers games. Her eyes grew really big and she shot me a look.

"What's Lamar Odom doing here?" she asked.

"I have no idea!" I said.

We watched Lamar walk in and find Khloé, and they started talking. Lisa and I found this all very interesting. I thought, *Wow, Khloé has a new friend*. She didn't talk about it much that day, but before I knew it, a week later she was asking me to go to dinner with her and Lamar. Then there was another dinner, and another.

Two weeks passed. We were shooting the first couple of days of Season Four when I had the shock of my life: On camera, Khloé and Lamar asked to take me to dinner, and at dinner, Lamar told me he wanted to marry Khloé. He basically asked for Khloé's hand in marriage. I was stunned and wildly excited—

"Mommy, I'm in love," she said. "Lamar is the guy for me. He's the love of my life. I just know it in my heart."

Lamar proposed to Khloé in our backyard, during a dinner with a bunch of our friends and family. Khloé was sitting in a chair in the backyard, and Lamar came over to her and went down on one knee. He pulled open a velvet box with a beautiful engagement ring, and everyone was shocked. Khloé was so excited.

It's funny. Now that I think back on it, I didn't doubt for a second that this was the love of Khloé's life. She had never told me she was in love before. She had never brought anybody home. She had never told me she was happy like that before. She had never said all the things she said to me then. That's all she needed to say to me. Honestly, the moment I met Lamar, I knew he was the one. He was delicious, and I knew he adored Khloé.

Still, as they say, I hadn't heard nothin' yet. Khloé and Lamar went on to explain to me that, for several reasons, they had decided they wanted to get married on September 27. They just *had* to get married before Lamar started his basketball season. It was their one-month anniversary. They had other reasons. When it all sunk in, I gasped.

"Wait a minute," I said, cameras rolling. "September 27 is in only nine days!"

"Yes, Mommy, we want to get married in nine days," said Khloé.

Oh. My. God. My mind instantly went crazy making lists. We needed a dress, a cake, a location, a pastor, a caterer, bridesmaids, a registry, flowers, invitations. I needed help. So I did the only thing I knew to do: I called my best friend, Shelli Azoff. Shelli said to call Sharon Sacks, the amazing wedding planner.

"Can you get over here right now?" I asked Sharon. "We have a nine-one-one wedding coming up. I have nine days to pull this off."

Sharon was there within the hour. Simultaneously, I was on the phone with Vera Wang, who, thank God, I'd met fifteen years prior, when she and Bruce were both judges at the Miss America Pageant. She and I had been friends ever since.

"Vera," I said, rattling on about the nine days and the lists rolling through my mind. "Can you help me?"

"Get Khloé on a plane today," Vera said. "I would love to design her dress, and I'll do all of the bridesmaids, and of course I'll do yours."

We made Khloé's reservations on the spot. Within an hour, cameras still rolling, we bought tickets for Khloé and a girlfriend and they were on their way to New York for fittings with Vera Wang. I stayed behind with Sharon to plan the wedding and to get Khloé organized. She returned home within forty-eight hours. Khloé just wanted to get married and she didn't care about a big party. She would have been happy going to Vegas. So I planned the whole wedding with Sharon. It was pretty much my dream wedding. You would have thought I was the bride.

Khloé was going to have the wedding of a lifetime, and, of course, we would be able to capture it on *Keeping Up with the Kardashians*.

Of course, the wedding featured the usual Kardashian chaos. During the pre-wedding prep, there was plenty of drama and absolute pandemonium, yet Khloé would actually send orders to me via her BlackBerry, even though she was usually standing right next to me. Kylie passed Khloé's BlackBerry back and forth between us.

The ceremony itself is what I'll always remember. I sat in the front row with Bruce. I was clutching Bruce's hand, with my handkerchief ready. Lamar had the biggest smile on his face as Bruce walked Khloé down the aisle. Khloé was surrounded by her sisters, now her bridesmaids, all wearing gorgeous lavender Vera Wang dresses. Khloé looked so, so beautiful, and Bruce walked her down the aisle and gave her away. It was one of the greatest moments of my life, watching my daughter get married to the man she loved. We will have these memories forever because of the show, which was the most-watched episode in the history of the network. Otherwise, we might not fully know what happened, because the nine-day wedding craziness was as chaotic as it was wonderful. It was fast and furious, but it was right—romantic and wonderful. If you had told me that I would be ecstatic about my daughter coming home and telling me she was getting married in nine days, I never would have believed you. But it has always been my dream for each of my daughters to get married and find happiness.

Finally, I could say that for at least one of them: Check!

Kourtney, meanwhile, had had someone special in her life for quite a while: Scott. Scott had been courting Kourtney back when we started shooting Season One. I wasn't sure about Scott. He was really handsome and really smooth, and he seemed like a little bit of a bad boy. I had had my share of bad boys myself, of course, so I knew one when I saw one. I wasn't going to let this kid come in and take my precious Kourtney for a wild ride. If there was anything that I could do to protect her heart, I was going to do it. I wanted him to know that I was paying attention.

As I got to know Scott a little bit better, our relationship evolved. Now I adore him, but it was a rocky road in the very beginning. He was still a kid. He's only twenty-six now, so when we started the show, he was more like twenty-two. A baby. I had some experience with twenty-two-year-old babies, and I think I might have taken that out a little bit on Scott. Looking at him, I thought, *Hmmm, this feels familiar.* I could not forget my experience with Ryan. But that wasn't Scott's fault.

Scott was also drinking then. His drinking culminated in an incident that was (of course) filmed in an episode of our show. The whole family had gone to Vegas for Kim's birthday. We had really been looking forward to letting our hair down and just being together. Scott got drunk. I had business associates with us, and I decided to cut him off. He asked the waiter for more alcohol, and I told the waiter, "Don't serve him. He's gone way too far." That really upset Scott, and he got so worked up that he shoved a $100 bill down the waiter's throat, demanding to be served.

It was a powerful moment, both for the show and for our family, and a definite wake-up call for Kourtney. She knew Scott needed help. We wanted Scott to be okay. I don't think that exactly came across in the show. But by that time, we had all fallen in love with Scott, and we didn't want someone we loved to be in trouble or hurting. When I talked to him I said, "I love you and want you to be a part of our family, because I think you are really a good person deep down—and, by the way, my daughter is in love with you. So what can we do to make you the best Scott you can be?" We all reached out that way and made sure that he knew he was loved but that he had to get it together.

You will remember that my mother was in a similar situation at one point with my stepdad, Harry, whom I adored. My mom had to tell Harry that she wasn't willing to be around him anymore until he cleaned up his act with alcohol. Suddenly, two generations later, Kourtney was facing the same dilemma. She loved Scott and wanted to give him another chance. She wanted to do everything she could to make the relationship work, and she wasn't willing to walk away from him yet. I really admired her for that. Scott got it together; I haven't seen him with a drink in over a year now.

Later that same year, we all went to Mexico on a vacation for Kourtney's birthday, which was an annual tradition. All of Kourtney's girlfriends were there with us. I remember looking at her while she was running around in her bikini and thinking, *If I didn't know my daughter better, I would say she's pregnant.* It wasn't that she was even showing, it was that I just sensed it. I just knew instinctively. A few weeks later, she came into work at Smooch.

"Oh my God, Mom, I have something to tell you. I'm pregnant!" she said.

I was so, so happy for her! I knew that she was going to make an amazing mom, and I was so excited, because of course this was going to be our first grandchild.

I never imagined that Kourtney would be the first of my daughters to have a baby, because she was really the least enthusiastic about small children. We had a children's store, and when people would come in with little kids, she got annoyed. She would say, "Ugh, they're bringing their baby in our store." I would say, "Well, we do have a kids' store. It's not really weird that somebody's bringing her kid in here." So seeing her so ecstatic about becoming a mother was great. She started reading every book she could get her hands on. I knew that Kourtney was going to be a great mom.

Kourtney started seeing the same OB/GYN, Paul Crane, who had delivered all six of my kids. Now he was going to deliver my first grandchild. The day Kourtney went into labor, we were all at my house, having a barbecue.

"Mom, I feel a little funny," she said. "I think I'm going to go home."

She went home to lie down and took Kylie and Kendall with her because she didn't want to be alone. Scott was at the barbecue, too, but you know, guys are different. He stayed at the house for a few minutes and hung out with us until the girls called us from the house and said, "I think we should go to the hospital." Kourtney thought her water had broken!

The birth began like almost everything else Kardashian: a little crazy and a little chaotic, and with the cameras rolling. We actually shot footage of Kourtney's water leaking in an episode of the show. Kendall and Kylie ran around, giddy, unable to contain themselves, while Scott took somewhat shaky footage of Kourtney preparing to leave for the hospital.

We were all crazy with excitement, but Kourtney seemed almost serene. She calmly put on her makeup and packed her bag. When they arrived at Cedars-Sinai, she even took a nap. Soon the rest of us arrived, me at midnight, then Khloé at 5:30 a.m., and Kim sometime afterward, her hair extensions only halfway in because she left in the middle of prepping for a photo shoot.

The hospital room was crowded but full of love. There were only supposed to be two family members in the room, so we had to get creative about where we stood. Kim peeked from the closet while the nurse checked Kourtney, and we all hid in various corners. Kourtney was in her hospital bed with a look of determination. The rest of us didn't really know what to do with ourselves. I even caught myself practicing my Lamaze breathing.

When Dr. Crane told her to push, we were with her: Scott, Kim, Khloé, and me. Khloé was able to help hold Kourtney's leg while she pushed, and I watched from the doorway as Kourtney's tiny body folded up on itself and the baby's little head appeared. Kim covered her mouth in amazement. We were all crying—everybody but Kourtney. She had a job to do. She was quiet, serious, working. Finally, Dr. Crane asked her if she wanted to pull the baby out. "Can I do that?" she asked. She was able to put her hands around the baby's torso and tug, gently, and finally Mason Dash Disick was on her chest, crying softly.

There wasn't a dry eye in the house. The miracle of birth never grows old and never ceases to completely amaze me. The birth of a baby can humble anyone. I watched Scott's face and how he reacted to the entire experience, and I saw him in a way I had never seen him before.

Afterward, Kourtney told our producers that Mason's birth was life-changing for her, the most amazing thing she had ever experienced. That's exactly how I would have described her birth so many years before. Watching your baby have a baby—it's one of those moments that makes life a miracle.

I've watched Kourtney become the most amazing mother in the world, totally devoted and dedicated to her baby on every level. She makes selfless decisions as she raises her baby, and doesn't go anywhere without him, nor does she slow down for a second. When I suggested, "Why don't you just take a couple of months off?" she wouldn't hear me out. She was determined to get back to work, even with a baby strapped to her back. I think Mason's first photo shoot was when he was maybe four days old.

Scott, meanwhile, turned around 180 degrees. He's an amazing partner, an amazing dad, and an amazing son. I've gotten to know his parents, and they're wonderful. I think Kourtney has shown all of us that she is going to do life her way. And I even have to admit, I respect her for not succumbing to my wishes for her to be married just because she has a baby. She kind of did it backward. It wasn't the way I did things, but it works for her.

As I write this, we're just finishing up Season Six of *Keeping Up with the Kardashians*. I thought I was done, and then all of a sudden, as in all things Kardashian and in any family with six kids, something new happened . . . Kim fell in love.

Kris Humphries (great first name, right?) was a basketball player for the New Jersey Nets. Kim had met him at the end of shooting our spin-off show *Kourtney & Kim Take New York*. She had been dating Kris for about six months. I had never seen Kim so happy, and I could tell Kris was different. One day, Kris came to Bruce and invited him to go golfing. While they were on the golf course, Kris asked Bruce for Kim's hand in marriage. Bruce and Kris came running home, where Kris asked *me* for Kim's hand. Then he asked my advice on how to best pop the question to Kim. He wanted to surprise her, but he wanted to do it in a really low-key and private way, which I thought was really cool. He planned this big surprise for her, and that same night I planned an engagement dinner.

He asked Kim to marry him at her house by taking dozens of red rose petals and spelling out "WILL YOU MARRY ME?" on the floor of Kim's bedroom. When she came home she didn't even know he was going to be there, but there he was, down on bended knee when she walked into her rose-strewn bedroom. Of course she said yes.

They came over to our house, where I had gathered the entire family.

"It's another nine-one-one!" I told everyone. "A nine-one-one barbecue," which translated to: "Get your ass over here right now."

Everybody came over immediately. I didn't tell them why they needed to come. It was important that we kept the proposal hidden until the last second, because *none* of us can keep a secret from one another.

Once the whole family was gathered outside at the dining room table, Kim and Kris walked in. Kim was wearing her huge diamond ring, and she just started flashing her hands around and casually running her fingers through her hair. At first no one noticed.

Then Kylie screamed, "Are you engaged?!"

"Yes!" Kim said.

Everybody started screaming, jumping up and down, and crying. It was just a great, great night. We had dinner, and once again I just sat around looking at my six children, my husband, my grandchild, and my three sons-in-law (one honorary and one future), thinking, *Life is so good.* We had a gorgeous pink Cinderella cake and as a joke, I had rented two mini-horses covered in glitter, and we all wore fake engagement rings.

Of course, the camera crew caught every second.

The Epiphany

I never imagined that a neck-lift would be a transcendental, life-changing experience for me at the age of fifty-five. People think about plastic surgery and they think "self-absorbed," not "life chang-ing." Yet my neck-lift surgery taught me some amazing lessons about life—and about love, friendship, loyalty, self-control, and the power of letting go. Most of all, it taught me about the importance of over-coming fear. My husband often says, "Fear is like fire: it can burn your house down, or it can keep you warm and cook your food."

It depends on how you look at it. I've looked fear in the eye and chosen to overcome it, and that applies to all kinds of facets of my life, from emotional to physical. But few things compared to the neck-lift I had last summer.

Since my first surgery in childhood, when I had the tumor in my leg removed, I have been terrified of going under anesthesia. When I went under anesthesia as a child, I wasn't sure if I would wake up with a leg or not. Going under for that surgery seemed like I was surrendering control of my life. I don't like surrendering control. *I am a control freak*. When I went under again for breast implant surgery in 1988, it was again a very frightening and disorienting experience. I also had a recent knee surgery from a torn meniscus, but that happened so fast, I didn't have a choice or a chance to really worry about it. Even though the surgery—both surgeries—were very successful, I woke up feeling terrible, throwing up in the car on the way home from the anesthesia and vowing: *I'll never do that again!*

I had been seeing my plastic surgeon, Garth Fisher, for years, but never for myself. One time, Kendall needed a little stitch. Then Bruce had his face-lift, and I went with him to his appointments. Another time, my son, Rob, was injured playing basketball and needed a stitch in his shoulder. Every time I was in Garth's office, I would barely get halfway down the hall before I would start taking my shirt off to show Garth my boobs and ask him if I needed them done again. He always told me I looked great and to relax.

Then, in the summer of 2011, I went back to Garth's office.

"Okay, I'm ready to have my boobs done again," I told him. "I think that they make me look matronly. They're too big. Now what do I do with these implants?"

My self-esteem was taking a beating because I was aging and I didn't feel as good about myself as I once did. I was also an absolute workaholic, obsessed with work, addicted to my office, and traveling like crazy. I was working hard all the time, not taking any time for myself, and I felt like doing something like this—just for me—might just give me a boost of confidence and make me feel better. I also knew that if I was ever going to be put to sleep again for surgery, I needed a surgeon I trusted 150 percent. That surgeon was Garth. I knew I could give my control over to Garth and be okay with it.

"You don't need your boobs done," he told me. "Why in the world would you mess with them? They look great."

Then he added, "But I will do your neck."

"What?!" I said. "You've been telling me all these years you would never touch my face."

"It's time," he said. "It's the perfect time. We can fix your neck. It's been bothering you for a while. So let's do it."

I was, like, *What*? Here I had just gotten up the nerve to redo my boobs after thirty years, and now he was telling me, "No, your boobs look great, but let's do your neck."

I walked out that day still in a fog. It was finally time. Then the fear took over: all I could think about was what would happen during the surgery. I would be put to sleep. I would lose control. I would be OUT. It was a visual I just could not get out of my head. I debated with myself for days, worried about something going wrong. I spent weeks preparing for the worst. It wasn't a medical procedure; it was elective surgery, something I didn't really *have* to do. Something I said I would *never* do.

I kept berating myself:

How selfish are you to do this for yourself when you are every-one else's manager?

What if, God forbid, you don't awake from the anesthesia? Who will take care of everybody? Who will be their manager? Who will drive the ship of Keeping Up with the Kardashians? *Who will take care of the brand?*

It was very hard for me to let things go. Fear became my en-emy. Fear was overwhelming and powerful.

Finally, I scheduled the surgery. By then it had become a challenge that I couldn't deny. Yes, it was something that I really wanted for myself. Still, it was something that also scared me to death. I had done my homework on the subject, and I had decided that I wanted to do it. I looked around. Lots of people have plastic surgery. So, yes, I wanted the surgery, and it just became a challenge for me to overcome my fear and do it.

Then something amazing happened: my children, family, and friends wrapped me in their arms and made me feel so loved.

As I was contemplating the surgery, I was also thinking about my relationships, both past and present. Even after all these years, I was still suffering from the loss of some of my closest friends during my divorce from Robert. That was very, very painful. Not only did I lose a spouse in my divorce, but I also found I could not replace or fix all the relationships I had undone in the process. There were people I let down, people I disappointed, and in the twenty years I have been remarried to Bruce, there were still wounds that never seemed to heal. Despite everything I had, there were still people missing in my life.

When I married Bruce, it took some time for me to reconnect with friends like Joyce and Larry Kraines and Sheila and Randy Kolker. After Robert passed away in 2003, we seemed to find one another again, and it has been one of the most amazing joys. A true awakening, and I feel blessed to have them in my life again.

When I had my boobs done in 1988, the two faces that were there to greet me when I woke up from surgery were Sheila's and Joyce's. They were the ones who drove me home from the hospital and put me into bed, who took care of me at the moment when I truly felt the worst I ever had. Making plans for this neck-lift reminded me again how important these girls, as well as my other friends, were and are to me, and I knew I needed them to be there for me again.

The morning of the surgery, the most spectacular thing happened: all of my best friends and all of my children surrounded me when I got to the hospital. I had asked a few of my girlfriends to be with me when I went into surgery since Bruce couldn't be there. So when I sat there in the waiting room, waiting for the nurse to call me in for the surgery, I looked around and I saw Shelli Azoff, Joyce Kraines, Sheila Kolker, and Lisa Miles, along with Kimberly, Kourtney, Khloé, and Rob. I felt like the luckiest girl in the world, blessed by love and friendship. I suddenly realized that this was the same group of girls who sat with me so many years ago, waiting for Rob to be born. I burst into tears, overcome with emotion. I almost forgot about being petrified.

With everyone standing around me in the operating room, most in scrubs, I was able to find a complete peace. I was so grateful for where I had been and how far I had come in my life, through drive, ambition, focus. Now I was able to let go, for the first time in twenty years, because I realized in that moment the power of friendship, the power of love, and the power of feeling complete.

There was another essential group of friends in that operating room: the entire camera crew from *Keeping Up with the Kardashians*. They were all in scrubs, too, doing their best to be invisible. A camera crew in the operating room? Absolutely. There is no way I would have had the operation without them. They had been through the last six years of my life, documenting every second. Although most people would cringe at the thought of having a surgery filmed, for me it wouldn't have been the same without them. This crew are members of my family now. They laugh with me and they cry with me. They have been with me every moment for the last six years. Why in the world would they miss this? As I promised in the beginning: *the cameras roll no matter what.*

I looked over at Farnaz Farjam, our wonderful and beautiful producer and now one of my best friends. She was in scrubs, too, and I thought she was going to cry. I looked over at all of my girlfriends, and I could see the love in their faces. I looked over at my kids; they were holding my hands.

As the anesthesiologist prepped me, I thought about the people in my life I had lost. I thought about how Robert Kardashian would surely get a good laugh out of all of us being together again in a room like this under these circumstances. He would have also surely loved to see us being silly and loving one another and being there for one another.

I thought about Cici, Robert's cousin and my longtime and ever-loving friend and closest confidante, who was in Houston and couldn't be there, and how much she was missed. I thought about her parents, Auntie Dorothy and Jack, who had been such a big part of my life. I thought about my girlfriend Mary Frann, and my girlfriend Stephanie Schiller. I thought about my grandparents, Lou and Jim and Mary Lee and True. I thought about Nicole, about how much I loved and missed her and how she would have loved to be there, to go through something like that with all of us. I thought about my stepfather who became my dad, Harry Shannon, and how much I loved him, and how excited I was that my mom was coming up to be with me right after the surgery.

I thought about everyone I'd loved, everyone I'd lost, and everyone who was there in the room with me that day. My whole life seemed to flash before my eyes as I thought about all the people who had joined me on the journey of my lifetime.

I was thinking about all of this as the nurses wheeled me into the operating room. They let me recline while the anesthesiologist administered the IV. Now my biggest fear—going under, losing control—was now my biggest challenge, and I was going to accept it, embrace it, and conquer it. I took a deep breath and exhaled.

"You've got about thirty seconds," said the anesthesiologist. "Then you will really start to feel this."

I looked back at my family and friends.

"Oh, I love you guys so much," I said.

I acknowledged everyone individually:

"I love you, Kourtney."

"I love you, Kim."

"I love you, Khloé."

"I love you, Rob."

I went through the entire list. Love, love, love, love, love, love, love. Six incredible kids, one incredible husband, a world of wonderful friends, an amazing life.

I took people for granted the first time around, in my first life. In my second life, I realized what I had missed so much and how special the people in my life are to me. Although I have always had so many girlfriends, it was this original little group being together again that was so powerful that day. We were all there, and we had all gone through so much. We had all lost a lot, but in spite of those losses, I couldn't help but think: *Wow, look at what we still have to look forward to. Even though we're getting older—we're in our fifties, not our twenties or thirties or forties anymore—life is going to be as fabulous as we make it. How lucky we all are to have each other!*

As I lost consciousness, I exhaled and, finally, I let go, trusting in God and my doctor that I would emerge from this experience better, stronger, and ready for the next challenge.

The next thing I knew, I opened my eyes. It had been a ten-hour surgery. But it seemed like only a moment had passed. It was midnight by then. Everyone was still there, including the camera crew, but the only faces I saw were those of my daughter Kim and my best friend, Shelli Azoff, standing over me.

"Mom, are you okay?" Kim said. "Mom, you look beautiful."

"Kris, I love you," said Shelli. "Everything went great."

Kim explained that we were going to get into the ambulance to take me to the recovery center, which was a beautiful private hotel.

I was wheeled out of the office. I felt a breeze outside. I remember the sirens starting and then I realized I was waking up in the middle of the night. For a moment I wondered where I was. I looked over and saw Kimberly sleeping on a rollaway bed on the floor, not a stitch of makeup on, in her pajama top, wearing a pair of leggings and these little socks she sleeps in. And I just thought, *Wow, you must have done something right, because here's your kid at three in the morning—a woman who has a lot of things on her mind today, including planning her own wedding—sleeping on the floor beside you because she doesn't want to leave your side.*

I closed my eyes, and I thought, *We can do anything together— me, my kids, my husband; my family and I—and all that matters in the whole world is being loved. That's what life is all about.*

Once again, I had that familiar feeling: *This is exactly where I'm supposed to be.*

Somehow, I made it through everything and ended up right here. I survived adversity and suffered enormous, tremendous personal loss. I grieved loved ones and drifted away from lifelong friends. But somehow, some way, through the grace of God, I made it through and ended up standing on my feet, stronger than ever.

I believe we are all God's children put here for a very specific reason, and I believe everything happens for a reason. We are here on this journey to help someone else, encourage someone else, and be a blessing to someone else. If I was put here on earth to only give birth to my babies, I would have been so happy and satisfied with that. But I am so grateful that I was able to do that and then so much more, to strive for perfection, to reach for the stars, to grow, nurture, mentor, befriend, advise, learn, admire, experience, and love. Wow, what a life it has been. What blessings I have received. What love I was able to give and to get. What an amazing world it is that has allowed a wife and mother like me to begin again at age fifty.

We all need a passion and a purpose. When I was young, it was having babies and raising kids. Now it's running my kids' careers and keeping up with my husband. My days are so full I don't know what to do, but I love every single second of it. I often listen to my mom tell me about her day at her children's shop, Shannon & Co., in La Jolla. I sit on the phone and commiserate with her about a long, hard day, while deep inside I am praising God that she has her work because I honestly believe it keeps her young. Our work and our passion light us up. One of my dear friends, Kathie Lee Gifford, tells me often that she remembers what her dad used to tell her: "Figure out what you love to do in life and then figure out a way to get paid for it." Those words were my mantra for many years and actually encouraged me to soldier on when I felt defeated if something didn't work out the way I had planned. I would often think to myself, *Okay, well, then, if this isn't my career path. So NEXT!* I know we will live longer and happier lives with a passion and a purpose. It's often said that life is a dance, and I am continually learning new steps.

My family and I have a platform. That's a privilege, and we don't ever want to abuse the support and love everyone has given us. Now, it will be up to each and every one of us in my family individually to decide what we want to do with that platform and how we can influence someone else in a positive way. With mine, I hope to encourage someone else to be a better mother, a better wife, a better lover, and a better friend. I hope to show women at *any* age that you can follow your dreams and still become whatever it is you set your mind to, no matter how big the dream. I would like to communicate that hard work and perseverance really do pay off.

As I've repeatedly written, all I ever wanted to do in my life was be a wife and mother and have six kids. Well, I'm living my dream, and I'm lucky enough for whatever reason to be living it on life's biggest stage: television! I love what I do, and I thank God every single day for these blessings. He obviously has a bigger plan for my life. My job and responsibility now is to pay attention and be a good steward with the gifts I have been given. To surround myself with good, positive energy and be ready for the next stage. One of the most important things I live by is by all means never to take myself too seriously and for goodness' sake have a sense of humor. I can't tell you how many times I stop myself cold in my tracks every day and remind myself to laugh . . . and to lighten up! Having a good sense of humor has helped me through so many trying times and honestly helped me with my stress level. My message is to Pay Attention! You never know what you are going to learn. I learned so much when I was young just sitting in on a business meeting, gaining information for my life to come, developing skills I never in a million years thought I would need to use. I am grateful to those who were kind to me, and especially those who have stopped along the way to lend a bit of encouragement or advice or offer even a hug.

I know people say we are "famous for being famous." But I know we are famous because we work hard and we never stop trying to be better people, have better television shows, create better stores, develop better clothing lines, forge amazing partnerships, and work hard at maintaining our beautiful personal relationships with family and friends. We are having the time of our lives in this fickle world of fame and fortune. But it's the work and the family, not the fame, that holds it all together. As one of our producers said in our *E! True Hollywood Story*, "Fame may come and go, but family is forever."

I get the game, and I am up for the challenges that lie ahead, just as long as they start with a *K*.

ACKNOWLEDGMENTS

To my wonderful collaborator, Mark Seal, who helped breathe life into my memoir.

Charles Suitt and Karen Hunter, who encouraged me to share my life and my story.

The amazing team at Simon & Schuster—Louise Burke, Brigitte Smith, Anthony Ziccardi, Sally Franklin, Jen Robinson, and Andrea DeWerd—for your hard work and the countless hours spent making my memoir a success.

My mother and father, Mary Jo and Harry Shannon. Without you, this book would not exist. Dad, I miss you every day.

Nicole Brown Simpson, who lives in my heart every day and her beautiful family—Judi, Lou, Tanya, Minnie, and Denise Brown. Your strength continues to inspire me.

My team at Jenner Communications, who I could not live without: Noelle Keshishian, Liz Roman, Karen Johnson, Jesse Daniels, and Ronda Kamihira. Thank you so much for supporting me each and every day. I love you all.

Cici Bussey for being the best cheerleader I have ever had. You are a shining light in my life.

Shelli Azoff for always standing by my side through thick and thin no matter what and for being the best friend a girl could ever have.

To my dolls, Sheila Kolker, Joyce Kraines, Lisa Miles, and Celeste Macer, for a lifetime of memories and your love and friendship.

To Kathie Lee Gifford, for your love, friendship, encouragement, prayer, and endless laughs and memories. I adore you.

To Ryan Seacrest for believing in us as a family and for your love and friendship.

My PR powerhouse Jill Fritzo at PMK°BNC. You are a rock star!

Of course, my Glam Squad: Alex Roldan and Joyce Bonelli. Thank you for making me look and feel fabulous every day!

To Farnaz Farjam and our producers at Bunim/Murray Productions—you are all truly my second family and I love you.

To E!: Lisa Berger, Suzanne Kolb, Jason Sarlanis, and Damla Dogan. Thank you for one of the most amazing journeys of a lifetime, and of course, for all of the priceless home movies! And to our PR team at E!: John Rizzotti and Christel Wheeler, for all of your hard work and dedication. I love you.

To Ted Harbert for saying, "YES," and really meaning it. My family truly loves you!

To my husband, Bruce, for twenty years of unwavering love, happiness and support. And to my children, Kourtney, Kimberly, Khloé, Rob, Kendall, and Kylie, and my grandson, Mason, for giving me my passion for life. And to my son-in-law Lamar for showing me perseverance and undeniable strength. I love you all.

And lastly, Robert Kardashian . . . thank you for being our guardian angel and watching over us from up above.